WITHDRAWN

Official Know-It-All Guide™

Coins 2004

Coins

2004

Dr. Roderick P. Hughes

Frederick Fell Publishers, Inc.
2131 Hollywood Blvd., Suite 305, Hollywood, FL 33020
Phone: (954) 925-5242   Fax: (954) 925-5244
Web Site: www.Fellpub.com

737.4973
H894c
2004
Library Use Only

Fell's Official Know-It-All Guide to Coins 2004
FREDERICK FELL PUBLISHERS, INC.

2131 Hollywood Boulevard - Suite # 305

Hollywood, Florida 33020

954-925-5242

e-mail: fellpub@aol.com

Visit our web site at www.fellpub.com

Library of Congress Cataloging-in-Publication Data

Hughes, Roderick P.
    Coins 2004: your absolute, quintessential, all you wanted to know, complete guide / Roderick P. Hughes, ISSN: 1541-8022
        p.   cm.-- (Fell's official know-it-all guide)
    ISBN 0-88391-109-4
    1. Coins--Collectors and collecting--Handbooks, manuals, etc. I. Title. II. Series.

    CJ81.h78-2000
    737.4'075--DC21

10 9 8 7 6 5 4 3 2 1   ISSN: 1541-8022

Interior and Cover Design by Chris Hetzer

TABLE OF CONTENTS

Table of Contents

Table of Contents

PREFACE

The prices for this 2004 Edition were compiled after meticulous checking of the actual prices for which U.S. Coins are trading. Prices represent 10% to 30% above wholesale dealer-to-dealer prices.

As a service to you, I will provide answers to coin-related questions. Should you wish to have a coin identified or need to know where to get an appraisal for a collection, answers may be obtained by sending a **self-addressed stamped envelope** to me at the following address:

Roderick P. Hughes, Ph.D.
Box 3, St. Bonaventure University
St. Bonaventure, NY 14778

For help in the preparation of this volume I would like to thank Chris Hetzer who did a terrific job as editor in redesigning this volume and St. Bonaventure University whose facilities could certainly have been put to better use.

To Mrs. Fran Funke who first exposed me to the joys of coin collecting, I offer a very tardy "thank you." This book is dedicated to you.

—*Roderick Hughes*

INTRODUCTION

This concise volume is meant to serve two groups of people. Its intention is to provide beginning collectors with all the basic information and necessities for the appreciation of numismatics and for the building of a collection that may well retain or increase its value.

The middle chapters provide accurate price information on virtually all coins of more than nominal value from half cents to $20 gold pieces.

Chapter 2 is meant to introduce most every relevant consideration for determining the worth of a coin. This section contains an initial discussion of what has come to be the most controversial area of the hobby—grading. The recent emergence of a number of grading and authentication services points up the degree to which even an experienced collector is unwilling to rely on his own expertise.

The vast price differences that can now be found, especially between the higher grades of uncirculated coins, has had a chilling effect on potential buyers, to say nothing of the substantial losses suffered by those who have for one reason or another purchased substantially—or even slightly—overgraded coins.

Later chapters survey the rudiments of coin collecting. Collecting accessories, where and how to acquire and sell coins, and sources for furthering one's knowledge of numismatics are some of the topics.

The second group for whom this volume may be of some help includes non-collectors — those who have come across an occasional coin that looks to be old and valuable. Often it is difficult to get some sense of real value even from friends and relatives who may be to some degree interested in coins. This volume will help non-collectors get a good idea about whether a professional opinion should be sought.

One especially troublesome situation is to find oneself responsible for a collection of a family member. Who to turn to? It seems unwise to trust completely in the judgment of another, whether he is a friend or not, until some idea is gotten concerning values.

Lastly, I caution the reader that even the inadvertent mishandling of moderately priced coins can seriously affect their value. I cannot think of one good reason to ever clean a coin.

This volume, therefore, can supply that preliminary opinion *before* wasting the time of a dealer regarding an item that is quite common in collecting circles and appears extraordinary only to the possessor.

ACKNOWLEDGEMENTS

Virtually all the coin photos for this volume were supplied to me by Numismatic Guaranty Corporation of America (NGC). Mr. David Stump and Ms. Tracy Gist handled my requests for high resolution digital photos quickly and expertly. I thank them very much for their generous help. I doubt that this volume could have been completed without them. The offices of NGC are located at Box 4776, Sarasota, Florida 34230. Telephone 941-360-3990 or 800-NGC-COIN. Fax 941-360-2553. I recommend the staff at NGC as consummate professionals for any of your coin authentication and certification needs.

COIN MARKET 2004

Generally Speaking

The coin market was very strong throughout 2003. Prices of key coins among the Morgan Dollars (especially those from the Carson City Mint), Walking Liberty Halves, Washington and Standing Liberty Quarters, Mercury Dimes, Buffalo and Liberty Nickels, Lincoln and Indian Cents, as well as the entire Barber series have increased on a monthly basis. Collector coins in the $20-$1000 range have not been this sought after since the early 1990's. Often I have had to buy good coins at what I had just sold them a month or two before. A nice 1916D Mercury Dime or 1923S Standing Liberty Quarter is sold before I can put it on my retail list. The 1932D and S Washington Quarters are wonderful sellers these days as more collectors are attempting to complete this series begun by interest in the State Quarters. The 1955 Franklin Half has nearly doubled in price in the last year.

These above coins are the staples of many U.S. collections. So even modest collections have seen some surprising price increases.

The State Quarters program is now beginning its sixth year. Every ten weeks a new state quarter is in the news. This presents collectors at all levels with reminders of their hobby. The United States Mint has done its part. Collectors are able to order their favorite state quarters, even in bag quantities, as well as current proof and mint sets containing the quarters. The ripple effect of the state quarter program has directly driven up the prices of early Washington quarters and the proof quarter varieties from the 1932's through the 90's.

Several other notable developments have taken place in 2003. First, several firms are now grading the GSA Dollars. These items have been extremely popular of late. Some of these coins are being graded in the original government holder. Others are given new encapsulations with a GSA designation on the holder. Prior to this, collectors were not able to buy the dollars with any sort of third-party opinion. This will only serve to make the market in these dollars more attractive and more easily priced. Secondly, a well-known firm is now publicly offering one million dollars for the fifth specimen of the 1913 Liberty Head Nickel that has not been seen for decades. Such an offer is a great marketing device, although the likelihood of this nickel being found is rather remote. This firm has further offered $10,000 just to be the first to see the coin. If the coin is still in the same condition as when it went missing, presumably its worth is well over $1,000,000. However, who knows what may have happened to the coin's condition in the intervening years.

Thirdly, during 2003 the spot price of gold went as high as $390/ounce. This greatly helped buoy the prices of gold coins—both collector pieces (minted prior to 1934) and Modern gold commemorative and bullion pieces. This is always a shot in the arm for the hobby. Prices have stayed strong, in the $350 range, which has simply added to a robust market.

Fourthly, I get dozens of letters inquiring about Wheat Cents. Common individual pieces (dated 1909-1958) are now being bought by dealers for 3 cents each. That is 50% more than these cents were worth two years ago. Bags (5000 coins) can be sold to dealers for $150 each. Dealers may be unwilling to pay three cents each in smaller quantities than a roll (50 coins). Some other comments are in order. The coins must not be discolored, corroded or damaged in any way. Unrusted "Steel" cents (dated 1943) are worth about 12 cents each. ""S"-mint and common coins dated before 1940 command a slightly better price. Also, better dates and mint marks are listed in the Lincoln Cent section of the volume.

The State Quarters

The state quarters remain extremely popular as the program moves into its sixth year. Quarters for Illinois, Alabama, Maine, Missouri, and Arkansas were minted for 2003. In most cases the designs for 2004 have not been finalized. Several of the first few issues (Delaware, Pennsylvania, Georgia and Tennessee) are already difficult to find in circulation, although mintages are even lower on some later issues. In fact, some issues are being minted in quantities in excess of 750 million to 1 billion coins for each of the two mint marks (Philadelphia and Denver). The proof versions from San Francisco are found in much smaller quantities, 2-3 million, and are not meant for circulation. A full set at the end of the program will be composed of 150 coins, 50 from each mint. Also, silver proofs are available in sets from the Mint. When these are added, the set will need 200 coins to be complete. The 1999-2002 silver proofs are already selling well above their issue price.

Where will this all go? The particulars of the Mint's plans can be found in the Washington quarter pricing section of this volume. The presumption is that over a 10-year period all of these coins will make their way into circulation. Consequently, the rest of the set, except for the proof issues, can be acquired for face value.

Other Areas of the Coin Market

Modern Mint commemoratives are being readily purchased by dealers at full Coin Dealer Newsletter bid prices. This represents an active market in these issues. However, the prices offered are in many cases lower than the original issue prices. Most dealers report that these items are being sold to other dealers representing TV promoters. Sales of such items are rarely made to traditional collectors.

Uncirculated platinum coins are trading reasonably well. First minted in 1997, the Platinum Eagles provide the only means in U.S. coinage to invest in this metal. Like the Gold Eagle, these coins come in 1/10, 1/4, 1/2, and 1-oz pieces. Total mintage is small by comparison to the gold counterparts. For example, only about 20,000 ½ oz. coins were minted in 1997. Mintages for 1998, 1999, 2001 and 2002 are small too. Whether these coins will ever have numismatic value remains to be seen. Currently, they are purchased as a convenient way to hold the metal and premiums over spot for the fractional denominations and proof issues are significant and, in my estimation, too high to make this a bullion investment. Overall the interest in these issues is minimal. But stranger things have happened in the coin market. If interest ever surges, the meager supply of these issues will quickly disappear, and prices will rise accordingly. **Proof platinum** pieces have astonishing low mintages. This could make them a very good bet.

The prices of Common circulated and uncirculated Morgan Dollars continue to strengthen. The buy programs for TV advertising to uneducated collectors to purchase common low grade 1921 and pre-1921 dollars continues. The 1921's have returned to the $8 level. Every dealer is looking for the pre-1921 coins in all grades from culls to AU coins. Fine grade, no-problem coins are actively bought by dealers at $10, AU coins at $13 and BU coins at around $17. Original BU rolls of the common pre-1921 dates are still quite actively sought at $440-$500/roll.

Nice looking better date coins in the Morgan dollar series continue to be difficult to acquire in VG to BU. Even low-grade S and CC minted dollars are actively sought. Carson City minted coins, the 1893s, 1894 and even some of the lesser keys are on every dealer's buy list. Key and semi-key dollars in all grades, even damaged coins, are in demand. I have been running buy ads for circulated CC dollars for over two years. My offering prices have moved up 100% in that short time for common circulated coins.

The GSA boxed Carson City issues are fast sellers by mail order and at shows. This I believe is due to the Carson City Mint's Old West mystique coupled with confidence that collectors can have in the quality of these issues, given that they are in the original government plastic holders. These boxed dollars sold by the General Services Administration during the Nixon days have steadily moved up in price. The cheapest ones (1883CC, 1884CC) are now on buy lists at $125. Sell prices are at $140-$150.

The dealer buy prices on common low-grade (VG-Fine) Peace Dollars have moved up to $7 @. Generally these coins are not as desirable as Morgans. However, most all the dates and mints after 1924 are getting more difficult to acquire. The entire set is being purchased by dealers at around $375 in VG+. Dealers are especially looking for the coins dated 1921 and 1928. All mint-marked issues in XF and above are being actively sought.

Common low-grade (good to fine) type coins continue to sell well. My experience has been that I rarely see such coins trading at coin shows to individual collectors. Rather they provide the stock in trade for flea markets and gun shows. Coins of this sort with no defects in G+ condition command the following retail prices: Half-Cents ($25), Large Cents ($11), Indian Head Cents ($1), 2-cent pieces ($10), 3-cent pieces ($10), half-dimes ($10), 20-cent pieces ($55), Standing Liberty Quarters ($2), Bust Halves ($30), Trade Dollars ($60). Seated and Barber coins are good sellers. G+ (full rims on both sides of the coin and undamaged) coins retail at 15 times face. Dealers purchase them at 11-12 times face. In grades of fine (all letters of "Liberty" in the headband on the obverse of the coin) and above, all Barber coins have advanced in price in the last year, some significantly. A nice XF Barber Half, for example, can easily command a price of $100 or so at retail.

This is a refrain of many years. Key coins continue to be much sought after. Dealers are happy to pay well for the tough Indian Head Cents (1869-1872, 1877, 1908s and 1909s), Lincolns (1909s, 1909svdb, 1914d, 1922, 1955 double die, 1972 double die), Liberty 5-cent (1885, 1886, 1912s), Buffalo Nickels (1913s and d of both types, 1914s, 1921s and virtually all pre-1930 mint marked coins in grades of fine to AU), Barber coins (all low mintage dimes, quarters and halves in full good to AU), Mercury Dimes (1916d, 1921 and 1921d, 1942/1 and 1942/1d), Liberty Standing Quarters (all dates and mints 1916-1924), Washington Quarters (1932, 1932d and s, all mint marked coins 1934-1940 in XF to BU), Walking Liberty Halves (1916pds, 1917ds on obverse, 1919pds, 1921pds and 1938d). And all low-mintage silver dollars, as mentioned earlier, are never found in quantities large enough to fill the demand.

Non-generic Gold coin prices have been strong in 2003. Rare date and very high-grade specimens, especially branch mint issues, continue to appreciate. The prices for such items begin in the thousands of dollars. Slight differences in grade can be a reason for huge price differences—sometimes 3 to 10 times the next lower grade. Should this type of item come into your possession, you had better ask for advice from a reputable dealer, and even then get a second opinion. Opinions concerning such coins, even among professionals, can vary.

Roderick Hughes

Coin questions?

Advice, appraisals or offers for selling coins or an entire collection? Write:

Dr. Roderick P. Hughes at Box 3,
St. Bonaventure University, Saint Bonaventure, NY 14778.
Please enclose a self-addressed stamped envelope.

Chapter 1

Coin Minting & Design Features

Metal Content, Weight & Fineness

The color of a coin is as good an indication as any of its composition. U.S. cents have traditionally been made of copper, although the content and amount of the metal has varied considerably over the years. The original Large cents 1793-1857 were made entirely of copper and were approximately the size of the half dollar.

Since the end of the Large cent era, the one-cent coin has been alloyed from time to time with nickel, zinc and tin. In 1943, due to the need for copper in the war effort, the cent was made of steel with a zinc coating. Since 1982, although the color of the cent does not vary much from previous years since it is still copper coated, the composition was changed to 97.5% zinc and 2.5% copper.

Two other copper coins are the half cent (100%) and the two-cent piece (95%).

All our "nickel" coins, including the "nickel" three-cent piece, are somewhat misnamed as they are 75% copper and only 25% nickel.

The only exception to the above is found in the war years (1942-1945) when the composition of the five-cent piece was changed to 56% copper, 35% silver and 9% manganese. The color of the circulated nickels is a dull gray, albeit a darker cast for the wartime alloys.

Generally, our silver coins have contained 90% of the white metal alloyed with 10% copper. From 1965-1970 the composition of the Kennedy half dollar was changed to 40% silver and 60% copper. This same composition is found in proof dollars (1971-1974) and for some bicentennial quarters, half dollars and dollars.

However, with these exceptions, after 1964 the composition of our coinage changed to a copper-nickel alloy. The nickel is found in the outside layers largely to retain a color similar to the previous silver issues. The layers of these coins become apparent when the coin is turned on edge.

Ninety percent gold and 10% copper is the most often found composition of most U.S. regular issue and commemorative gold coins.

The gold U.S. Eagle bullion coin is composed of 91.67% gold, 3% silver and 5.33% copper. The silver Eagle is 99.93% silver and .07% copper. Each of these coins, however, contains a full ounce of precious metal.

The composition and weight of U.S. coins was, until the 1850s, such that the actual metal content value was virtually identical to and sometimes even greater than the coin's face value.

The effect was to drive out of circulation what few minor coins had not been melted and to give rise to a number of alternative units of exchange—tokens, fractional currency, and the foreign coins from many nations.

In 1853 the problem of a diminished supply of circulating coins was addressed by reducing the weight of the half dime, dime, quarter and half dollar. This weight reduction was evidenced by the addition of arrows at the date and/or rays on the reverse of coins dated 1853-1855.

After the mints had made concerted efforts to provide a large supply of minor coins for exchange purposes, the arrows and rays were removed. At about this time half cents and Large cents had finally reached the end of their usefulness. These coins had simply become too cumbersome and costly for continued use in general circulation. Consequently, the size of the cent was greatly reduced, and the copper in its composition has become less and less, so that our most current cents are composed of only 2.5% of the metal.

As confidence was lost in paper currency with the impending Civil War, all types of coins began to quickly disappear from circulation. All manner of ingenious alternatives were substituted. Again tokens, fractional currency, even postage stamps were used in everyday transactions.

By 1873, although fractional coins were now available for circulation, arrows next to the date again became necessary to indicate a slight rise in the weight of dimes, quarter dollars and half dollars.

Also at about this time a special silver dollar sized coin known as a "Trade Dollar" was minted to compete with Mexican and other foreign dollar sized coins in the Orient. To place this coin on a competitive footing, the weight (and thereby amount of silver) was raised by about 2% above the standard silver dollar.

With many minor changes in weights and compositions for individual denominations in the intervening years, the final blow to intrinsic value was struck by the Coinage Act of 1965. This act called for the elimination or reduction of silver from the coins of general circulation and was made necessary by the upward pressure of the free market price of silver. Until the 1960s, the Treasury was willing to sell silver at $1.2929 an ounce. With the depletion of the Treasury's stockpile of silver dollars and bullion, however, by 1967 it became apparent that restrictions on such sales had become necessary. The refusal of the Treasury to continue sales combined with its prohibition on the melting of the hoards of coins withdrawn by the general public further escalated the price rises in the metal.

In a few short years, silver coins had completely disappeared from circulation and Gresham's Law had been obeyed. The government saw the futility of minting additional silver coins.

3

Coin Dating

Another readily noticeable feature of virtually every United States coin is the date of issue. Usually found on the obverse side of the coin, the date with some exceptions indicates the year in which the coin was minted. In some years, no coins of some denominations were minted at all. In 1815, for example, no half cents, cents, half dimes or dimes were produced by the mint.

Especially in the early days of coinage, it was not uncommon for dies to be re-engraved so that a later date is found engraved over an earlier one. This practice gave rise to many varieties of overdates. Dramatic examples of such superimpositions are found on the 1807 over 6 cent and even on the relatively recent 1942 over one dime. Much research had been conducted as to the circumstances that surrounded overdating techniques and decisions. Collectors have even been known to specialize in the uncovering of new varieties of this sort and to build collections with overdating as the focus.

In a particularly famous exception to dating coins in the year of mintage, silver dollars dated 1804 are generally believed to have been minted in the 1830s, mainly as souvenirs for presentation sets. This date also appears on a number of restrikes struck for collectors as late as 1859.

An even more common practice in the early days of the mint was to use dies until they were no longer serviceable without regard to the actual years in which the coins were being struck. Mintage figures by year for this period are notoriously unreliable.

In 1964, with the drain of silver coins from circulation and consequent shortage, the Treasury sought to respond by doubling the various mints' annual production of coins. Congress aided this effort by permitting the 1964 date on coins regardless of year minted. It was supposed that such high mintage figures would discourage any thought of these coins becoming collectors' items. Intrinsic value of course was soon to defeat this plan for coins struck in silver. However, the initial clad coins (dated 1965-1967) were often struck in a year later than the date found on the coin.

My own introduction to coin collecting was sparked by the 1960 "small date" craze. That year, two somewhat different sized numerals are found on the Lincoln cent. The smaller of the two dates, especially those from the Philadelphia mint, were initially seen as quite valuable and were much sought after. In retrospect the frenzy seems quite unwarranted. Examples of the "small date" minted

in Denver can easily be had for 5-10 cents each. The scarcer one from Philadelphia sells for $2 and demand for it has all but vanished.

Our earliest coinage provides all sorts of varieties of date sizes and numeral styles of interest mainly to specialists.

This is not to say that such considerations as those above have no significant impact on coin prices and overall desirability. Undoubt-

4

edly, the 1960 small date cents were not as rare as originally thought. And the value of many "varieties" can be quite ephemeral. I can remember when the price difference between the small and large date variety of the 1857 Large Cent was much more marked. Today the price gap seems to have all but closed.

The price of overdates and other varieties in the date on a coin is much more a function of rarity and popularity than of other components. Even then the scarcity of some items can long go unrecognized or become buried in an unpopular series. Most often relatively small differences in date design are completely ignored.

More will be said about pricing and value considerations in Chapter 2.

Mint Marks

The mint mark is an important feature in the design of a coin because it shows which mint struck a particular coin and also is quite necessary in determining a coin's value. Since eight different mints have produced coins, small letters are placed on a coin in various locations to indicate the mint of origin.

Philadelphia, Pa.	"P"	1793 to present
Charlotte, N.C.	"C"	1838 – 1861
Dahlonega, Ga.	"D"	1838-1861
New Orleans, La.	"O"	1838-1861, 1879-1909
San Francisco, Ca.	"S"	1854-1955, 1968 to present
Carson City, Nev.	"CC"	1870-1893
Denver, Colo.	"D"	1906 to present
West Point, N.Y.	"W"	1984 to present

The location of the mint mark can be either the obverse or reverse of a coin dated before 1968. Since 1968 all mint marks are found on the coin's obverse.

Until recently, with the exception of a few years of wartime nickel production (1942-1945), coins produced at the Philadelphia mint bear no mint mark.

The following rules of thumb will be helpful in determining the existence and/or location of a mint mark on each of the various denominations:

Half Cents—no mint mark (Philadelphia).

Cents (through 1907)—no mint mark (Philadelphia)
.

Indian Cents (1908 & 1909)—"S" mint mark on reverse, bottom center.

Lincoln Cents (1909 to present)—"S" or "D" mint marks obverse below date.

Two-Cents—no mint mark (Philadelphia).

Nickel Three-Cents—no mint mark (Philadelphia).

Shield Nickels—no mint mark (Philadelphia).

Liberty Nickels (1912)—"D" or "S" on reverse lower left between "Cents" and "United."

6   **Buffalo Nickel**—"D" or "S" on reverse bottom center along rim.

Jefferson Nickel (1939-1964)—"D" or "S" on reverse right center along rim. (1942-1945)—"P," "S," or "D," on reverse large letter above Monticello.   (1965-1967)—no mint mark (Philadelphia). (1968 to date)—"P," "D," or "S," on obverse below date along rim.

Silver Three-Cents (In 1851)—"O" on reverse right center at the opening of the design.

Half Dimes (1838-1873)—"O," or "S" on reverse lower center within or outside wreath.

Early Dimes (to 1916)—"O," "CC," "S," or "D" as above on half dimes until Mercury type.

Mercury Dimes (1916-1945)—"D" or "S" on reverse lower left along rim between "One" and "Dime."

Roosevelt Dimes (1946-1964)—"D" or "S" on reverse lower left above "E" in "One." (1965-1967)—no mint mark (Philadelphia). (1968 to date)—"P," "D," or "S," on obverse above date.

Coin Minting & Design Features

Twenty Cents—"CC" on reverse below eagle.

Early Quarters (to 1916)—"O," "S," "CC," or "D" on reverse below eagle.

Standing Liberty Quarters (1916-1930)—"D" or "S" on obverse left of date.

Washington Quarters (1932-1964)—"D" or "S" on reverse below branch. (1965-1967)—no mint mark (Philadelphia). (1968 to date)—"P," "D," or "S" on obverse above date.

Early Halves (1838-1839)—"O" on obverse above date. (1840-1915)—"O," "S," "CC," or "D" on reverse below eagle.

Walking Liberty Halves (1916)—"D" or "S" on obverse below "In God we Trust." (1917)—as above and also on reverse along rim at 7 o'clock. (1918-1947)—"D" or "S" on reverse as above.

Franklin Halves (1948-1963)—"D" or "S" on reverse under "States".

Kennedy Halves (1964)—"D" on reverse below eagle's left claw. (1965-1967)—no mint mark (Philadelphia). (1968 to date)—"P," "D," or "S" on obverse below neck of Kennedy.

Early Dollars (to 1873)—"O," "CC," or "S" on reverse below eagle.

Trade Dollars (1873-1855)—"CC" or "S" on reverse below eagle.

Morgan Dollars (1878-1921)—"O," "CC," "S," or "D" on reverse below wreath.

Peace Dollars (1921-1935)—"D" or "S" on reverse along rim under "One."

Eisenhower Dollars (1971-1978)—"D" or "S" on obverse below neck.

Anthony Dollars (1979-1981)—"P," "D," or "S" on obverse on Anthony's right shoulder.

$1 Gold (1849-1870)—"C," "D," "O," or "S" on reverse under wreath.

$2.50 Gold (1839)—"C," "D," or "O" on obverse above date. (1840-1907)—"C," "D," "O," or "S" on reverse at bottom above "2½" (1908-1929)"D" on reverse lower left along rim.

$3 Gold (1854-1870)—"D" "O," or "S" on reverse below wreath.

$4 Stella—no mint mark (Pattern coins).

$5 Gold (Early issues to 1837)—no mint mark (Philadelphia). (1838-1839)—"C" or "D" on obverse above date. (1840-1907)—"C," "D," "O," "S," or "CC" on reverse at bottom above "Five." (1908-1929)—"D," "S," or "O" on reverse lower left along rim.

$10 Gold (to 1907)—"O," "S," or "CC" on reverse above "Ten." (1907-1933 (Indian))—"D" or "S" on reverse along rim at 7 o'clock.

8

$20 Gold (Liberty type to 1907)—"O," "S," or "CC" on reverse above "Twenty."

Saint-Gaudens Type (1907-1933)—"D," or "S" on obverse above near date.

Commemorative Coins—Various locations. Recent commemoratives have obverse mint marks.

BULLION COINS
$1 Silver Eagle (1986 to date)—"S" on reverse left of eagle's tail.

$5 1/10 oz. Gold Eagle (1987 to date)—"P" on obverse within lower right rays (on proofs only).

$10 1/4 oz. Gold Eagle (1987 to date)—"P" on obverse within lower right rays (on proofs only).

$25 1/2 oz. Gold Eagle (1987 to date)—"P" on obverse within lower right rays (on proofs only).

$50 1 oz. Gold Eagle (1986 to date)—"W" on obverse within lower right rays.

Obverse and Reverse

The obverse, or front, of a coin is the side which presents the most important design features. Generally, a coin series will take on the name of this feature. (There are some exceptions, notably the "Buffalo" nickel.) Most often the obverse is comprised of a bust or head of a famous or fictional person. Heads of presidents, Indians and, of course, The Goddess of Liberty—sitting, standing, walking, head left and head right—have been most popular.

As mentioned before, the date is generally found on the obverse side of a coin.

The reverse or back side of a coin is defined as the side opposite the important design feature. The eagle, in any number of poses, has been selected most often to grace this side of our coinage. Fasces, wreaths, buildings and the Liberty Bell are distant seconds in this competition.

The denomination of most coins and sometimes the mint mark, and assorted inscriptions and mottos is found on the reverse.

A list of mottos, inscriptions and other miscellaneous design features   follows:

9

MOTTOS

E Pluribus Unum—Found on the reverse of early coins as part of the Great Seal. Literally, it means "From Many, One" and is undoubtedly a reference to the union of the original and subsequent states. This motto is now a standard feature of all current coins. Its history as a design feature has not been an uninterrupted one. For years it was found absent from our coinage.

In God We Trust—First appearing on two-cent coins in 1864, this motto now appears on all U.S. coins. Briefly, in 1907, there was a flap when, through the effort of President Theodore Roosevelt, the motto was removed from the $10 and $20 gold coin as inconsistent with official church-state separation. As might have been expected, a huge public outcry ensued and the motto was restored in 1908.

INSCRIPTIONS

United States of America—Was to be placed on the reverse of all coins under the same law which established the Mint. On many commemorative coins this inscription is found on the obverse.

Liberty—To be placed on the obverse of all coins under the same law that established the Mint. Often found in Liberty's hair and, ironically, one of the first devices to wear away on a circulating coin.

OTHER DEVICES

Designer's Initials—Not found on U.S. coins until the 1849 $1 gold coin, the initials of the engraver are often quite inconspicuous and may appear on either the obverse or reverse of a coin. On our most recent coinage these initials can be found as follows:

Cent—V.D.B. (Victor D. Brenner)—on the obverse along the rim under Lincoln's shoulder.

Five-Cent—F.S. (Felix Schlag)—now located on the obverse along the rim under Jefferson's shoulder.

Dime—J.S. (John Sinnock)—found on the obverse under the forward portion of Roosevelt's neck.

Quarter—J.F. (John Flanagan)—located on the obverse at the base of Washington's neck.

Half Dollar—G.R. (Gilroy Roberts)—designed the obverse. His initials are found on the lower portion of the neck of Kennedy's bust.

F.G. (Frank Gasparro)—designed the reverse. His initials are found on the reverse at the right of the eagle's tail.

Anthony Dollar—F.G. (Frank Gasparro)—found on the reverse beneath the eagle.

Major Portraits, Places, & Symbols on U.S. Coinage

The Goddess Liberty—Appears throughout the history of U.S. coinage as a symbol of unextinguished freedom. She is dressed in a war bonnet on the obverse of the $10 gold piece beginning in 1907.

Six Presidents—Lincoln (Cent), Jefferson (Five-Cent), Roosevelt (Dime), Washington (Quarter), Kennedy (Half Dollar), Eisenhower (Dollar).

Coin Minting & Design Features

Benjamin Franklin and Susan B. Anthony—With the exception of the presidents mentioned above, Franklin and Anthony are the only other actual persons to have found their way onto regularly issued coinage. Franklin, of course, holds a special place as a statesman and founder of our country. Anthony was a prominent pioneer of women's rights. Heightened sensitivity to women's issues in the 1970s undoubtedly led to her appearance on the dollar coin. Regrettably, the coin has seen very little circulation.

Buildings—The Lincoln Memorial was placed on the reverse of the Lincoln cent beginning in 1959. Jefferson's home, Monticello, is found on the reverse of the five-cent piece.

The Eagle—The national bird has been the most popular and recurring symbol found on the reverse of our coinage. (It also appears as an obverse device on the cents of 1856-1858 and the Gobrecht Dollar of 1836-1839.) Found even on the very recent bullion silver and gold coins, some particularly majestic examples grace later gold coins and silver dollars. However, the example found on early $5 gold pieces appears extremely scrawny and unattractive.

The Shield—This device is often found on the reverse of our coinage, upon the eagle's breast, or on the obverse resting against the seated Liberty.

Arrows and Olive Branches—Usually found in the talons of the full-faced eagle, symbolizing at the same time a readiness for war and a hope for peace.

Indian Princess—Found on the one-cent coin of 1859-1909 and the $1 gold coin from 1854 to 1889 among others. The model for these coins is reputed to have been the engravers daughter, Sarah Longacre.

The Indian Chief—The obverse of the five-cent "Buffalo" nickel, as it is sometimes called, is actually a composite portrait of three Indian Chiefs (Iron Tail, Two Moons and John Tree). An unidentified chief sat for the $2.50 and $5 gold coins of 1908-1929.

The Buffalo—"Black Diamond" was the model for the reverse of the five-cent piece of 1913-1938.

The Wreath—Another very popular reverse, especially for our early coinage, the wreath is sometimes found alone as a device, as on the Large cent; at other times it appear with another symbol, as with the shield on the Indian cent of 1860-1909. The wreath most often appears to be composed of oak or laurel branches, but is identified as a composite of tobacco, cotton, wheat and corn on the Flying Eagle cent of 1856-1858.

Fasces—Found on the reverse of the Winged Liberty dime of 1916-1945, the fasces is a bundle of rods encasing an ax with its head protruding meant to symbolize officialdom.

Liberty Bell—Found as the prominent device on the reverse of the Franklin half dollars (1948-1963), and later superimposed upon the moon on the reverse of the Eisenhower dollar commemorating the Bicentennial.

Victory Torch and Branches—This design is presented on the reverse of the Roosevelt dime. The torch symbolizes liberty. The oak branch on the right and the olive branch on the left remind us of strength and peace respectively.

12

Presidential Coat of Arms—This symbol graces the reverse of the Kennedy half dollar (1964 to Present).

Misc. Symbols	Where Found	Symbolizes
Chain	Large Cents 1793 (Reverse)	Strength of Union
Wheat Ears	Lincoln Cents 1909-1958 (Reverse)	Prosperity
13 Rays	1866 Shield Nickel (Reverse)	13 Original States
13 Stars	Shield Nickels 1866-1883 (Reverse)	13 Original States
Sun	Saint-Gaudens $20 Gold 1907-1933	Exact origin unclear
Six Pointed Star	Three-Cent Silver Coins 1851-1864 (Obverse)	Exact origin unclear
Five Pointed Star	$4 Gold (Reverse)	Exact origin unclear

Bicentennial Designs	Denomination
Colonial Drummer	Quarter (Reverse)
Independence Hall	Half Dollar (Reverse)
Liberty Bell and Moon	Dollar (Reverse)

Coin Relief and High Points

Coin relief refers to the relation the features of a coin have to the field. On virtually all U.S. coins minted over the years the design features are raised, sometimes called "bas-relief." They extend above the field and, thereby, these high points of the design show the most wear on a circulated coin.

An extreme example of bas-relief occurred on some 1907 $20 Saint-Gaudens gold coins. The relief was so pronounced that stacking the coins was impractical. A few proofs were minted as pattern pieces with an extremely high relief such that the coin has an almost concave appearance.

The Indian Head $2.50 and $5 gold coins are different from all other U.S. coins in just the opposite way that high relief coins are. They have a recessed or incused design. The design features are below the field.

When grading coins, an absolute necessity is a familiarity with what portions or features of the design experience the inevitable wearing as the coin changes hands in circulation. Even slight wear on the very highest points of the design can make huge differences in grading and price. It is conceivable that simply sliding a high grade uncirculated coin across a table can subtract thousands of dollars from its value to a collector.

Coin Edges and Milling

There is more to a coin than its obverse or reverse. What? Surprisingly, the edges of coins are vastly different. Currently, one-cent and five-cent pieces have plain edges. And generally minor coins, those composed of base metals, have been minted without the reeded edges found on the clad dimes, quarters and halves that circulate today.

Coins minted of precious metals have been known to encourage certain abuses. One obvious one involves scraping small quantities of the

13

metal from the edge of a coin and then passing it along at full face value. The scrapings could then be sold.

To lessen the likelihood of this, practice steps were taken to make tampering of this sort more difficult. Plain edges would not accomplish this. Consequently, U.S. silver and gold coins, almost from the beginning, were minted with small, vertical serrations on the edge, called "reeds."

Notable exceptions are found on 50-cent pieces where stars and lettering along with intermittent reeding can be found, depending on the date of the half dollar, up until 1836. Early silver dollars through 1803 also have lettered edges with decorations attesting to the denomination of the issue.

The very earliest half cents and Large cents have various designs and lettering on the edges. Ten-dollar gold pieces, minted from 1907-1933, can be found with the number of stars corresponding to the states in the Union at the time. The Saint-Gaudens $20 gold pieces of 1907 have the date inscribed on the rim as well as on the obverse. In fact, the rarer variety presents the date in Roman numerals.

14

One would expect that the reeding, especially on later coins, would be fairly uniform. A small number of studies have shown otherwise. Wide variances in the number of reeds have even been found on the Roosevelt dime.

Coin Manufacturing

The process of minting coins is much like that of any firm that stamps or fashions small parts. The Mint must, of course, proceed with much greater care since its products are legal tender and since "rejects," if security is lax, may well enter the collector market as valuable mint errors.

Simply put, from mine to Federal Reserve Bank, a coin is made through an eight-step process.

1. A mining company extracts the ore (copper, nickel, silver, gold or iron) from the ground.

2. The metal is smelted or refined and the finished product in the form of coils of strip metal or planchets is shipped to the Mint.

3. The Mint cleans, weighs and then punches the metal into blanks which are slightly larger than the finished coin will be.

4. These blanks are annealed, which is a heating process used to make the metal more receptive to striking and thereby cause less wear and tear on the dies.

5. These blanks then go through a process called "upsetting" which provides the coin with a raised rim. This allows for a more uniform feeding and striking process.

6. These planchets are fed into a coin press where both the obverse and reverse of the coin are struck from dies. These dies are the products of the original design for the coin and are fashioned in a lengthy process from models to master dies. At the same time the coin is being struck by the obverse and reverse dies, a collar, in effect an "edge die," fashions a smooth or reeded edge on the coin depending on the denomination being struck.

15

7. The finished products are inspected. All coins must meet specifications with regard to weight, size and fineness. Coins not within certain tolerance limits or coins which are defective in some way due to misstriking are rejected.

8. Finally, acceptable coins are counted and bagged for ultimate shipment to your pocket or purse through the banking system.

A Note on Mintage Figures

As you can imagine, coins cost the government less to make than their actual value as legal tender. This is especially true now that precious metals have all but disappeared from U.S. coins. The difference in the cost of production and face value of coins is called "seigniorage." It represents the profit the government makes by minting coins.

Sometimes, as has happened several times in the history of U.S. coinage, the intrinsic value or metal worth of coins increases to a level at or above the coin's face value. When this happens the coins quickly disappear from circulation.

Most recently this happened with all our 90% and 40% silver coins.

Close calls have come even with pennies of late. The price of copper per pound nearly crept over the point where melting cents would be marginally profitable.

How many coins are minted in a year?

Recently released figures from the Mint give the totals shown below by denomination for 2000. This total of around 28 billion coins compares with about 21 billion in 1999, 3.3 billion in 1961, and roughly 1.4 billion in 1951. Since the very beginning of official coinage in the U.S., the Mint has produced approximately 350 billion coins.

Cents	14.26 Billion
Nickels	2.35 Billion
Dimes	3.66 Billion
Quarters	6.47 Billion
Dollars & Gold	1.29 Billion

Estimates have been given that as many as 1/3 of all gold coins minted were melted into bars in 1933-1934. No reliable estimates have ever been produced for the "great silver melt" that began in the middle 1960s and may well continue today since the silver value of many coins is well above their numismatic and face value.

But putting aside any adjustments for the melting of coins which has happened officially and unofficially throughout the history of U.S. coinage, we might still venture estimates for how many coins have been minted per capita.

If we divide the population of the U.S. into a rough estimate of the number of coins "out there," we may be astounded to realize that the mint has produced about 1000 coins for each of us. In fact, each of us should have about 600 cents somewhere in our possession. In 1993 alone, the Mint arranged to supply everyone in the U.S. with 48 pennies. Where have they all gone?

When we realize that 30 years ago we were getting along with cent productions of one-tenth those of today, and that the production itself accumulates, the need for current production levels seems incredible.

One way to account for part of the drain of cents from circulation can be found when we realize that all Lincoln cents through 1958 (the wheat cents) have a slight numismatic value and therefore no longer circulate.

Even then, 192 billion cents have been produced. Are significant numbers lost? Or saved in drawers and piggy banks and seen as not worth carrying around? No one seems to know. As a personal reckoning you might try to count all the pennies you have around the house. Are you above or below the per capita penny wealth level of the U.S.?

Mint Errors

With all the billions of coins produced at the Mint, a few substandard coins escape the inspection process. Sometimes these defective coins are the result of dramatic errors in the production process. Most often they are due to very minor variations in die or striking conditions.

Essentially, there are three types of errors that may occur in the minting process. Coins of course, may be altered or damaged outside the mint; however, we will reserve the term "error" for governmental alteration or damage.

PLANCHET & BLANKING ERRORS

17

This sort of error is usually due to a defect in the "raw material" of the minting process. The planchet may be either overweight or underweight, or be the wrong metal for the denomination being struck. With the current clad coinage the planchet may more readily split or flake. Such errors occurred much less frequently with earlier coinage.

STRIKING ERRORS

Coins can be struck off-center when the planchet is not completely lined up with the die.

Double strikes occur when a coin is not expelled from the collar after the initial striking. Should a coin remain stuck in the die, it will produce an incused design on subsequent planchets that are fed into the press. These are called "capped die strikes."

Another type of doubling can happen if various parts of the production machinery are not tightly fitted so than a "bouncing" of the coin takes place giving the design a blurred appearance in whole or in part.

If two coins enter the collar at the same time, each will be struck on just one side. The remaining side will be blank.

Weak strikes are the result of worn dies or at the end of a striking run when lower coining pressures occur as a result of the presses being turned off.

DIE ERRORS

Due to the extreme pressure needed for the coining process, the coin die experiences a great deal of stress. These stresses result in damage to the die in the form of cracks, chips and scratches. Such damage to the dies is evident on a coin since metal from the planchet will, under pressure, fill any indentations on the die, thus leaving a raised area on the coin.

A "cud" is a die broken to such an extent that a piece of the die actually breaks off. As the planchet is struck metal flows into the empty area and a ppears as a blob of metal on the resulting coin.

The opposite problem occurs when portions of the die are filled with debris. On coins struck under these circumstances areas of the design will be missing or weak.

When care is not taken in the alignment of the dies, the obverse and reverse side of a coin can be rotated outside the normal 180 degrees alignment called for by mint specifications. This is called a rotated die error.

Changes made to existing dies, while not errors as such, result in coin oddities. Engraved over-dates and mint marks are the most common design feature changes that are made on existing dies, although lettering and portrait changes occur often also.

Most mint errors are surprisingly inexpensive. The existing supply of dramatic errors is quite small. But demand is not great either.

From our proceeding discussion I have listed major types of errors with a range of prices dependent mainly on the denomination and age of the series. Older coins and higher denomination coins are generally more expensive. Prices listed are for coins that otherwise might grade XF or better.

Nickel Struck on a Dime Planchet

18

Improper Planchet—$25 to $2,000. (Probably the most expensive error. Especially valuable on obsolete and recent $1 coins.)

Split Planchet or Lamination Errors—$1 to $50. (Splitting of planchet must be considerable.)

Incomplete Planchet—$1 to $100. (Again, missing portion must be considerable.)

Quarter Struck off-Center

Off-Center Strike—$1 to $1,000.
Very dependent on percentage of design missing. The minimum requirement for the value of the error to be significant is 25 to 50%.

Multiple Strike Sacagawea

Double Strike—$10 to $500. (Additional strikes add to the value of the error.)

1979 Lincoln Capped Die Strike

Capped Die Strikes—$25 to $200. (Image of other strikes is clear on most valuable specimens of this error.)

One-Sided Strike—$10 to $500.

Blank Planchet—$1 to $200.

Weak Strikes—Usually <u>decreases</u> the value of the coin.

Cuds and Die Breaks—$5 to $250.

Filled Die—$1 to $25. (Certain exceptions exist, for example the 1922 cent, where the mint mark was filled. When errors become recognized and cataloged their prices increase considerably.)

Rotated Dies—$1 to $25.

Re-engravings—Very dependent on date and recognition accorded to the re-engraving.

Chapter 2

Determining A Coin's Value

What's it worth? The question seems simple—the answer is not. Let us look at some of the ways the question of worth can be answered and turn to factors that, when taken together, determine value.

Catalogue value—This is the price listed in a book like this one. It is an attempt to set out the average price for which a coin retails and is arrived at by comparing the prices at which many sellers are willing to part with a particular coin. It is not, however, an offering price since the author of the catalogue may not even be a dealer and, consequently, have no coins for sale. Further, since catalogues are printed far less frequently than a dealer's price list, it is often the case that a catalogue price can become dated. Also, it is not unusual for a dealer to offer coins at a percentage of catalogue price. You can see then how unrealistic it would be to think that the price you have found in the catalogue is the one you will eventually or easily receive for your coin. Better to think of this price as a "ballpark" figure from which a deal can be struck.

Retail value—This is the price at which a dealer may offer a coin. There may be considerable variance in this price from dealer to dealer. Such a price is dependent on many factors including how much was paid for the coin, when it was purchased, how many of the particular item the dealer may possess, how many coins are being purchased in the deal, how large the overall transaction is, how hard the buyer is willing to bargain to acquire the coin, etc. Further, this is the value that will probably be placed on your coins if you ask for an appraisal or ask to have your collection valued for insurance purposes. Retail price is the closest to the replacement value of a coin.

Wholesale value—This is the price at which a dealer would expect to purchase a coin from a fellow dealer. The term is also used at times to indicate a quantity price at which a seller or buyer may be willing to exchange a large number of a particular item. Should a dealer make an offer on a coin or collection, it only makes sense that the offer will be somewhat below what he knows he would have to pay a supplier or wholesaler. The reason for this has to do with the fact that when the offer is made to the dealer, it is unlikely that this one coin will be something for which he has an immediate need. Also in buying a collection there will always be particular pieces that the dealer has little interest in buying. His lack of interest will be reflected in the offer he makes.

Buy price—This is the price that a dealer is most likely to quote you when you persist in asking what your coin or collection is worth. You can see by now that this price will be substantially below what the dealer believes he can ask as a retail price. Most coins will have a buy price of something on the order of 50-75% of the price at which a dealer would retail the coin. If a coin is especially desirable, the offer may be as high as 90% of retail. Many coin publications have a section of want ads, where dealers nationwide place offers for coins that they especially need. Once you are able to properly identify the coins you have, these ads will give you a good idea of what you can expect to receive for them should you wish to sell.

Factors Determining Value

Essentially, there are four factors that influence or determine the market price of a coin.

MINTAGE

A common mistake made by the novice collector is to think that "old" means "rare" and, therefore, "valuable." Actually, this is a confusion of categories. Older coins generally have lower mintages, but it is really the number of coins of an issue that were minted (or currently survive, which is also a function of age) that determines a coin's value.

Many Large cents of the early 1800s can be purchased for $10 to $200. Their mintages often run from 6-10 million. The 1857 issue, the last one, has a very low mintage at only one-third of a million. Though a later date, it is considerably more scarce than many earlier dates and commands a retail price of $46 or so in very good condition.

A small number of fairly recent coins are quite valuable because of low mintages. The 1931S Lincoln cent, the 1950D Jefferson nickel, and the 1932D and S Washington quarters are all keys to their series.

Simply by consulting mintage figures one could probably get a fairly good idea as to whether a coin is valuable. There is a confounding variable, however. The surviving number of some issues is considerably less than the quantity originally minted. This is because of melting, loss, or destruction of some other sort. For instance, the mintage of the 1903O Morgan dollar is quite high at 4.5 million. A fine specimen can retail for $200—10 to 15 times the price of silver dollars of far less mintage. Speculation has it that a large portion of this issue was melted under the Pittman Act of 1918. An exact figure on the number of extant 1903O dollars is, of course, not known. But if price is any indication, the number of coins of this issue that survive must be something well below a half million.

During the time around 1980, when silver soared to as high as $50 an ounce, many of the most recent silver coins were sent to the smelters. There have been any number of attempts by those who were buying large quantities of silver coins at that time to give, on the basis of their own sample, an estimate of how the melt might have gone on a date by date basis. It could well turn out that many coins thought to be very common are not so. It is doubtful that any rarities were created, but the unreliability of the mintage figures is nevertheless intriguing.

CONDITION

If the secrets to real estate value are location, location, and location, then the most overlooked factors in coin value are condition, condition, and condition. How well preserved a coin is, how close to its original mint state, how well it was struck, all these greatly affect the value of a coin. For example, a 1921S Walking Liberty half dollar can easily be purchased for $22-$30 in good to very good condition. In mint state 65 (MS-65) you may well have to pay $25,000 for it. So few have survived in such pristine condition that a truly superb specimen can command such a large sum.

To complicate matters, it is difficult, if not impossible for the novice collector to tell the difference between a "super coin" such as the one described above and an MS-60 specimen (the lowest uncirculated grade) which sells for something on the order of $8,000.

Grading differences are found among circulated coins also, although here the price differences are moderate. This entire discussion is meant to drive home the point about how critical it is for the collector to gain experience in learning how to grade coins. This volume can only serve as an introduction to this art/science. Before you purchase or sell your first coin, you should obtain a good book on grading, preferably one with extensive drawings or photos.

The next step is to seek out someone who is knowledgeable about coins, preferably someone who does not desire to buy your coins or sell any to you. A coin club is usually a good place to find such a person. Ask to be shown a coin of the same series in each of the grades that are listed below. Nothing can take the place of this hands-on experience. The point here is to determine what passes for extremely fine condition when a disinterested party grades a coin *before* you realize the coin you bought actually grades far less. Especially at first, my advice would be to go very slowly, ask a lot of questions, compare the judgments of several people, and then take the plunge with low-priced coins where a mistake will not mean a severe monetary loss.

Grading is a very controversial area. Legitimate differences about how well preserved or worn a coin is can occur. And grading standards have shifted over the years even within the most prestigious grading bodies. The American Numismatic Association Certification Service is far stricter now than it was just a few years ago. Why this happened is anybody's guess, but I believe in part it was due to more educated buyers entering what had become a buyer's market. The tendency is always there to push the coins one has for sale a grade or two higher. After all, everyone wants to realize the best price they can get. Likewise, when buying, it is not uncommon to talk the coin down. These are some of the things that we come to expect in many of life's transactions. However, once these tendencies are recognized, your strategy should be not to buy or sell unless you and the other person can pretty much agree on the coin's grade. And this means you must do some homework. You must seek to close the advantage in grading knowledge that the other party in the transaction may have.

What follows are generic descriptions of the condition of U.S. coins. Each coin series or type has certain peculiarities regarding high points, etc., by which wear can be detected and calculated.

Fair/Poor (FA)—Most of the design and date of the coin will be obliterated by extreme wear.

25

About Good (AG)—Rims will be worn into the field of the coin. The date and the design will be partly worn away.

Good (G)—Rims are fully distinct from the field. All of the large design features and dates are intact.

Very Good (VG)—Rims, date and large design features are strong.

Fine (F)—Medium-sized design features specific to the design are clear and distinct. All letters in "Liberty" show on appropriate coins.

Very Fine (VF)—Slight wear apparent on the highest features. All lettering is sharp.

Extremely Fine (XF)—Large and medium design features are sharp. Some mint luster remains.

Almost Uncirculated (AU)—All original design features are sharp. Only slight wear or light rubbing is visible on the highest features. Mint luster is almost completely intact.

Uncirculated (UNC) or (MS60)—No wear or rubbing can be found on the most prominent design features. Luster is intact, although there may be many small marks and scratches evident in the field of the coin.
Choice Uncirculated (CU) or (MS63).

Gem Uncirculated (GU) or (MS65)—A well struck uncirculated coin. Bag marks and other abrasions are minimal. Full mint luster has been retained.

Proof (PR)—A description often included in the grading of coins. However, this description better refers to a special striking process in which care has been taken to bring about an especially well-struck coin, not permitted to come into contact with other coins, and consequently free of all marks and abrasions. Such a coin, of course, can have been mishandled at the mint or afterward (usually referred to as "impaired.") Some have even been known to circulate. Consequently, there can be different grades of proof coins.

The following photos show the Walking Liberty half dollar in each of the grades from about good to uncirculated.

About Good

26

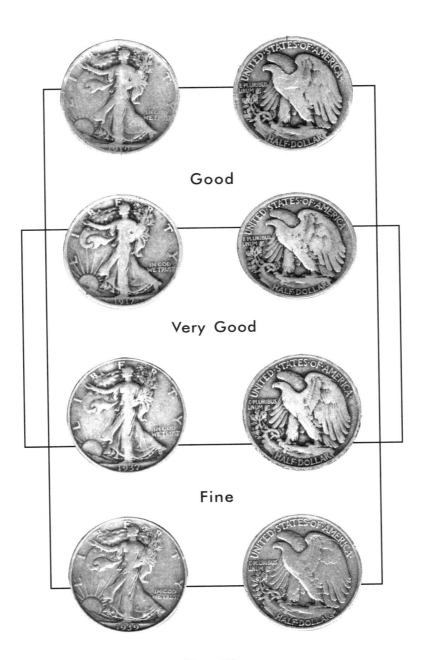

Good

Very Good

Fine

Very Fine

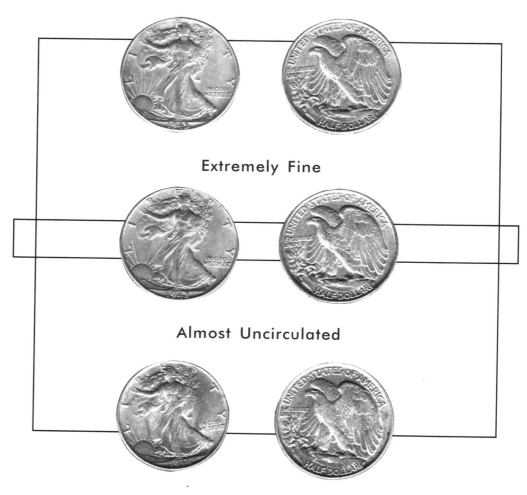

Extremely Fine

Almost Uncirculated

Uncirculated

When assessing the condition of a coin there are other important aspects beyond the wear that the coin may have undergone. Below is a handy check list. Listed first are things that detract from a coin's appearance and value.

Cleaned—It is almost never the case that the normal cleaning agents for copper, nickel, silver or gold can be used on coins. If a coin looks cleaned its worth is less.

Copper cleaner, for instance, gives copper coins a shiny appearance, but since it is an abrasive, the coin's surface suffers greatly. A silver coin, when dipped in silver cleaners, takes on an unnatural appearance that no experienced collector would mistake for luster. Once a coin is pitted or dark there is not much that can be done about it. Cleaning will only make things worse. Most coins must be dropped a grade or two if cleaning has taken place. It is almost always a good idea to avoid purchasing such coins. Wait for one with no problems to come along. In the long run, it will be much easier to sell.

Scratches, rim nicks, abrasions, dents—All seriously affect a coin's value.

Weak strike—When a great many coins are struck from the same die, the clarity of the impression gradually lessens. Even an uncirculated coin may lack certain high relief features because of this. In extreme cases large elements of the design may be very unclear.

Spots, discolorations, carbon spots—Copper coins especially suffer from exposure to the elements. Corrosion and pitting must be looked for on early copper coins. And, strange as it seems, even very recent coins can be affected. Proof sets, sealed in their original government packaging sometimes develop white spots on the silver coins and carbon spots on the cent.

Holes—When coins have been used as jewelry often a hole has been drilled in them so that they can be worn on a chain. To disguise this the hole may be filled. However, in every case, the value of the coin is greatly affected.

The absence of all of the previously listed defects combined with some or all of the following features listed usually enhance a coin's value.

Strong strike—Early strikes from a die show more of the detail of the design. Coins with evidence of a full strike are much sought after and command considerable premiums. Full steps on the reverse of the Jefferson nickel, a full split band on the reverse of the Mercury dime, a full head on the obverse of the Standing Liberty quarter dollar, full bell lines on the reverse of the Franklin half dollar are all evidence of strong strikes.

29

Toning—A very small number of mostly uncirculated coins react to the elements such that the surface of the coin takes on a mellow, even quality that at times can even be iridescent. Where the toning is uneven the eye appeal and, thereby, value of the coin is lessened.

POPULARITY

In 1960, when I first began to collect coins, Lincoln pennies were the rage. Everyone, it seemed, wanted to fill the penny boards that provided a hole for each date and mint mark. Since then not only has the lowly Lincoln fallen from favor, but date collecting itself has given way to other styles of collecting. Today silver dollars, gold, and type coins are quite popular. Silver dollars never seem to lose favor with the collecting public. Especially in the uncirculated grades, a silver dollar will often sell for much more than a coin from another series that is of a comparable grade and mintage. For example, one can only imagine how much an 1871 silver three-cent piece would command if the series were as popular as Morgan dollars. The mintage of this coin was only 4,360 and yet it retails for around $750 in the lowest uncirculated grade. Hardly anyone collects this series by date and so the demand for a coin of any particular year is very low. Typically, a collector would want such a coin only as an instance of the type it represents.

Fads come and go in coin collecting as in everything else. Sometimes it pays to stay off the beaten path and simply collect what interests you. Who knows, maybe popularity will eventually coincide with your interests and you will be on the ground floor price-wise.

METAL CONTENT

Every U.S. silver and gold coin has what can be called a "floor" value or "junk" value based on its metal content. Presumably, a coin cannot be worth less than this unless part of it is missing or the coin is so worn that its metal content (by weight or fineness) is not clear. Or, as we shall see directly, the transaction involving it is so inconsequential as not to be worth the time of the buyer.

On the other hand, many silver coins have no significant value <u>over</u> the silver content. Consequently, the junk value and the price at which one would realistically expect to sell that same coin to a dealer (its numismatic value) are the same.

Let us take some examples which will permit us to elaborate on the chart that follows.

 **Case #1**

We find a badly worn 1934P Walking Liberty half dollar. It is discolored and has some small dents in the rim. In this condition common silver coins have no numismatic value. However, if the spot price of silver for today is $5.00/oz., we can calculate the silver value of the half dollar by multiplying the weight of the coin, 192.9 grains (about .4 oz. since there are 480 grains per ounce) times the fineness (the metal content of the coin is 90% silver) times the going price of silver.

$$.402 \text{ oz.} \times .90 \times \$5 = \$1.80$$

So that ugly half dollar is worth roughly 3.5 times its face value. Why roughly? Well, we should not lose sight of the fact that this is only one coin. Could we fault a dealer who offered us only $1.50 or even $1.25 for the coin? I think not. After all, we are still talking about less than a $1 profit for the dealer. Is such a transaction really worth his time? Should we have $100 face of comparable silver coins, it becomes more realistic to expect something very close to $360—the value of the silver alone in such coins.

Actually, in bag ($1,000 face) quantities, silver coins at times carry a small premium over the silver content, although this has not been true for the last several years. The premium, when there is one, probably derives from the ease with which the bags can be traded, the magic of owning silver pieces that were officially minted and actually circulated, or some such thing. However, there are times when this premium has disappeared and, in fact, as strange as it may sound, there are times when it is very difficult to obtain the full silver-content price for silver coins. Let me explain. The price for silver coin bags might be called somewhat "inelastic" especially when the price of silver rises or falls dramatically. During the phenomenal run-up of the price of silver in 1980, when it peaked at around $50/oz., dealers were quite unwilling to pay much more than 20 to 25 times face. (If we use our chart we can see that

31

even at $40/oz. silver coins should have commanded something like 28 times face—about $14 for a half dollar!)

Dealers claimed they were having difficulty receiving payments on a timely basis from smelters. And, when you think about it, this makes sense. At the time everybody was trying to have their coins melted into bars or other fabricated products, the smelters became backlogged and were unwilling to take the risk that prices would remain high. Dealers likewise began to lay off some of the risk through the lower prices they were willing to pay.

Quick price rises (and in some cases declines) are not necessarily going to be reflected immediately in the coin bag quotes you will receive. When the volatility ends, the bag price once again comes into line. A dealer, especially a small one, is naturally going to minimize his exposure to risk. If one wants better elasticity in price, then one might better hold silver bars, or silver stocks.

One easy way to keep abreast of "junk" silver coin bag prices is to consult *The Wall Street Journal*. On the commodities page, at the bottom of the column titled "Cash Prices," can be found a listing for "Coins, wholesale, $1,000 face value." Most large dealers would normally be willing to sell at this price and buy at from $200 to $300 less. Bag prices quoted in coin newspaper and magazine dealer ads will typically be several weeks or more out of date. The price in any actual transaction will almost always have to be negotiated by phone or in person that very day. Prices change hourly. So if you have an investment in this area, it is of paramount importance to find some way to keep current on prices.

Also, trading in smaller than bag quantities will mean a wider buy/sell price spread. Increasingly, dealers have sought to make distinctions in types of "junk" silver coins. As you might imagine, a bag of very worn silver coins will contain less silver than a bag containing coins that have seen little circulation. A spot check might be necessary to uncover this. Recently, half dollars, and coins from the earlier series (Mercury dimes and Walking Liberty halves) have become more desirable and command a slight additional premium of about $100 to $300 per bag. Common uncirculated silver coins are traded at a premium of from 5-20% over regular bag prices.

Case #2

Your aunt has given you a 1921 silver dollar. The date is the year of his birth and he had it until he passed away. You don't wish to sell the coin but you do want to know its value so as to make a decision concerning how best to care for it.

The first thing you must do is correctly identify the piece. There were two types of silver dollars issued in 1921. The Peace type, in almost any condition has a numismatic value beyond its silver content. More likely, however, the dollar is of the Morgan type. In this case, unless the coin is in one of the highest grades, its value will be determined largely by the going price of silver. Dollars, because of their extreme popularity, have carried a significant premium above silver content making their price even more inelastic than other silver coins. Dollar bags, for which the 1921 Morgan is a staple, are quoted on the basis of 1,000 piece lots. With silver at $5/oz., bags trade in the $7,000-$7,300 area. The silver-content value for the bag would be something on the order of $3,750—making dollars a somewhat unsuitable way to invest in silver.

As you can see, your aunt coin demands no special precautions be taken for its care. You could expect to receive something around $5-$6 for it from a dealer, although I am sure your aunt would like you to keep the coin to remember him by. In fact, _most_ people have trouble understanding how a piece they have prized for a lifetime commands such a paltry sum. You could easily buy one like it for around $8, however.

Case #3

A small coin accumulation, assembled by your grandmother has been given to you. Included are three rolls of Kennedy half dollars. They do not look to be silver coins so you decide to spend them. But wait! Even though other denominations ceased being regularly issued in silver after 1964, half dollars were minted for general circulation with a 40% silver content from 1965-70. This part of your inheritance can be calculated as follows:

Weight		Silver Content		Spot Price		Value
.37 oz.	x	.40 fine	x	$5/oz.	=	$.74

Your rolls ($10 face each) are worth about $14.80 each. Putting them in with your pocket change would certainly have been foolish.

 **Case #4**

One other coin is often traded on the basis of its "junk" silver value. From 1942-45, due to a projected wartime shortage of nickel, the composition of the five-cent piece was changed to include 35% silver. Circulated pieces are identifiable by their darker gray color and the change in the placement and size of the mint mark. Both types of five-cent pieces were minted in 1942. So not every coin with that date will have silver value. In high grades these "silver nickels" have a numismatic value beyond the silver value. The value of   low-grade coins can be computed:

Weight		Silver Content		Spot Price		Value
.16 oz.	x	.35 fine	x	$5/oz.	=	$.28

Quantities of less than a roll are of little interest to a dealer. With silver at $5/oz. expect to sell at about $8/roll and buy $11+/roll.

 **Case #5**

While remodeling your house, you find a $5 Indian gold piece behind the woodwork. The rim has a number of large dents and the coin has been defaced from what appear to be a number of deep scratches. Should you be tickled with your find?

Well, gold coins, too, have a "junk" value. However, unlike silver coins, very few gold coins fall into this category. A gold coin must either be damaged or very severely worn not to have some numismatic value. Even then, such coins are good candidates for use in jewelry. The purchaser of a ring or pendant is usually not as concerned about a coin's condition since often only one side will show or the rim can be obscured by the setting.

Consequently, the floor price, calculated below and on our chart, represents the absolute lowest price an identifiable, complete $5 gold coin can be worth. Your baseboard find is a good one!

Weight		**Gold Content**		**Spot Price**	**Value**
.269 oz.	x	.90 fine	x	$375/oz. =	$90.78

All the above calculations have been based on:

480 grains/troy oz.   1 gram=.0322 troy oz.
31.104 grams/troy oz.   1 gram=15.4342 grains

35

Bullion Value of Silver Coins
(Per $1.00 Face Value)

Spot Price	Low Grade/ Circulated 10c, 25c, 50c	40% Silver 50c	Low Grade/ Circulated Silver War 5c	Low Grade/ Damaged Silver $1.00
$ 4.00	$2.90	$1.18	$4.40	$3.09
$ 5.00	3.60	1.48	5.60	3.87
$ 6.00	4.40	1.78	6.80	4.64
$ 7.00	5.10	2.08	8.00	5.42
$10.00	7.20	2.96	11.20	7.73
$15.00	10.90	4.46	17.00	11.60
$20.00	14.40	5.92	22.40	15.48
$30.00	21.60	8.88	33.60	23.19
$50.00	36.00	14.80	56.00	38.69

Bag Quantities (Wholesale price includes usual premium)

Spot Price	Low Grade/ Circulated 10c, 25c, 50c ($1000 Face)	40% Silver 50c ($1000 Face)	Low Grade/ Circulated Silver War 5c ($1000 Face)	Low Grade/ Damaged Silver $1.00 ($1000 Face)
$4.00	$3000-$3300	$1200-$1300	$3200-$3400	$5300-$5500
$5.00	3700-4000	1500-1600	3800-4200	5400-57500
$6.00	4500-4800	1800-2000	4700- 6000	6500-8000
$8.00	6000-6300	2400-2600	6300-6800	6700-8000
$9.00	6800-7100	2700-2900	7000-7400	8000-8200
$10.00	7500-7800	3000-3200	7700-8100	8300-8500
$11.00	8200-8500	3300-3500	8400-8800	9000-9200
$12.00	8900-9200	3600-3800	9100-9500	10000-11000
$13.00	9700-10000	3900-4100	9900-10300	11000-11500
$14.00	10400-10700	4200-4400	10600-11000	11500-12000
$15.00	11200-11500	4500-4700	11400-11800	12000-12500

Bullion Value of Gold Coins
(Assumes the coin is damaged or otherwise uncollectable)

Denomination

Spot Price	$1.00	$2.50	$5.00	$10.00	$20.00
$250.00	$12.10	$30.25	$60.50	$121.00	$242.00
$300.00	14.50	36.25	72.50	145.00	290.00
$350.00	17.00	42.50	85.00	170.00	339.00
$400.00	19.35	48.00	96.25	193.50	387.00
$500.00	24.20	60.50	121.00	242.00	484.00
$600.00	29.00	72.50	145.00	290.00	580.00
$900.00	43.40	108.50	217.00	434.00	868.00

Value as a Function of Time and Knowledge

Some, I suppose, would argue that in many cases a coin's value is a function of work (time) and knowledge. There is some truth to this—a truth that is often lost on a novice buyer or seller. Let me explain.

With regard to many inexpensive coins, the cost of the time and work involved in identifying, pricing, packaging, marketing, etc., often exceed any intrinsic worth that the coin may have. When one purchases a coin for $2 it may well be that the entire value of the coin can be written off to the costs of selling it. The real value of the coin consequently is derived from getting it to a point where a sale can be made. To speak in terms of resale then is to miss the point. How much is a roll of AU 1950D cents worth beyond its face value? Would it be out of the question for a dealer to charge 25 cents each for such a coin? And what portion of that price might one expect to recover upon a resale? Twenty-five cents does not represent the value of the coin in any sense other than the cost of selling it. One should expect to recover almost nothing with any attempt at resale.

Secondly, and somewhat more controversial, is the part that knowledge should play in the determination of worth. If I were to spend considerable time researching the relative scarcity of various types of early Large cents, am I obligated to make that knowledge available to all who request an offer for their collection? Is my knowledge worth something? And is the value of that scarce variety I discover a product of my recognizing it as such?

These questions may well border on the area of business ethics; and therefore may well be outside the scope of this volume. But that is not to say that they will have no bearing on an actual transaction. Rather, I think, the average dealer expects to be compensated for his or her knowledge and experience. *How* that is to be done often remains fairly unclear to the party in the transaction who lacks the knowledge.

Chapter 3

U.S. MINOR COINAGE

This chapter attempts to assess the value of U.S. coins composed of base metals (copper and nickel), as opposed to precious metals. Recent clad coinage is discussed in Chapter 4, along with the silver coinage these clad coins were meant to replace.

Values of Minor Coins

Half Cents Minted 1793/1857

Liberty Cap Type   Liberty Cap Type
                          (Flowing Hair)

Liberty Cap 1793-1797

	G	VG	F	VF	XF	AU	MS60
1793 Head Left	1800.00	2820.00	4020.00	6000.00	10560.00	17520.00	28800.00
1794 Head Right	330.00	420.00	710.00	1320.00	2940.00	5700.00	12000.00
1795 Lettered Edge, with Pole	330.00	420.00	710.00	1260.00	2940.00	5160.00	7200.00
1795 Lettered Edge, Punct. Date	330.00	440.00	720.00	1260.00	3000.00	6000.00	8640.00
1795 Plain Edge, Punct. Date	330.00	420.00	690.00	1200.00	2640.00	4560.00	7200.00
1795 Plain Edge, No Pole	330.00	420.00	710.00	1230.00	2760.00	6000.00	10200.00
1796 With Pole	7380.00	9840.00	12000.00	16200.00	24000.00	33000.00	54000.00
1796 No Pole	13800.00	22200.00	37200.00	51000.00	66000.00	93600.00	150000.00
1797 Lettered Edge	900.00	1680.00	3360.00	7200.00	21000.00	36000.00	48000.00
1797 Plain Edge	340.00	450.00	780.00	1440.00	2820.00	4620.00	8160.00
1797 Gripped Edge	15600.00	38400.00	48000.00	60000.00	72000.00	90000.00	
1797 1 Above 1, Plain Edge	330.00	420.00	690.00	1200.00	2880.00	4680.00	8400.00

Draped Bust Type

Draped Bust 1800-1808

	G	VG	F	VF	XF	AU	MS60
1800	45.00	59.00	84.00	168.00	348.00	540.00	1320.00
1802 2/0 Reverse of 1800	12600.00	20400.00	30000.00	42000.00	72000.00	96000.00	
1802 2/0 2nd Reverse	480.00	948.00	2400.00	5700.00	15000.00	27600.00	
1803	46.00	59.00	90.00	210.00	600.00	990.00	2220.00
1804 Plain 4- with Stems	45.00	72.00	120.00	222.00	558.00	1380.00	2520.00
1804 Plain 4-Stemless	44.00	58.00	76.00	114.00	96.00	396.00	900.00
1804 Crosslet 4 w/Stems	44.00	58.00	76.00	108.00	90.00	390.00	840.00
1804 Crosslet 4 - Stemless	44.00	58.00	76.00	108.00	96.00	414.00	840.00
1804 Spiked Chin	44.00	58.00	78.00	114.00	96.00	402.00	990.00
1805 Medium 5- Stemless	44.00	58.00	78.00	114.00	96.00	390.00	840.00
1805 Small 5 - w/Stems	468.00	990.00	1980.00	3900.00	7200.00	12000.00	
1805 Large 5 - w/Stems	44.00	58.00	76.00	114.00	96.00	390.00	840.00
1806 Small 6 - w/Stems	42.00	300.00	498.00	780.00	720.00	4200.00	6960.00
1806 Small 6 - Stemless	44.00	58.00	76.00	108.00	210.00	390.00	810.00
1806 Large 6 - w/Stems	44.00	58.00	78.00	114.00	210.00	390.00	810.00
1807	44.00	58.00	78.00	114.00	378.00	600.00	1230.00
1808 8 over 7	96.00	192.00	420.00	930.00	2820.00	6960.00	10200.00
1808 Normal Date	44.00	58.00	78.00	114.00	264.00	618.00	1260.00

Classic Head Type

Classic Head 1809-1829

	G	VG	F	VF	XF	AU	MS60
1809 Normal Date	32.00	39.00	52.00	66.00	90.00	180.00	348.00
1809 9 over 6	34.00	72.00	78.00	90.00	72.00	540.00	660.00
1809 Circle inside 0	32.00	39.00	54.00	96.00	240.00	378.00	660.00
1810	32.00	50.00	90.00	156.00	360.00	720.00	1140.00
1811	126.00	204.00	378.00	1170.00	3300.00	4500.00	6000.00
1825	30.00	39.00	52.00	66.00	120.00	312.00	600.00
1826	30.00	39.00	52.00	66.00	96.00	168.00	348.00
1828 13 Stars	30.00	39.00	52.00	60.00	72.00	132.00	186.00
1828 12 Stars	30.00	39.00	52.00	72.00	36.00	258.00	840.00

Classic Head 1809-1829

1829	30.00	39.00	52.00	63.00	102.00	168.00	240.00

Classic Head 1831-1836

	G	VG	F	VF	XF	AU	MS60
1831	3600.00	3900.00	4200.00	4800.00	6600.00	9600.00	11400.00
1832	30.00	38.00	480.00	60.00	72.00	132.00	198.00
1833	30.00	38.00	480.00	60.00	72.00	126.00	186.00
1834	30.00	38.00	480.00	60.00	72.00	126.00	198.00
1835	30.00	38.00	480.00	60.00	72.00	126.00	186.00
1836 Proof Only						Proof 63	3600.00

Braided Hair Type

Braided Hair 1840-1857

	G	VG	F	VF	XF	AU	MS60
1840 Proof Only							
1841 Proof Only							
1842 Proof Only			Original and Restrikes				
1843 Proof Only			for 1840-1849 Issues				
1844 Proof Only			Proof 63 $3,500				
1845 Proof Only							
1846 Proof Only							
1847 Proof Only							
1848 Proof Only							
1849 Sm Date, Proof Only							
1849 Large Date	38.00	42.00	50.00	66.00	84.00	138.00	240.00
1850	32.00	40.00	50.00	66.00	102.00	144.00	300.00
1851	28.00	38.00	48.00	60.00	72.00	118.00	162.00
1852 Proof Only (Restrike)						Proof 63	3500.00
1853	28.00	38.00	50.00	60.00	72.00	118.00	162.00
1854	28.00	38.00	48.00	54.00	60.00	72.00	120.00
1855	28.00	38.00	48.00	54.00	60.00	72.00	120.00
1856	28.00	39.00	48.00	54.00	63.00	78.00	132.00
1857	44.00	48.00	60.00	66.00	84.00	108.00	162.00

Cents Minted 1793-Date
Large Cents Minted 1793/1857

Flowing Hair Type
(Chain Reverse)

Chain Type

	G	VG	F	VF	XF	AU	MS60
1793 "AMERL" In Legend	4800.00	6600.00	10560.00	16800.00	33000.00	54000.00	90000.00
1793 "AMERICA"	4440.00	6360.00	8400.00	15000.00	26400.00	45000.00	78000.00
1793 Periods After "LIBERTY"	4680.00	6480.00	10200.00	16200.00	31200.00	49200.00	84000.00

42

Flowing Hair Type
(Wreath Reverse)

Flowing Hair 1793

Wreath Type

	G	VG	F	VF	XF	AU	MS60
1793 Vine/Bars Edge	1320.00	1800.00	3300.00	4980.00	20400.00	8400.00	12600.00
1793 Lettered Edge	1380.00	1920.00	3420.00	5100.00	21000.00	8640.00	12960.00
1793 Strawberry Leaf	90000.00	120000.00	168000.00				

Liberty Cap Type

Liberty Cap 1793-1796

	G	VG	F	VF	XF	AU	MS60
1793 Liberty Cap Type	1760.00	4400.00	6600.00	15400.00	32450.00	66000.00	
1794 Head of 1793	860.00	1320.00	1870.00	5170.00	9240.00	14850.00	
1794 Head of 1794	270.00	360.00	520.00	1090.00	2150.00	3630.00	5670.00
1794 Head of 1795	270.00	350.00	510.00	1090.00	2150.00	3630.00	5500.00
1794 Starred Reverse	7150.00	9900.00	20900.00	30800.00	60500.00	93500.00	
1795 Lettered Edge	270.00	360.00	520.00	1090.00	2420.00	4130.00	6330.00
1795 Plain Edge	270.00	350.00	510.00	1080.00	2090.00	3580.00	3960.00
1795 Reeded Edge	115500.00	165000.00	247500.00				
1795 Jefferson Head	3850.00	8250.00	14300.00	26400.00	66000.00		
1796	270.00	360.00	690.00	1320.00	2970.00	7260.00	20350.00

43

Draped Bust Type

Draped Bust 1796-1807

	G	VG	F	VF	XF	AU	MS60
1796 Reverse of 1794	100.00	210.00	490.00	1040.00	2460.00	3480.00	
1796 Reverse of 1796	100.00	250.00	480.00	1270.00	2640.00	3600.00	
1796 Reverse of 1797	100.00	180.00	380.00	840.00	1980.00	2880.00	4680.00
1796 "LIHERTY" Error	180.00	440.00	670.00	1840.00	5640.00	11400.00	
1797 Gripped Edge - '96 Rev	100.00	180.00	300.00	510.00	1920.00	3300.00	
1797 Plain Edge -'96 Rev	110.00	180.00	290.00	640.00	2160.00	3360.00	
1797 '97 Rev.- Stems	100.00	170.00	250.00	340.00	990.00	2040.00	3060.00
1797 '97 Rev. - Stemless	110.00	200.00	340.00	750.00	2760.00	3900.00	
1798 8 over 7	110.00	200.00	310.00	1040.00	3600.00	4740.00	
1798 Reverse of 1796	90.00	160.00	270.00	780.00	3000.00	4200.00	
1798 1st Hair Style	60.00	80.00	140.00	280.00	900.00	1590.00	2640.00
1798 2nd Hair Style	70.00	80.00	180.00	320.00	1320.00	3000.00	4800.00

	G	VG	F	VF	XF	AU	MS60
1799 9 over 8	1330.00	2420.00	5180.00	18400.00	48000.00	204000.00	
1799	1210.00	2420.00	4890.00	16100.00	36000.00		
1800 over 1798 - Style 1 Hair	50.00	70.00	180.00	610.00	2400.00	4200.00	
1800 80 over 79 - Style 2 Hair	60.00	100.00	160.00	400.00	1440.00	2640.00	
1800 Normal Date		50.00	90.00	140.00	340.00	1200.00	2400.00
1801 Normal Reverse	50.00	80.00	130.00	230.00	870.00	1740.00	2640.00
1801 3 Errors	100.00	150.00	460.00	1010.00	3900.00	7320.00	
1801 Fraction 1/000	50.00	60.00	140.00	320.00	1170.00	1980.00	3000.00
1801 1/100 over 1/000	60.00	60.00	150.00	440.00	1200.00	2400.00	3960.00
1802 Normal Reverse	50.00	60.00	140.00	220.00	738.00	1140.00	2400.00
1802 Fraction: 1/000	50.00	70.00	150.00	350.00	1260.00	2280.00	3840.00
1802 Stemless	40.00	60.00	120.00	220.00	750.00	1350.00	2100.00
1803 Small Date, Small Fraction	50.00	60.00	130.00	220.00	732.00	1110.00	2220.00
1803 Small Date, Large Fraction	40.00	60.00	130.00	220.00	750.00	1110.00	2100.00
1803 Large Date, Small Fraction	4320.00	6900.00	12600.00	19200.00			
1803 Large Date, Large Fraction	50.00	70.00	210.00	410.00	1560.00	2880.00	
1803 1/100 over 1/000	40.00	60.00	160.00	290.00	900.00	1560.00	2160.00
1803 Stemless Wreath	40.00	60.00	120.00	250.00	780.00	1350.00	2100.00
1804	480.00	920.00	1440.00	2360.00	5400.00	10200.00	42000.00
1804 Restrike of 1860		360.00	390.00	420.00	462.00	528.00	
1805	50.00	60.00	120.00	250.00	738.00	1230.00	2220.00
1806	60.00	70.00	130.00	290.00	1080.00	2220.00	6300.00
1807 Small 7 over 6, Blunt 1	1380.00	2530.00	6040.00	9200.00	21000.00	42000.00	
1807 Large 7 over 6	50.00	70.00	110.00	220.00	720.00	1110.00	1920.00
1807 Small Fraction	40.00	60.00	110.00	220.00	720.00	1110.00	1920.00
1807 Large Fraction	40.00	60.00	110.00	220.00	720.00	1110.00	2040.00
1807 "Comet" Variety	40.00	60.00	140.00	440.00	1770.00	3780.00	6300.00

44

Classic Head Type

Classic Head 1808-1814

	G	VG	F	VF	XF	AU	MS60
1808	44.00	115.00	190.00	440.00	980.00	2070.00	2990.00
1809	87.00	179.00	290.00	870.00	1040.00	3800.00	6330.00
1810 10 over 09	35.00	75.00	190.00	490.00	980.00	2020.00	3740.00
1810 Normal Date	43.00	81.00	190.00	490.00	950.00	1380.00	3170.00
1811 1 over 0	64.00	110.00	340.00	950.00	3280.00	7480.00	11500.00
1811 Normal Date	64.00	110.00	270.00	780.00	1210.00	2250.00	4140.00
1812	41.00	69.00	190.00	440.00	840.00	1730.00	2420.00
1813	35.00	81.00	190.00	490.00	950.00	1930.00	3220.00
1814 Plain 4	40.00	72.00	200.00	410.00	840.00	1900.00	2990.00
1814 Crosslet 4	35.00	69.00	190.00	440.00	900.00	1330.00	2760.00

Coronet Type
(Matron Head, 1816-1839)

Coronet Head 1816-1839

	G	VG	F	VF	XF	AU	MS60
1816	13.00	20.00	27.00	69.00	144.00	259.00	345.00
1817 13 stars	14.00	17.00	21.00	58.00	104.00	196.00	248.00
1817 15 stars	15.00	18.00	22.00	75.00	432.00	777.00	1380.00
1818	13.00	17.00	25.00	49.00	104.00	179.00	242.00
1819 9 over 8	13.00	18.00	27.00	58.00	242.00	357.00	506.00
1819	13.00	17.00	21.00	52.00	98.00	161.00	259.00
1820 20 over 19	15.00	18.00	21.00	64.00	271.00	432.00	633.00
1820	14.00	17.00	21.00	60.00	101.00	184.00	259.00
1821	22.00	41.00	87.00	328.00	748.00	2358.00	5750.00
1822	13.00	18.00	32.00	78.00	156.00	426.00	690.00
1823 3 over 2	49.00	92.00	225.00	420.00	1668.00	4025.00	
1823	58.00	110.00	259.00	489.00	2157.00	6210.00	
1824 4 over 2	16.00	21.00	46.00	253.00	870.00	1560.00	3480.00
1824	14.00	18.00	23.00	150.00	330.00	480.00	900.00
1825	14.00	19.00	32.00	83.00	270.00	504.00	918.00
1826 6 over 5	16.00	23.00	58.00	156.00	720.00	1320.00	1920.00
1826	13.00	18.00	23.00	69.00	156.00	330.00	720.00
1827	13.00	18.00	28.00	87.00	120.00	228.00	360.00
1828	13.00	18.00	23.00	69.00	150.00	300.00	432.00
1829	13.00	18.00	21.00	87.00	126.00	240.00	396.00
1830	13.00	17.00	22.00	58.00	114.00	222.00	348.00
1831	13.00	17.00	21.00	50.00	90.00	162.00	240.00
1832	13.00	17.00	21.00	53.00	108.00	198.00	360.00
1833	13.00	17.00	21.00	49.00	102.00	174.00	270.00
1834 Lg 8 & Strs, Med Let	64.00	104.00	133.00	219.00	540.00	870.00	
1834	15.00	20.00	23.00	58.00	120.00	192.00	270.00
1835	13.00	17.00	21.00	53.00	78.00	156.00	252.00
1836	13.00	17.00	21.00	43.00	90.00	162.00	252.00
1837	13.00	17.00	21.00	43.00	78.00	156.00	204.00
1838	13.00	17.00	21.00	43.00	78.00	156.00	204.00
1839	13.00	17.00	22.00	46.00	90.00	162.00	270.00

Mature Head)
(1839-1857)

Braided Hair 1839-1857

	G	VG	F	VF	XF	AU	MS60
1839 Braided Hair	13.00	17.00	18.00	29.00	49.00	180.00	258.00
1840	13.00	17.00	18.00	26.00	46.00	156.00	228.00
1841	13.00	17.00	18.00	26.00	46.00	168.00	240.00
1842	13.00	17.00	18.00	26.00	44.00	126.00	198.00
1843	13.00	17.00	18.00	26.00	44.00	126.00	198.00
1844	13.00	17.00	18.00	23.00	46.00	138.00	198.00
1844 over 81	14.00	19.00	22.00	52.00	87.00	222.00	600.00
1845	13.00	17.00	18.00	21.00	41.00	120.00	153.60
1846	13.00	17.00	18.00	21.00	41.00	120.00	153.60
1847	13.00	17.00	18.00	21.00	41.00	120.00	153.60
1847 7 over Small 7	14.00	18.00	23.00	35.00	87.00	126.00	228.00
1848	13.00	17.00	20.00	22.00	41.00	120.00	153.60
1849	13.00	17.00	20.00	22.00	44.00	126.00	180.00
1850	13.00	17.00	20.00	22.00	41.00	114.00	150.00
1851	13.00	17.00	20.00	22.00	41.00	114.00	150.00
1851 over 81	13.00	18.00	26.00	37.00	104.00	162.00	420.00
1852	13.00	17.00	20.00	22.00	41.00	114.00	150.00
1853	13.00	17.00	20.00	22.00	41.00	114.00	150.00
1854	13.00	17.00	20.00	22.00	41.00	114.00	150.00
1855	13.00	17.00	18.00	21.00	43.00	120.00	156.00
1855 "Knob on Ear"	13.00	17.00	18.00	35.00	58.00	168.00	282.00
1856	13.00	17.00	18.00	21.00	41.00	114.00	150.00
1857	29.00	46.00	52.00	64.00	75.00	156.00	240.00

Flying Eagle Type
Minted 1856-58

Flying Eagle Cent

	G	VG	F	VF	XF	AU	MS60
1856	5290.00	6095.00	6555.00	7245.00	7475.00	8395.00	8740.00
1857	18.00	20.00	27.00	36.00	110.00	138.00	248.00
1858	18.00	20.00	27.00	36.00	110.00	138.00	248.00

46

Indian Head Type
Minted 1859-1909

Indian Head Cent

	G	VG	F	VF	XF	AU	MS60
1859	11.00	13.00	15.00	41.00	98.00	173.00	207.00
1860	7.00	9.00	10.00	14.00	46.00	81.00	150.00
1861	18.00	26.00	33.00	41.00	104.00	161.00	184.00
1862	6.00	7.00	9.00	12.00	29.00	58.00	92.00
1863	7.00	10.00	11.00	12.00	23.00	46.00	69.00
1864	15.00	20.00	29.00	35.00	58.00	75.00	156.00
1864 Bronze	7.00	11.00	17.00	29.00	52.00	60.00	89.00
1864 L Variety			98.00	133.00	213.00	242.00	345.00
1865	6.00	10.00	17.00	21.00	33.00	46.00	87.00
1866	35.00	46.00	63.00	87.00	167.00	230.00	259.00
1867	37.00	51.00	66.00	104.00	167.00	230.00	271.00
1868	37.00	41.00	51.00	81.00	150.00	184.00	259.00
1869	52.00	81.00	184.00	288.00	345.00	414.00	489.00
1870	41.00	69.00	156.00	230.00	288.00	345.00	489.00
1871	64.00	75.00	213.00	259.00	322.00	437.00	460.00
1872	69.00	87.00	259.00	288.00	345.00	432.00	575.00
1873	19.00	27.00	41.00	48.00	138.00	156.00	184.00
1874	14.00	19.00	29.00	41.00	92.00	127.00	184.00
1875	14.00	26.00	41.00	45.00	87.00	121.00	184.00
1876	26.00	33.00	43.00	58.00	138.00	161.00	202.00
1877	518.00	604.00	863.00	1093.00	1265.00	2070.00	2415.00
1878	27.00	36.00	51.00	75.00	133.00	173.00	202.00
1879	6.00	10.00	13.00	29.00	64.00	69.00	75.00
1880	3.00	6.00	9.00	10.00	23.00	41.00	75.00
1881	3.00	5.00	7.00	10.00	19.00	29.00	46.00
1882	3.00	5.00	7.00	10.00	19.00	29.00	46.00
1883	3.00	5.00	7.00	10.00	19.00	29.00	46.00
1884	3.00	5.00	7.00	10.00	23.00	35.00	67.00
1885	6.00	7.00	14.00	23.00	58.00	69.00	104.00
1886	4.00	6.00	12.00	29.00	104.00	115.00	138.00
1887	2.00	2.00	4.00	6.00	15.00	25.00	51.00
1888	2.00	2.00	4.00	6.00	18.00	25.00	46.00
1889	2.00	2.00	4.00	6.00	12.00	23.00	41.00
1890	2.00	2.00	4.00	6.00	12.00	23.00	41.00
1891	2.00	2.00	4.00	6.00	12.00	23.00	41.00
1892	2.00	2.00	4.00	6.00	12.00	23.00	41.00
1893	2.00	2.00	4.00	6.00	12.00	23.00	35.00
1894	2.00	4.00	7.00	12.00	20.00	35.00	68.00
1895	2.00	2.00	4.00	6.00	12.00	23.00	35.00
1896	2.00	2.00	4.00	6.00	12.00	23.00	35.00
1897	2.00	2.00	4.00	6.00	12.00	23.00	35.00
1898	2.00	2.00	4.00	6.00	12.00	23.00	35.00
1899	2.00	2.00	4.00	6.00	12.00	23.00	35.00
1900	2.00	2.00	2.00	3.00	9.00	19.00	25.00
1901	2.00	2.00	2.00	3.00	9.00	19.00	25.00

47

Indian Cents

	G	VG	F	VF	XF	AU	MS60
1902	2.00	2.00	2.00	3.00	9.00	19.00	25.00
1903	2.00	2.00	2.00	3.00	9.00	19.00	25.00
1904	2.00	2.00	2.00	3.00	9.00	19.00	25.00
1905	2.00	2.00	2.00	3.00	9.00	19.00	25.00
1906	2.00	2.00	2.00	3.00	9.00	19.00	25.00
1907	2.00	2.00	2.00	3.00	9.00	19.00	25.00
1908	2.00	2.00	2.00	3.00	9.00	19.00	25.00
1908S	51.00	53.00	60.00	64.00	104.00	150.00	230.00
1909	2.00	3.00	4.00	5.00	10.00	21.00	35.00
1909S	276.00	317.00	368.00	403.00	460.00	518.00	621.00

Indian Head Type
Minted 1859-1909

Lincoln Cent Type
(Wheat Reverse to 1957)

*The designer's initials (Victor D. Brenner) are found on the bottom inside rim on the reverse in 1909. They were discontinued from 1909-1917 and replaced below Lincoln's shoulder from 1918 to date.

Lincoln Cents

Wheat Reverse

	Good	VG	Fine	VF	XF	AU	MS60
1909	0.90	1.10	1.70	2.20	2.50	8.80	14.30
1909VDB	3.30	3.60	4.20	4.40	5.00	5.50	9.90
1909S	44.00	60.50	74.80	110.00	132.00	181.50	192.50
1909SVDB	440.00	495.00	577.50	627.00	726.00	770.00	902.00
1910	0.30	0.30	0.40	0.60	2.20	5.50	14.30
1910S	6.60	7.70	8.80	11.00	22.00	55.00	66.00
1911	0.30	0.40	0.60	2.20	4.40	6.60	16.50
1911D	4.40	5.50	7.70	12.10	36.30	60.50	88.00
1911S	15.40	18.70	22.00	27.50	41.80	77.00	148.50
1912	1.40	1.50	1.70	4.40	8.80	14.30	27.50
1912D	5.50	5.50	7.70	14.30	41.80	66.00	137.50
1912S	9.90	13.20	15.40	17.60	44.00	71.50	110.00

48

Lincoln Cents
Wheat Reverse

	Good	VG	Fine	VF	XF	AU	MS60
1913	0.70	0.70	1.40	3.30	12.10	15.40	27.50
1913D	2.80	2.80	3.30	6.60	24.20	55.00	88.00
1913S	6.10	6.60	7.70	11.00	30.80	66.00	137.50
1914	0.50	0.70	1.40	3.30	9.90	26.40	44.00
1914D	93.50	126.50	176.00	231.00	495.00	880.00	1155.00
1914S	9.90	11.00	13.20	19.80	44.00	121.00	247.50
1915	1.40	2.20	3.30	9.90	36.30	60.50	82.50
1915D	1.70	2.00	2.20	2.80	11.00	27.50	66.00
1915S	6.60	7.70	8.80	11.00	36.30	66.00	137.50
1916	0.20	0.30	0.50	1.40	3.90	4.40	11.00
1916D	0.40	0.50	1.10	2.20	8.80	13.20	49.50
1916S	1.10	1.30	1.40	2.20	8.80	16.50	60.50
1917	0.20	0.30	0.50	1.70	3.90	4.40	9.90
1917D	0.30	0.40	1.00	2.20	7.70	11.00	55.00
1917S	0.50	0.60	1.00	1.70	5.50	14.30	55.00
1918	0.20	0.30	0.50	1.40	3.90	5.50	9.90
1918D	0.30	0.40	1.10	2.20	6.60	13.20	55.00
1918S	0.50	0.60	0.90	2.20	6.60	15.40	55.00
1919	0.20	0.20	0.30	0.50	1.70	4.40	7.70
1919D	0.40	0.40	0.60	2.20	6.60	11.00	44.00
1919S	0.20	0.30	0.50	0.90	1.70	8.80	27.50
1920	0.20	0.20	0.30	0.50	1.70	4.40	8.80
1920D	0.30	0.40	0.60	2.20	6.60	8.80	49.50
1920S	0.30	0.40	0.40	1.10	3.30	11.00	82.50
1921	0.30	0.40	0.60	1.70	5.50	11.00	38.50
1921S	1.30	0.90	1.40	3.30	11.00	49.50	104.50
1922 No "D" Faulty Die	330.00	440.00	550.00	605.00	1430.00	2970.00	4070.00

*Filled die on the 1922D cent obscured the mint mark on some strikes.

1922D	7.70	6.60	7.70	11.00	18.70	44.00	77.00
1923	0.30	0.30	0.40	1.70	3.30	4.40	11.00
1923S	1.70	2.00	2.50	4.40	19.80	66.00	187.00
1924	0.30	0.30	0.40	1.70	5.50	6.60	19.80
1924D	9.90	11.00	12.10	18.70	49.50	110.00	247.50
1924S	1.00	1.10	1.40	2.20	8.80	33.00	110.00
1925	0.20	0.20	0.30	0.90	2.20	4.40	8.80
1925D	0.40	0.50	0.60	1.10	6.60	12.10	49.50
1925S	0.40	0.40	0.50	1.10	3.30	13.20	60.50
1926	0.20	0.20	0.30	0.90	1.10	3.30	6.60
1926D	0.30	0.40	0.60	1.10	4.40	8.80	33.00
1926S	2.20	3.30	3.90	5.00	11.00	49.50	99.00
1927	0.20	0.20	0.30	0.90	2.20	4.40	6.60
1927D	0.30	0.30	0.40	0.90	3.30	6.60	33.00
1927S	0.60	0.70	1.70	2.80	6.60	16.50	66.00
1928	0.20	0.20	0.30	0.90	2.20	4.40	7.70
1928D	0.30	0.30	0.40	0.70	2.20	6.60	19.80
1928S	0.50	0.60	0.70	1.70	3.30	8.80	44.00
1929	0.20	0.20	0.30	0.70	1.10	3.30	5.50
1929D	0.20	0.20	0.30	0.50	2.00	3.30	14.30
1929S	0.20	0.20	0.30	1.10	1.30	2.20	7.70
1930	0.20	0.20	0.30	0.50	1.40	2.20	3.30
1930D	0.20	0.20	0.30	0.50	1.70	4.40	11.00
1930S	0.20	0.20	0.30	0.60	1.70	3.30	4.40
1931	0.60	0.70	0.80	1.10	2.20	5.50	16.50
1931D	2.80	3.30	3.90	4.40	6.60	24.20	49.50
1931S	38.50	46.20	49.50	52.80	55.00	66.00	77.00
1932	1.10	1.70	2.00	2.20	3.30	8.80	18.70

	Good	VG	Fine	VF	XF	AU	MS60
1933	1.10	1.40	1.70	2.00	3.30	8.80	16.50
1933D	1.70	2.20	2.50	2.80	4.40	11.00	16.50
1934	0.10	0.10	0.20	0.20	0.70	1.10	2.20
1934D	0.10	0.20	0.30	0.30	1.70	5.50	16.50
1935	0.10	0.10	0.20	0.20	0.70	1.10	1.10
1935D	0.10	0.20	0.30	0.30	0.70	3.30	3.30
1935S	0.10	0.20	0.30	0.30	1.70	4.40	7.70
1936	0.10	0.10	0.20	0.20	0.70	1.10	1.10
1936D	0.10	0.20	0.30	0.30	0.70	1.10	1.10
1936S	0.10	0.20	0.30	0.30	0.70	1.10	2.20
1937	0.10	0.10	0.20	0.20	0.70	1.10	0.90
1937D	0.10	0.20	0.30	0.30	0.70	1.10	1.70
1937S	0.10	0.20	0.30	0.30	0.70	1.10	1.70
1938	0.10	0.10	0.20	0.20	0.70	1.10	1.70
1938D	0.10	0.20	0.30	0.30	0.70	1.10	1.70
1938S	0.20	0.30	0.50	0.60	0.70	1.10	1.70
1939	0.10	0.10	0.20	0.20	0.30	0.40	0.60
1939D	0.20	0.30	0.50	0.60	0.70	1.40	2.20
1939S	0.10	0.20	0.30	0.30	0.70	1.10	1.10
1940	0.10	0.10	0.30	0.20	0.30	0.40	0.90
1940D	0.10	0.10	0.20	0.20	0.30	0.40	0.90
1940S	0.10	0.10	0.20	0.20	0.30	0.40	0.90
1941	0.10	0.10	0.20	0.20	0.20	0.30	0.80
1941D	0.10	0.10	0.20	0.20	0.20	0.90	1.70
1941S	0.10	0.10	0.20	0.20	0.20	1.70	2.20
1942	0.10	0.10	0.20	0.20	0.20	0.30	0.50
1942D	0.10	0.10	0.20	0.20	0.20	0.30	0.50
1942S	0.10	0.10	0.20	0.20	0.20	1.10	3.30
1943	0.10	0.10	0.20	0.20	0.20	0.50	0.70
1943D	0.10	0.10	0.20	0.20	0.20	0.60	0.90
1943S	0.10	0.10	0.20	0.20	0.30	0.60	1.10
1944	0.10	0.10	0.20	0.20	0.20	0.20	0.40
1944D	0.10	0.10	0.20	0.20	0.20	0.20	0.40
1944S	0.10	0.10	0.20	0.20	0.20	0.30	0.40
1945	0.10	0.10	0.20	0.20	0.20	0.30	0.40
1945D	0.10	0.10	0.20	0.20	0.20	0.30	0.60
1945S	0.10	0.10	0.20	0.20	0.20	0.30	0.40
1946	0.10	0.10	0.20	0.20	0.20	0.20	0.30
1946D	0.10	0.10	0.20	0.20	0.20	0.20	0.40
1946S	0.10	0.10	0.20	0.20	0.20	0.20	0.50
1947	0.10	0.10	0.20	0.20	0.20	0.20	0.80
1947D	0.10	0.10	0.20	0.20	0.20	0.20	0.40
1947S	0.10	0.10	0.20	0.20	0.20	0.20	0.40
1948	0.10	0.10	0.20	0.20	0.20	0.20	0.40
1948D	0.10	0.10	0.20	0.20	0.20	0.20	0.40
1948S	0.10	0.10	0.20	0.20	0.20	0.20	0.40
1949	0.10	0.10	0.20	0.20	0.20	0.20	0.40
1949D	0.10	0.10	0.20	0.20	0.20	0.20	0.40
1949S	0.10	0.10	0.20	0.20	0.20	0.20	0.80
1950	0.10	0.10	0.20	0.20	0.20	0.20	0.40
1950D	0.10	0.10	0.20	0.20	0.20	0.20	0.40
1950S	0.10	0.10	0.20	0.20	0.20	0.20	0.60
1951	0.10	0.10	0.20	0.20	0.20	0.20	0.60
1951D	0.10	0.10	0.20	0.20	0.20	0.20	0.60
1951S	0.10	0.10	0.20	0.20	0.20	0.20	0.60
1952	0.10	0.10	0.20	0.20	0.20	0.20	0.60
1952D	0.10	0.10	0.20	0.20	0.20	0.20	0.60
1952S	0.10	0.10	0.20	0.20	0.20	0.20	0.60
1953	0.10	0.10	0.20	0.20	0.20	0.20	0.60
1953D	0.10	0.10	0.20	0.20	0.20	0.20	0.60
1953S	0.10	0.10	0.20	0.20	0.20	0.20	0.60
1954	0.10	0.10	0.20	0.20	0.20	0.20	0.60
1954D	0.10	0.10	0.20	0.20	0.20	0.20	0.30
1954S	0.10	0.10	0.20	0.20	0.20	0.20	0.30

Lincoln Cents

Wheat Reverse

	Good	VG	Fine	VF	XF	AU	MS60
1955	0.10	0.10	0.20	0.20	0.20	0.20	0.30
1955 Double Die Obverse	385.00	440.00	495.00	550.00	605.00	660.00	1210.00
1955D	0.10	0.10	0.20	0.20	0.20	0.20	0.30
1955S	0.30	0.30	0.30	0.30	0.30	0.40	0.50
1956	0.10	0.10	0.10	0.10	0.10	0.10	0.10
1956D	0.10	0.10	0.10	0.10	0.10	0.10	0.10
1957	0.10	0.10	0.10	0.10	0.10	0.10	0.10
1957D	0.10	0.10	0.10	0.10	0.10	0.10	0.10
1958	0.02	0.05	0.05	0.05	0.05	0.05	0.05
1958D	0.02	0.05	0.05	0.05	0.05	0.05	0.05

Lincoln Cent Type
(Memorial Reverse 1958-Date)

Memorial Reverse

	Good	VG	Fine	VF	XF	AU	MS60
1959	0.02	0.05	0.05	0.05	0.05	0.05	0.05
1959D	0.02	0.05	0.05	0.05	0.05	0.05	0.05
1960	0.02	0.05	0.05	0.05	0.05	0.05	0.05
1960 Sm. Date				1.00	1.50	1.75	2.00
1960D Sm. Date	0.02	0.05	0.05	0.05	0.05	0.05	0.10
1960D			0.10	0.15	0.20	0.20	
1961	0.02	0.02	0.02	0.02	0.02	0.02	0.02
1961D	0.02	0.02	0.02	0.02	0.02	0.02	0.02
1962	0.02	0.02	0.02	0.02	0.02	0.02	0.02
1962D	0.02	0.02	0.02	0.02	0.02	0.02	0.02
1963	0.02	0.02	0.02	0.02	0.02	0.02	0.02
1963D	0.02	0.02	0.02	0.02	0.02	0.02	0.02
1964	0.02	0.02	0.02	0.02	0.02	0.02	0.02
1964D	0.02	0.02	0.02	0.02	0.02	0.02	0.02

Dates and mintmarks after 1964 to date (except for S-mint coins from proof sets) have only nominal value.

Lincoln One Cent - Proof Coins

Proof Coins	Proof 64	Proof Coins	Proof 64
1968S	0.75	1986S	4.00
1969S	0.75	1987S	2.00
1970S	0.75	1988S	2.00
1971S	0.75	1989S	2.00
1972S	0.75	1990S	3.00
1973S	0.75	1991S	5.00
1974S	0.75	1992S	3.00
1975S	3.00	1993S	4.00
1976S	2.00	1994S	4.00
1977S	1.00	1995S	5.00
1978S	1.00	1996S	4.00
1979S	1.00	1997S	5.00
1980S	0.75	1998S	4.00
1981S	1.00	1999S	4.00
1982S	1.00	2000S	4.00
1983S	2.50	2001S	5.00
1984S	2.00	2002S	4.00
1985S	2.00	2003S	3.00

52

1943 the alloy of the Lincoln cent was changed to zinc-coated steel. These coins are easily recognized by their color, ranging from a bright steel to dark steel gray. In 1959 the Lincoln Memorial was placed on the reverse side of the cent to commemorate the 150th anniversary of Lincoln's birth. The coin has undergone further minor modifications since that time. Many other varieties exist due to differing mint mark sizes and metal alloys used. Since 1975, cents minted at San Francisco were produced for proof sets only.

Dates and mint marks after 1964 to date (except for S-mint coins from proof sets) have only nominal value.

Two-Cent Coins
Minted 1864-1873

Two-Cent Piece

Two-Cent Pieces

	Good	VG	Fine	VF	XF	AU	MS60
1864 Small Motto	63.00	80.00	91.00	180.00	260.00	360.00	630.00
1864 Large Motto	10.00	11.00	15.00	22.00	44.00	70.00	100.00
1865	10.00	11.00	15.00	22.00	44.00	70.00	100.00
1866	10.00	11.00	18.00	33.00	44.00	70.00	100.00
1867	10.00	11.00	18.00	33.00	44.00	80.00	140.00
1868	10.00	11.00	18.00	33.00	44.00	80.00	180.00
1869	10.00	15.00	24.00	33.00	44.00	100.00	180.00
1870	13.00	15.00	24.00	44.00	88.00	150.00	240.00
1871	13.00	17.00	24.00	55.00	88.00	150.00	260.00
1872	91.00	136.00	181.00	286.00	396.00	510.00	800.00
1873	Proof Only			Impaired		850.00	910.00

Nickel Three-Cent Coins
Minted 1865-1889

Nickel Three-Cent Piece

	Good	VG	Fine	VF	XF	AU	MS60
1865	10.00	11.00	13.00	15.00	18.00	44.00	110.00
1866	10.00	11.00	13.00	15.00	18.00	44.00	110.00
1867	10.00	11.00	13.00	15.00	18.00	44.00	110.00
1868	10.00	11.00	13.00	15.00	18.00	44.00	110.00
1869	10.00	11.00	13.00	15.00	18.00	44.00	130.00
1870	10.00	11.00	13.00	15.00	18.00	44.00	130.00
1871	10.00	11.00	13.00	15.00	18.00	55.00	130.00
1872	10.00	11.00	13.00	15.00	18.00	55.00	130.00
1873 Closed 3	10.00	11.00	13.00	15.00	18.00	55.00	130.00
1873 Open 3	10.00	11.00	13.00	15.00	18.00	44.00	130.00
1874	10.00	11.00	13.00	15.00	18.00	55.00	130.00
1875	10.00	11.00	13.00	15.00	29.00	66.00	180.00
1876	13.00	15.00	18.00	24.00	29.00	77.00	180.00
1877 Proof Only			Impaired			Proof	1070.00
1878 Proof Only			Impaired			Proof	1130.00
1879	55.00	66.00	77.00	88.00	99.00	150.00	260.00
1880	77.00	88.00	100.00	110.00	140.00	180.00	260.00
1881	10.00	11.00	13.00	15.00	18.00	50.00	110.00
1882	80.00	90.00	100.00	110.00	130.00	170.00	260.00
1883	160.00	170.00	190.00	200.00	260.00	290.00	400.00
1884	350.00	360.00	380.00	400.00	460.00	510.00	570.00
1885	400.00	410.00	460.00	500.00	540.00	600.00	740.00
1886 Proof Only			Impaired			Proof	460.00
1887/6 Proof Only			Impaired			Proof	460.00
1887	260.00	280.00	300.00	320.00	350.00	400.00	510.00
1888	44.00	44.00	55.00	66.00	77.00	130.00	290.00
1889	77.00	77.00	88.00	99.00	110.00	130.00	290.00

Nickel Five-Cent Coins
Minted 1866-Date

Shield Five-Cent Piece

Shield Nickels

54

	Good	VG	Fine	VF	XF	AU	MS60
1866	16.00	17.00	24.00	41.00	130.00	170.00	240.00
1867 With Rays	16.00	18.00	27.00	51.00	140.00	240.00	320.00
1867 W/O Rays	10.00	11.00	14.00	16.00	33.00	70.00	130.00
1868	10.00	11.00	14.00	16.00	33.00	70.00	130.00
1869	10.00	11.00	14.00	16.00	44.00	70.00	130.00
1870	11.00	14.00	18.00	19.00	44.00	80.00	130.00
1871	36.00	41.00	58.00	81.00	130.00	210.00	320.00
1872	11.00	14.00	15.00	20.00	44.00	80.00	140.00
1873	11.00	14.00	15.00	27.00	55.00	90.00	150.00
1874	13.00	15.00	18.00	27.00	55.00	90.00	150.00
1875	14.00	16.00	27.00	36.00	66.00	100.00	180.00
1876	13.00	15.00	28.00	36.00	66.00	90.00	160.00
1877 Proof Only			Impaired		1122.00	1150.00	1270.00
1878 Proof Only			Impaired		572.00	610.00	640.00
1879	290.00	360.00	410.00	470.00	520.00	580.00	700.00
1880	320.00	380.00	410.00	470.00	580.00	640.00	720.00
1881	180.00	240.00	290.00	360.00	470.00	520.00	580.00
1882	11.00	13.00	14.00	18.00	36.00	60.00	130.00
1883	13.00	18.00	20.00	24.00	41.00	60.00	110.00
1883/2		110.00	150.00	240.00	270.00	320.00	400.00

Liberty Type
Minted 1883-1913

Liberty Five-Cent Piece

Liberty Nickels

		Good	VG	Fine	VF	XF	AU	MS60
1883	No "Cents"	3.30	4.40	4.40	6.60	7.70	14.30	35.20
1883	With "Cents"	7.70	8.80	14.30	20.90	39.60	69.30	103.40
1884		7.70	9.90	12.10	23.10	46.20	69.30	132.00
1885		248.00	303.00	440.00	550.00	688.00	798.00	1018.00
1886		88.00	110.00	160.00	248.00	330.00	413.00	550.00
1887		7.70	9.90	12.10	14.30	28.60	57.20	132.00
1888		11.00	12.10	14.30	23.10	40.70	80.30	121.00
1889		5.50	6.60	11.00	15.40	28.60	69.30	110.00
1890		5.50	6.60	11.00	15.40	28.60	69.30	110.00
1891		4.40	5.50	11.00	15.40	28.60	69.30	110.00
1892		4.40	5.50	11.00	15.40	28.60	69.30	110.00
1893		4.40	5.50	11.00	15.40	28.60	69.30	110.00
1894		6.60	8.80	28.60	63.80	132.00	143.00	209.00
1895		3.30	3.30	6.60	12.10	28.60	57.20	99.00
1896		4.40	5.50	9.90	15.40	35.20	74.80	110.00
1897		3.30	3.30	4.40	6.60	17.60	57.20	110.00
1898		2.20	2.30	4.40	6.60	17.60	57.20	88.00
1899		1.10	1.30	4.40	5.50	15.40	46.20	88.00
1900		1.10	1.30	4.40	5.50	15.40	46.20	88.00
1901		1.10	1.30	4.40	5.50	15.40	46.20	88.00
1902		1.10	1.30	4.40	5.50	15.40	46.20	88.00
1903		1.10	1.30	4.40	5.50	15.40	46.20	88.00
1904		1.10	1.30	4.40	5.50	15.40	46.20	88.00
1905		1.10	1.30	4.40	5.50	15.40	46.20	88.00
1906		1.10	1.30	4.40	5.50	15.40	46.20	88.00
1907		1.10	1.30	4.40	5.50	15.40	46.20	88.00
1908		1.10	1.30	4.40	5.50	15.40	46.20	88.00
1909		2.20	1.30	5.50	6.60	16.50	57.20	88.00
1910		1.10	1.30	4.40	5.50	15.40	46.20	88.00
1911		1.10	1.30	4.40	5.50	15.40	46.20	88.00
1912		1.10	1.30	4.40	5.50	15.40	46.20	88.00
1912D		2.20	1.30	4.40	7.70	38.50	103.40	187.00
1912S		77.00	99.00	121.00	330.00	528.00	660.00	770.00
1913		Only 5 known to exist. Est. $1,000,000+.						

BuffaloType
Minted 1913-1938

Buffalo Five-Cent Pieces

Buffalo Nickels

		Good	VG	Fine	VF	XF	AU	MS60
1913	On Mound	5.50	6.10	6.60	7.70	13.00	25.00	37.00
1913D	On Mound	7.70	9.90	12.10	15.40	25.00	49.00	66.00
1913S	On Mound	12.10	13.20	18.70	28.60	46.00	61.00	77.00
1913	No Mound	5.50	5.50	6.60	7.70	16.00	25.00	31.00
1913D	No Mound	35.20	40.70	55.00	60.50	73.00	121.00	198.00
1913S	No Mound	88.00	121.00	154.00	176.00	242.00	330.00	363.00

Buffalo Nickels

		Good	VG	Fine	VF	XF	AU	MS60
1914		6.60	6.60	7.70	8.80	17.00	31.00	49.00
1914D		28.60	46.20	55.00	72.60	121.00	154.00	231.00
1914S		6.60	7.70	15.40	24.20	39.00	55.00	121.00
1915		3.30	4.40	5.50	6.60	13.00	31.00	49.00
1915D		7.70	9.90	20.90	36.30	61.00	85.00	187.00
1915S		12.10	17.60	30.80	72.60	154.00	242.00	473.00
1916		2.20	2.20	2.20	3.30	8.00	17.00	43.00
1916D		6.60	7.70	11.00	28.60	55.00	85.00	154.00
1916S		4.40	5.50	7.70	22.00	49.00	85.00	176.00
1917		2.20	2.20	2.20	5.50	10.00	29.00	47.00
1917D		6.60	8.80	15.40	45.10	91.00	132.00	297.00
1917S		6.60	8.80	16.50	48.40	121.00	220.00	308.00
1918		2.20	2.20	3.30	6.60	19.00	37.00	61.00
1918D		6.60	8.80	17.60	72.60	187.00	275.00	363.00
1918/17D		429.00	550.00	990.00	2420.00	4840.00	7810.00	11990.00
1918S		5.50	6.60	17.60	72.60	163.00	240.00	308.00
1919		1.10	2.20	2.20	3.30	8.00	25.00	43.00
1919D		6.60	8.80	17.60	72.60	187.00	308.00	550.00
1919S		4.40	6.60	9.90	72.60	187.00	275.00	484.00
1920		1.10	1.10	2.20	3.30	8.00	25.00	49.00
1920D		4.40	7.70	15.40	72.60	231.00	308.00	484.00
1920S		3.30	4.40	8.80	55.00	154.00	220.00	396.00
1921		2.20	2.20	3.30	6.60	22.00	49.00	97.00
1921S		16.50	25.30	55.00	363.00	781.00	968.00	1089.00
1923		1.10	2.20	2.20	3.30	7.00	19.00	37.00
1923S		3.30	3.30	6.60	90.20	187.00	242.00	363.00
1924		2.20	2.20	2.20	3.30	9.00	31.00	55.00
1924D		3.30	4.40	7.70	60.50	154.00	242.00	308.00
1924S		5.50	7.70	29.70	429.00	1210.00	1540.00	1925.00
1925		1.10	2.20	2.20	3.30	8.00	22.00	35.00
1925D		5.50	8.80	19.80	60.50	132.00	211.00	363.00
1925S		3.30	6.60	7.70	55.00	169.00	240.00	429.00
1926		1.10	1.10	1.10	2.20	6.00	19.00	33.00
1926D		3.30	4.40	15.40	66.00	121.00	187.00	231.00
1926S		6.60	7.70	15.40	330.00	880.00	1100.00	2640.00
1927		1.10	1.10	1.10	2.20	6.00	19.00	33.00
1927D		2.20	2.30	4.40	13.20	43.00	73.00	154.00
1927S		1.10	2.20	2.20	17.60	66.00	121.00	451.00
1928		1.10	1.10	1.10	2.20	6.00	19.00	33.00
1928D		1.10	2.20	2.20	4.40	16.00	29.00	33.00
1928S		1.10	1.10	2.20	3.30	13.00	35.00	187.00
1929		1.10	1.10	1.10	2.20	6.00	19.00	33.00
1929D		1.10	2.20	2.20	4.40	14.00	31.00	47.00
1929S		1.10	1.10	2.20	2.20	9.00	25.00	43.00
1930		1.10	1.10	1.10	2.20	6.00	19.00	31.00
1930S		1.10	1.10	1.10	2.20	8.00	29.00	37.00
1931S		5.50	7.70	8.80	9.90	14.00	31.00	43.00
1934		1.10	1.10	1.10	1.10	5.00	13.00	22.00
1934D		1.10	1.10	1.10	2.20	6.00	19.00	37.00
1935		1.10	1.10	1.10	1.10	5.00	9.00	19.00
1935D		1.10	1.10	1.10	1.10	5.00	22.00	32.00
1935S		1.10	1.10	1.10	1.10	5.00	13.00	27.00
1936		1.10	1.10	1.10	1.10	5.00	9.00	16.00
1936D		1.10	1.10	1.10	1.10	5.00	11.00	19.00
1936S		1.10	1.10	1.10	1.10	5.00	13.00	19.00
1937		1.10	1.10	1.10	1.10	5.00	8.00	16.00
1937D		1.10	1.10	1.10	1.10	5.00	10.00	16.00
1937D	3-Legged"	154.00	253.00	308.00	357.50	479.00	616.00	1293.00
1937S		1.10	1.10	1.10	1.10	5.00	10.00	16.00
1938D		1.10	1.10	1.10	1.10	5.00	9.00	16.00

Jefferson Type
Minted 1938-Date

Jefferson Five-Cent Piece

	Good	VG	Fine	VF	XF	AU	MS60
1938	0.30	0.40	0.50	0.80	1.00	2.00	3.00
1938D	0.50	0.75	0.90	1.00	1.50	2.00	3.00
1938S	1.00	1.25	1.50	1.75	2.00	2.50	3.50
1939	0.10	0.10	0.20	0.25	1.00	1.50	2.00
1939D	2.00	2.50	3.00	3.50	5.00	17.00	24.00
1939S	0.25	0.40	0.50	1.00	2.00	6.00	13.00
1940					0.25	0.50	0.75
1940D	Pieces not priced generally sell at				0.25	1.00	2.00
1940S	or close to face value.				0.25	1.00	2.00
1941					0.25	0.40	0.60
1941D					0.25	1.00	2.00
1941S					0.25	2.00	3.00
1942					0.25	1.00	1.00
1942D					1.00	5.00	15.00

35% Silver Content
1942-1945S

	Good	VG	Fine	VF	XF	AU	MS60
1942P	0.30	0.50	0.70	1.00	1.25	4.00	10.00
1942S	0.30	0.50	0.70	1.00	1.25	2.00	8.00
1943P	0.30	0.50	0.70	1.00	1.25	2.00	3.00
1943D	0.50	0.80	1.00	1.00	1.25	2.00	2.00
1943S	0.30	0.50	0.70	1.00	1.25	2.00	3.00
1944P	0.30	0.50	0.70	1.00	1.25	2.00	3.00
1944D	0.30	0.50	0.70	1.00	1.25	3.00	6.00
1944S	0.30	0.50	0.70	1.00	1.25	3.00	5.00
1945P	0.30	0.50	0.70	1.00	1.25	2.00	3.00
1945D	0.30	0.50	0.70	1.00	1.25	1.00	2.00
1945S	0.30	0.50	0.70	1.00	1.25	1.00	2.00
1946	Pieces not priced generally sell at or close						0.30
1946D	to face value.						0.50
1946S							0.50
1947							0.30
1947D							0.50
1947S							0.50
1948							0.30
1948D							0.75
1948S							0.75
1949							0.75
1949D							0.75
1949S							1.00	1.50

Jefferson Nickels

	Good	VG	Fine	VF	XF	AU	MS60
1950							
1950D	4.00	5.00	5.25	5.50	5.75	6.00	6.50
1951							0.75
1951D							0.75
1951S							1.00
1952							0.30
1952D		Pieces not priced generally sell at or close					0.30
1952S		to face value.					0.30
1953							0.30
1953D							0.30
1953S							0.30
1954							0.20
1954D							0.20
1954S							0.20
1955							0.20
1955D							0.20

Pieces minted after 1955 have a value of 10-20 cents each in uncirculated condition. Proof pieces from proof sets are priced below.

Jefferson Five-Cent - Proof Coins

Proof Coins	Proof 64	Proof Coins	Proof 64
1968 S	0.50	1985 S	3.00
1969 S	0.50	1986 S	4.00
1970 S	0.50	1987 S	1.00
1971 S	1.00	1988 S	2.00
1972 S	1.00	1989 S	2.00
1973 S	1.00	1990 S	2.00
1974 S	1.00	1991 S	3.00
1975 S	1.00	1992 S	2.00
1976 S	1.00	1993 S	2.00
1977 S	1.00	1994 S	2.00
1978 S	1.00	1995 S	3.00
1979 S	1.00	1996 S	1.25
1980 S	1.00	1997 S	1.25
1981 S	1.00	1998 S	1.25
1982 S	1.00	1999 S	1.25
1983 S	1.00	2000 S	1.25
1984 S	3.00	2001 S	1.25
		2002 S	1.25

The price of the entire set, Circ./Unc./Proof, (1938-2003) is only about $50.00. Such a reasonable price provides a new collector a good place to begin.

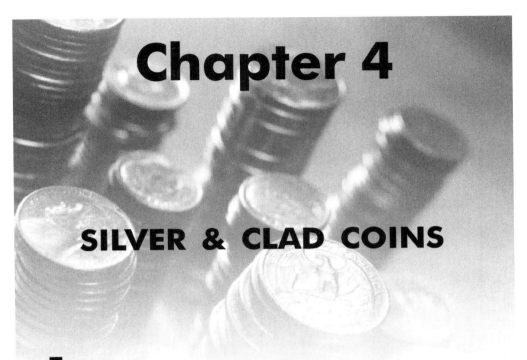

Chapter 4

SILVER & CLAD COINS

In 1966 (coins dated 1965), the United States began minting clad coinage to replace the silver dimes, quarters and half dollars that had circulated for more than 150 years. The effect was immediate, although not noticed by the general public at first. For various reasons many people began looking through their change, taking out the silver coins and putting them away. Some felt that the silver coins would become collector's items, others feared the end to "hard cash," still others speculated that the rising price of silver would inevitably push up the value of these 90% silver coins. To some extent everybody was right. As silver zoomed to $50/oz. by 1980, tons of coins came out from hiding and headed to the smelter.

Most of the best, however, have been saved for collectors. This chapter offers some assessments of the value of silver coins and the subsequent clad coins that replaced them. Such evaluations are especially tentative given that increases and decreases in the price of silver can affect values so easily. Minimum prices given are predicated on current wholesale silver coin prices—about 3-4 times face value. Chapter 2 gives a reasonably complete explanation concerning the refiguring of prices based on changes in the price of silver.

Values of Silver and Clad Coins
Silver Three-Cent Coins
Minted 1851-1873

Silver Three-Cent Piece

Silver Three-Cent Pieces

	Good	VG	Fine	VF	XF	AU	MS60
1851	15.00	18.00	24.00	29.00	60.00	140.00	170.00
1851O	19.00	24.00	36.00	70.00	130.00	240.00	360.00
1852	15.00	18.00	24.00	29.00	60.00	140.00	170.00
1853	15.00	18.00	24.00	29.00	60.00	140.00	170.00
1854	15.00	18.00	29.00	47.00	100.00	270.00	360.00
1855	24.00	32.00	52.00	86.00	170.00	280.00	470.00
1856	17.00	24.00	29.00	47.00	100.00	180.00	240.00
1857	15.00	18.00	24.00	47.00	100.00	240.00	320.00
1858	15.00	18.00	24.00	41.00	100.00	180.00	250.00
1859	15.00	18.00	24.00	41.00	70.00	140.00	170.00
1860	18.00	18.00	24.00	41.00	70.00	140.00	170.00
1861	15.00	18.00	24.00	41.00	70.00	140.00	170.00
1862/1				41.00	70.00	150.00	190.00
1862	18.00	24.00	29.00	41.00	70.00	140.00	170.00
1863/2						Proof	580.00
1863						580.00	700.00
1864		1863-1872 issues				580.00	700.00
1865		Seldom seen in grades				580.00	700.00
1866		lower than AU				580.00	700.00
1867						580.00	700.00
1868						580.00	700.00
1869						640.00	750.00
1870						640.00	750.00
1871						640.00	750.00
1872						640.00	810.00
1873	Proof Only					Proof	750.00

Half Dimes
Minted 1794-1873

Half Dimes

Flowing Hair 1794-1795

	Good	VG	Fine	VF	XF	AU	MS60
1794	860.00	1010.00	1350.00	2140.00	3970.00	5860.00	9760.00
1795	580.00	710.00	1040.00	1590.00	2870.00	4880.00	7080.00

60

Draped Bust Type

Draped Bust Type 1796-1805

	Good	VG	Fine	VF	XF	AU	MS60
1796 6 over 5	890.00	1070.00	1590.00	2690.00	5130.00	6840.00	17080.00
1796	800.00	950.00	1410.00	2440.00	4760.00	6100.00	9640.00
1796 "LIKERTY"	830.00	980.00	1440.00	2510.00	4880.00	6530.00	11900.00
1797 15 Stars	740.00	920.00	1350.00	2380.00	4730.00	6040.00	9280.00
1797 16 Stars	830.00	980.00	1410.00	2570.00	5010.00	6100.00	9520.00
1797 13 Stars	1350.00	1530.00	1900.00	2870.00	5370.00	9030.00	18300.00

Draped Bust Type
(Eagle & Shield Reverse)

Heraldic Eagle Reverse

	Good	VG	Fine	VF	XF	AU	MS60
1800	430.00	570.00	890.00	1220.00	3050.00	5490.00	6960.00
1800 "LIBEKTY"	440.00	580.00	980.00	1350.00	3240.00	5620.00	7320.00
1801	550.00	690.00	1100.00	1470.00	3420.00	6100.00	9150.00
1802	9150.00	15250.00	24400.00	39650.00	54900.00	85400.00	
1803 Large 8	580.00	710.00	950.00	1350.00	3240.00	5620.00	7200.00
1803 Small 8	740.00	890.00	1130.00	2020.00	4030.00	6410.00	9150.00
1805	710.00	860.00	1070.00	1770.00	3910.00	6410.00	10980.00

Capped Bust Type

Capped Bust 1829-1837

	Good	VG	Fine	VF	XF	AU	MS60
1829	22.00	27.00	31.00	60.00	120.00	190.00	260.00
1830	21.00	27.00	31.00	61.00	120.00	190.00	260.00
1831	20.00	26.00	27.00	55.00	110.00	190.00	260.00
1832	20.00	26.00	27.00	55.00	110.00	190.00	260.00
1833	20.00	27.00	29.00	55.00	100.00	190.00	260.00
1834	20.00	26.00	27.00	55.00	100.00	190.00	260.00
1835	20.00	26.00	31.00	55.00	100.00	190.00	260.00
1836	20.00	26.00	35.00	55.00	100.00	190.00	260.00
1837 Small 50	24.00	31.00	43.00	86.00	140.00	310.00	800.00
1837 Large 50	21.00	29.00	37.00	55.00	100.00	190.00	260.00

Liberty Seated Type
Minted 1837-1873

Liberty Seated Half Dime

No Stars

	Good	VG	Fine	VF	XF	AU	MS60
1837 Small Date	25.00	30.00	47.00	86.00	160.00	330.00	600.00
1837 Large Date	25.00	33.00	47.00	86.00	160.00	330.00	600.00
1838 O	68.00	98.00	159.00	324.00	600.00	890.00	1470.00

Stars with no drapery

	Good	VG	Fine	VF	XF	AU	MS60
1838	11.00	12.00	13.00	19.00	55.00	130.00	240.00
1838 Small Stars	13.00	24.00	37.00	80.00	147.00	300.00	540.00
1839	11.00	12.00	13.00	19.00	49.00	130.00	240.00
1839 O	12.00	13.00	15.00	22.00	68.00	150.00	520.00
1840	12.00	13.00	15.00	22.00	49.00	130.00	240.00
1840 O	12.00	14.00	16.00	25.00	68.00	210.00	610.00

62

Stars on obverse

1840 Drapery	16.00	27.00	43.00	86.00	165.00	300.00	380.00
1840 O Drapery	22.00	43.00	86.00	141.00	354.00	860.00	2750.00
1841	11.00	12.00	13.00	21.00	43.00	110.00	150.00
1841 O	12.00	15.00	19.00	37.00	92.00	250.00	600.00
1842	11.00	12.00	14.00	18.00	43.00	110.00	150.00
1842 O	21.00	30.00	47.00	110.00	440.00	710.00	920.00
1843	11.00	13.00	14.00	18.00	43.00	110.00	150.00
1844	11.00	12.00	13.00	18.00	43.00	110.00	150.00
1844 O	61.00	86.00	147.00	409.00	915.00	1710.00	4880.00
1845	11.00	12.00	13.00	19.00	43.00	110.00	150.00
1846	165.00	269.00	458.00	610.00	1647.00	3360.00	7320.00
1847	11.00	12.00	13.00	18.00	43.00	110.00	160.00
1848 Medium Date	11.00	12.00	13.00	18.00	43.00	110.00	210.00
1848 Large Date	14.00	19.00	30.00	43.00	104.00	240.00	450.00
1848 O	12.00	14.00	21.00	40.00	86.00	220.00	340.00
1849 9 over 6	11.00	14.00	16.00	35.00	90.00	190.00	370.00
1849 9 over 8	12.00	15.00	21.00	46.00	92.00	170.00	370.00
1849	11.00	12.00	13.00	19.00	43.00	110.00	150.00
1849 O	20.00	29.00	61.00	171.00	366.00	740.00	1830.00
1850	11.00	12.00	13.00	18.00	43.00	110.00	150.00
1850 O	11.00	13.00	17.00	42.00	88.00	250.00	650.00
1851	11.00	12.00	13.00	18.00	43.00	110.00	150.00
1850	11.00	13.00	18.00	35.00	92.00	190.00	460.00
1852	11.00	12.00	13.00	18.00	43.00	110.00	150.00
1852 O	20.00	27.00	49.00	104.00	214.00	430.00	740.00
1853 No Arrows	22.00	31.00	49.00	96.00	177.00	330.00	630.00
1853 O No Arrows	122.00	177.00	287.00	458.00	1098.00	2290.00	4520.00

Arrows at date

	Good	VG	Fine	VF	XF	AU	MS60
1853	11.00	12.00	13.00	15.00	43.00	120.00	190.00
1853 O	11.00	12.00	13.00	16.00	49.00	120.00	210.00
1854	11.00	12.00	13.00	15.00	43.00	120.00	190.00
1854 O	11.00	12.00	16.00	20.00	61.00	130.00	220.00
1855	11.00	12.00	13.00	15.00	43.00	120.00	190.00
1855 O	13.00	17.00	25.00	43.00	110.00	190.00	540.00

Stars on Obverse

	Good	VG	Fine	VF	XF	AU	MS60
1856	11.00	12.00	13.00	18.00	43.00	110.00	150.00
1856 O	12.00	13.00	16.00	36.00	80.00	250.00	490.00
1857	11.00	12.00	14.00	18.00	43.00	110.00	150.00
1857 O	12.00	13.00	16.00	30.00	49.00	180.00	300.00
1858	11.00	12.00	14.00	18.00	43.00	110.00	150.00
1858 Over Inverted Date	22.00	37.00	49.00	74.00	165.00	250.00	610.00
1858 O	11.00	13.00	16.00	35.00	61.00	120.00	230.00
1859	12.00	14.00	19.00	31.00	61.00	120.00	200.00
1859 O	12.00	15.00	21.00	35.00	98.00	190.00	250.00

Legend on Obverse

	Good	VG	Fine	VF	XF	AU	MS60
1860	11.00	12.00	13.00	15.00	30.00	64.00	118.00
1860 O	11.00	12.00	13.00	16.00	35.00	74.00	159.00
1861	11.00	12.00	13.00	14.00	30.00	64.00	118.00
1861 1 over 0	19.00	25.00	49.00	110.00	232.00	366.00	488.00
1862	11.00	12.00	13.00	15.00	30.00	64.00	118.00
1863	122.00	153.00	190.00	257.00	391.00	458.00	574.00
1863 S	19.00	26.00	31.00	35.00	110.00	257.00	671.00
1864	244.00	354.00	427.00	580.00	732.00	854.00	976.00
1864 S	35.00	40.00	76.00	104.00	214.00	366.00	580.00
1865	214.00	269.00	342.00	427.00	549.00	586.00	751.00
1865 S	19.00	27.00	33.00	49.00	135.00	427.00	854.00
1866	214.00	244.00	342.00	397.00	519.00	580.00	684.00
1866 S	19.00	29.00	33.00	49.00	116.00	275.00	366.00
1867	354.00	397.00	488.00	580.00	671.00	732.00	885.00
1867 S	18.00	22.00	29.00	53.00	116.00	244.00	488.00
1868	41.00	49.00	86.00	141.00	244.00	379.00	592.00
1868 S	11.00	15.00	19.00	21.00	35.00	98.00	275.00
1869	11.00	13.00	15.00	21.00	35.00	104.00	196.00
1869 S	11.00	13.00	14.00	19.00	35.00	98.00	275.00
1870	11.00	12.00	13.00	14.00	30.00	64.00	118.00
1870 S (Unique)							305000.00
1871	11.00	12.00	13.00	14.00	32.00	64.00	118.00
1871 S	11.00	19.00	25.00	48.00	61.00	153.00	232.00
1872	11.00	12.00	13.00	14.00	30.00	64.00	118.00
1872 S, S Above Bow	11.00	12.00	13.00	14.00	30.00	64.00	118.00
1872 S, S Below Bow	11.00	12.00	13.00	15.00	30.00	64.00	118.00
1873	11.00	12.00	14.00	15.00	30.00	64.00	118.00
1873 S	11.00	12.00	13.00	15.00	32.00	64.00	118.00

63

Dimes
Minted 1796-Date

Early Types Minted 1796/1837

Draped Bust Type

Draped Bust 1796-1807

	Good	VG	Fine	VF	XF	AU	MS60
1796	950.00	1680.00	1900.00	2630.00	4400.00	6100.00	7810.00
1797 16 stars	1010.00	1710.00	1960.00	2810.00	5370.00	7630.00	8910.00
1797 13 stars	1010.00	1710.00	1960.00	2810.00	5370.00	7690.00	8420.00

64

Draped Bust Type

(Eagle & Shield Reverse)

Heraldic Eagle

	Good	VG	Fine	VF	XF	AU	MS60
1798/97 16 Star Reverse	460.00	540.00	830.00	1070.00	2140.00	3050.00	4580.00
1798/97 13 Star Reverse	860.00	1470.00	2200.00	3660.00	4820.00		
1798	430.00	520.00	740.00	1010.00	2020.00	2570.00	3970.00
1798 Small 8	550.00	740.00	1190.00	1930.00	2930.00	4760.00	7570.00
1800	410.00	510.00	740.00	1130.00	2140.00	2810.00	4640.00
1801	400.00	490.00	950.00	1590.00	3540.00	6710.00	
1802	610.00	770.00	1320.00	2140.00	4820.00	7690.00	10860.00
1803	400.00	490.00	790.00	1010.00	2930.00	6590.00	
1804	1040.00	1290.00	2320.00	3540.00	10680.00	24400.00	
1805	310.00	460.00	610.00	810.00	1470.00	2140.00	3660.00
1807	310.00	460.00	610.00	810.00	1470.00	2140.00	3660.00

Capped Bust Type

Capped Bust 1809-1837

	Good	VG	Fine	VF	XF	AU	MS60
1809	86.00	135.00	260.00	470.00	890.00	1650.00	2750.00
1811 over 9	49.00	74.00	210.00	420.00	980.00	1350.00	2570.00
1814 Small Date	37.00	55.00	86.00	190.00	370.00	860.00	1350.00
1814 Large Date	24.00	26.00	46.00	104.00	310.00	520.00	830.00
1820 Large 0	21.00	24.00	37.00	92.00	290.00	520.00	830.00
1820 Small 0	20.00	22.00	35.00	92.00	290.00	520.00	830.00
1821 Small Date	21.00	25.00	44.00	104.00	350.00	710.00	1040.00
1821 Large Date	21.00	25.00	40.00	92.00	290.00	520.00	830.00
1822	310.00	520.00	770.00	1100.00	2050.00	3910.00	8850.00
1823 3 over 2	20.00	22.00	33.00	83.00	270.00	520.00	980.00
1824 4 over 2	21.00	35.00	74.00	269.00	520.00	1020.00	1470.00
1825	20.00	22.00	33.00	83.00	270.00	510.00	830.00
1827	20.00	22.00	33.00	83.00	270.00	510.00	830.00
1828 Lg Date, curl 2	31.00	49.00	98.00	196.00	490.00	860.00	1710.00

Capped Bust (Reduced)

	Good	VG	Fine	VF	XF	AU	MS60
1828	22.00	37.00	68.00	116.00	320.00	490.00	950.00
1829	20.00	23.00	29.00	55.00	180.00	320.00	680.00
1830 30 over 29	25.00	43.00	86.00	153.00	340.00	520.00	950.00
1830	20.00	22.00	27.00	49.00	160.00	310.00	630.00
1831	20.00	22.00	27.00	49.00	160.00	310.00	630.00
1832	20.00	22.00	27.00	49.00	160.00	310.00	630.00
1833	20.00	22.00	27.00	49.00	160.00	310.00	630.00
1834	20.00	22.00	27.00	49.00	160.00	310.00	630.00
1835	20.00	22.00	27.00	49.00	160.00	310.00	630.00
1836	20.00	22.00	27.00	49.00	160.00	310.00	630.00
1837	20.00	22.00	27.00	49.00	160.00	310.00	680.00

Liberty Seated Type
Minted 1837-1891

Liberty Seated Ten-Cent Piece

Liberty Seated 1837-1891

	Good	VG	Fine	VF	XF	AU	MS60
No Stars Obverse							
1837 Large Date	25.00	31.00	61.00	86.00	464.00	680.00	950.00
1837 Small Date	31.00	37.00	61.00	86.00	464.00	680.00	950.00
1838 O	27.00	49.00	92.00	305.00	610.00	1100.00	2440.00

Liberty Seated 1837-1891

	Good	VG	Fine	VF	XF	AU	MS60
Stars on Obverse with No Drapery							
1838 Small Stars	16.00	22.00	38.00	61.00	147.00	350.00	580.00
1838 Large Stars	11.00	12.00	13.00	18.00	55.00	160.00	280.00
1839	11.00	12.00	13.00	25.00	49.00	160.00	280.00
1839 O	11.00	12.00	13.00	26.00	68.00	190.00	360.00
1840	11.00	12.00	13.00	18.00	49.00	160.00	280.00
1840 O	11.00	13.00	16.00	43.00	80.00	230.00	800.00
Stars on Obverse with Drapery							
1840	24.00	43.00	74.00	141.00	226.00	330.00	790.00
1841	11.00	12.00	13.00	18.00	35.00	110.00	260.00
1841 O	11.00	13.00	16.00	31.00	55.00	190.00	680.00
1842	11.00	12.00	13.00	15.00	31.00	110.00	240.00
1842 O	11.00	14.00	18.00	43.00	183.00	1100.00	2200.00
1843	11.00	12.00	13.00	19.00	37.00	110.00	240.00
1843 O	27.00	42.00	86.00	196.00	519.00	920.00	1830.00
1844	171.00	275.00	421.00	641.00	976.00	1470.00	2440.00
1845	11.00	12.00	13.00	15.00	30.00	110.00	240.00
1845 O	15.00	20.00	40.00	153.00	427.00	860.00	2140.00
1846	55.00	86.00	141.00	305.00	793.00	1960.00	4400.00
1847	11.00	19.00	29.00	49.00	98.00	310.00	860.00
1848	12.00	13.00	15.00	37.00	61.00	130.00	490.00
1849	12.00	13.00	14.00	26.00	37.00	110.00	250.00
1849 O	12.00	13.00	33.00	98.00	244.00	650.00	2080.00
1850	12.00	13.00	14.00	15.00	43.00	110.00	240.00
1850 O	12.00	13.00	18.00	42.00	76.00	180.00	860.00
1851	12.00	13.00	14.00	15.00	30.00	110.00	310.00
1851 O	12.00	21.00	27.00	55.00	122.00	400.00	1830.00
1852	11.00	12.00	13.00	15.00	30.00	110.00	240.00
1852 O	14.00	18.00	32.00	104.00	214.00	310.00	1220.00
1853 No Arrows	32.00	68.00	98.00	159.00	244.00	370.00	650.00
Arrows at Date							
1853	11.00	12.00	13.00	15.00	40.00	130.00	260.00
1853 O	11.00	13.00	14.00	35.00	74.00	240.00	860.00
1854	11.00	12.00	13.00	15.00	40.00	130.00	260.00
1854 O	11.00	12.00	13.00	19.00	47.00	150.00	260.00
1855	11.00	12.00	13.00	18.00	43.00	140.00	310.00
Stars on Obverse							
1856 Large Date	11.00	12.00	14.00	16.00	40.00	130.00	240.00
1856 Small Date	11.00	12.00	13.00	15.00	30.00	110.00	240.00
1856 O	11.00	13.00	14.00	19.00	49.00	210.00	610.00
1856 S	74.00	129.00	275.00	470.00	732.00	950.00	2190.00
1857	11.00	12.00	13.00	15.00	30.00	110.00	240.00
1857 O	11.00	12.00	13.00	19.00	43.00	180.00	370.00
1858	11.00	12.00	13.00	15.00	30.00	110.00	240.00
1858 O	13.00	18.00	32.00	68.00	110.00	280.00	520.00
1858 S	68.00	110.00	147.00	257.00	549.00	950.00	2320.00
1859	11.00	12.00	13.00	25.00	43.00	120.00	240.00
1859 O	11.00	12.00	13.00	25.00	61.00	190.00	330.00
1859 S	57.00	80.00	177.00	354.00	671.00	890.00	4880.00
1860 S	20.00	26.00	43.00	104.00	226.00	390.00	1650.00

66

Liberty Seated 1837-1891
Legend on Obverse

	Good	VG	Fine	VF	XF	AU	MS60
1860	11.00	12.00	13.00	25.00	29.00	70.00	180.00
1860 O	244.00	440.00	702.00	1068.00	2318.00	3660.00	8540.00
1861	11.00	11.00	12.00	15.00	22.00	70.00	140.00
1861 S	26.00	40.00	86.00	141.00	299.00	410.00	1260.00
1862	12.00	12.00	13.00	16.00	25.00	70.00	160.00
1862 S	29.00	36.00	55.00	129.00	196.00	260.00	980.00
1863	232.00	366.00	464.00	598.00	690.00	770.00	950.00
1863 S	26.00	33.00	43.00	80.00	141.00	310.00	920.00
1864	165.00	226.00	336.00	470.00	671.00	800.00	890.00
1864 S	19.00	25.00	35.00	74.00	104.00	260.00	800.00
1865	196.00	281.00	470.00	629.00	720.00	860.00	980.00
1865 S	19.00	22.00	38.00	108.00	183.00	550.00	1830.00
1866	226.00	324.00	488.00	653.00	732.00	950.00	1100.00
1866 S	32.00	41.00	61.00	98.00	171.00	240.00	920.00
1867	336.00	513.00	702.00	854.00	976.00	1100.00	1220.00
1867 S	22.00	31.00	55.00	98.00	183.00	460.00	950.00
1868	11.00	13.00	20.00	31.00	49.00	130.00	250.00
1868 S	11.00	17.00	27.00	59.00	92.00	160.00	320.00
1869	13.00	18.00	30.00	59.00	68.00	150.00	360.00
1869 S	11.00	12.00	16.00	24.00	52.00	130.00	350.00
1870	11.00	11.00	12.00	19.00	43.00	100.00	180.00
1870 S	200.00	240.00	310.00	370.00	480.00	770.00	1160.00
1871	11.00	11.00	12.00	16.00	37.00	140.00	250.00
1871 CC	890.00	1220.00	1900.00	3360.00	5160.00	7020.00	13420.00
1871 S	16.00	27.00	41.00	61.00	110.00	210.00	460.00
1872	11.00	11.00	12.00	15.00	19.00	70.00	130.00
1872 CC	290.00	510.00	1040.00	2140.00	4820.00	9150.00	24400.00
1872 S	13.00	18.00	68.00	68.00	165.00	320.00	1100.00
1873 Closed 3	11.00	11.00	12.00	16.00	25.00	80.00	130.00
1873 Open 3	14.00	21.00	43.00	55.00	98.00	180.00	520.00
1873 CC Unique							

Arrows at Date

	Good	VG	Fine	VF	XF	AU	MS60
1873	11.00	13.00	18.00	43.00	110.00	260.00	430.00
1873 CC	610.00	1350.00	2690.00	3760.00	5040.00	7630.00	13420.00
1873 S	11.00	15.00	25.00	49.00	147.00	350.00	830.00
1874	11.00	13.00	15.00	37.00	110.00	270.00	430.00
1874 CC	920.00	1620.00	3300.00	8060.00	14100.00	24400.00	32330.00
1874 S	16.00	31.00	55.00	86.00	183.00	440.00	800.00

Legend on Obverse

	Good	VG	Fine	VF	XF	AU	MS60
1875	11.00	11.00	12.00	15.00	20.00	70.00	130.00
1875 CC Below Bow	11.00	12.00	14.00	26.00	51.00	90.00	210.00
1875 CC Above Bow	11.00	12.00	14.00	18.00	34.00	70.00	190.00
1875 S Below Bow	11.00	11.00	12.00	15.00	21.00	70.00	130.00
1875 S Above Bow	11.00	11.00	12.00	15.00	29.00	70.00	130.00
1876	11.00	11.00	12.00	15.00	19.00	70.00	130.00
1876 CC	11.00	12.00	14.00	18.00	34.00	80.00	180.00
1876 S	11.00	13.00	15.00	18.00	31.00	70.00	130.00
1877	11.00	11.00	12.00	15.00	19.00	70.00	130.00
1877 CC	11.00	12.00	14.00	18.00	31.00	80.00	180.00
1877 S	11.00	13.00	15.00	20.00	36.00	70.00	130.00
1878	11.00	11.00	12.00	15.00	19.00	70.00	130.00
1878 CC	37.00	61.00	94.00	160.00	310.00	430.00	970.00
1879	150.00	190.00	220.00	310.00	370.00	400.00	420.00

Legends on obverse

	Good	VG	Fine	VF	XF	AU	MS60
1880	92.00	159.00	208.00	250.00	310.00	400.00	520.00
1881	110.00	160.00	200.00	250.00	310.00	350.00	390.00
1882	11.00	11.00	13.00	15.00	19.00	70.00	130.00
1883	11.00	11.00	12.00	15.00	19.00	70.00	130.00
1884	11.00	11.00	12.00	15.00	19.00	70.00	130.00
1884 S	14.00	18.00	24.00	41.00	80.00	270.00	650.00
1885	11.00	11.00	12.00	15.00	19.00	70.00	130.00
1885 S	340.00	490.00	680.00	1290.00	2050.00	3540.00	5010.00
1886	11.00	11.00	12.00	15.00	19.00	70.00	130.00
1886 S	19.00	31.00	37.00	68.00	86.00	160.00	490.00
1887	11.00	11.00	12.00	15.00	19.00	70.00	130.00
1887 S	11.00	11.00	12.00	15.00	19.00	70.00	130.00
1888	11.00	11.00	12.00	15.00	19.00	70.00	130.00
1888 S	11.00	11.00	12.00	15.00	21.00	90.00	190.00
1889	11.00	11.00	12.00	15.00	19.00	70.00	130.00
1889 S	11.00	13.00	19.00	33.00	55.00	140.00	340.00
1890	11.00	11.00	12.00	15.00	19.00	70.00	130.00
1890 S	11.00	13.00	20.00	37.00	61.00	140.00	300.00
1891	11.00	11.00	12.00	15.00	19.00	70.00	130.00
1891 O	11.00	11.00	12.00	15.00	21.00	70.00	140.00
1891 S	11.00	11.00	12.00	15.00	21.00	70.00	130.00

68

Liberty Head Type
Minted 1892-1916

Liberty Ten-Cent Piece
(Barber Dime)

Barber Dimes

	Good	VG	Fine	VF	XF	AU	MS60
1892	3.00	5.00	14.00	19.00	24.00	60.00	100.00
1892O	6.00	9.00	25.00	32.00	42.00	70.00	150.00
1892S	27.00	67.00	126.00	168.00	195.00	230.00	360.00
1893	6.00	11.00	16.00	24.00	35.00	70.00	150.00
1893O	16.00	27.00	95.00	105.00	126.00	150.00	260.00
1893S	7.00	15.00	24.00	32.00	45.00	120.00	240.00
1894	8.00	16.00	90.00	105.00	130.00	150.00	260.00
1894O	35.00	74.00	158.00	210.00	290.00	580.00	1030.00
1894S						MS64 $150,000-$200,000	

Barber Dimes

	Good	VG	Fine	VF	XF	AU	MS60
1895	58.00	95.00	320.00	400.00	450.00	470.00	630.00
1895O	170.00	270.00	660.00	950.00	1740.00	2310.00	3050.00
1895S	21.00	32.00	100.00	147.00	170.00	230.00	460.00
1896	8.00	14.00	42.00	55.00	70.00	110.00	150.00
1896O	45.00	76.00	210.00	289.00	370.00	580.00	790.00
1896S	42.00	66.00	189.00	237.00	290.00	450.00	740.00
1897	2.00	3.00	7.00	9.00	24.00	70.00	130.00
1897O	37.00	69.00	221.00	284.00	340.00	530.00	790.00
1897S	8.00	18.00	74.00	84.00	100.00	190.00	400.00
1898	2.00	3.00	8.00	11.00	21.00	60.00	110.00
1898O	5.00	12.00	71.00	90.00	126.00	190.00	420.00
1898S	5.00	9.00	24.00	32.00	53.00	110.00	330.00
1899	2.00	2.00	7.00	9.00	21.00	60.00	110.00
1899O	5.00	8.00	58.00	79.00	116.00	210.00	360.00
1899S	5.00	9.00	13.00	18.00	32.00	90.00	320.00
1900	2.00	3.00	7.00	9.00	19.00	60.00	110.00
1900O	6.00	12.00	78.00	100.00	158.00	280.00	580.00
1900S	3.00	4.00	9.00	12.00	25.00	70.00	170.00
1901	2.00	3.00	7.00	9.00	19.00	60.00	110.00
1901O	3.00	4.00	12.00	18.00	42.00	130.00	370.00
1901S	37.00	53.00	237.00	315.00	394.00	600.00	840.00
1902	2.00	3.00	7.00	9.00	19.00	60.00	110.00
1902O	3.00	5.00	11.00	21.00	37.00	120.00	340.00
1902S	5.00	8.00	42.00	63.00	79.00	140.00	330.00
1903	2.00	3.00	7.00	9.00	19.00	60.00	110.00
1903O	3.00	4.00	10.00	14.00	26.00	90.00	260.00
1903S	27.00	48.00	315.00	420.00	735.00	900.00	1040.00
1904	2.00	3.00	7.00	9.00	19.00	60.00	110.00
1904S	21.00	37.00	116.00	158.00	252.00	450.00	580.00
1905	2.00	3.00	7.00	9.00	19.00	60.00	110.00
1905O	3.00	5.00	32.00	42.00	58.00	110.00	260.00
1905S	3.00	4.00	7.00	13.00	27.00	80.00	230.00
1906	2.00	3.00	7.00	9.00	19.00	60.00	110.00
1906D	3.00	4.00	8.00	13.00	27.00	80.00	170.00
1906O	4.00	6.00	42.00	58.00	74.00	130.00	230.00
1906S	3.00	4.00	12.00	16.00	37.00	90.00	250.00
1907	2.00	3.00	7.00	9.00	19.00	60.00	110.00
1907D	3.00	4.00	9.00	12.00	30.00	90.00	270.00
1907O	3.00	3.00	32.00	42.00	58.00	80.00	210.00
1907S	3.00	4.00	9.00	13.00	37.00	100.00	320.00
1908	2.00	3.00	7.00	9.00	19.00	60.00	110.00
1908D	2.00	3.00	6.00	10.00	24.00	70.00	130.00
1908O	3.00	5.00	42.00	53.00	69.00	130.00	270.00
1908S	3.00	4.00	9.00	13.00	27.00	90.00	270.00
1909	2.00	3.00	7.00	9.00	19.00	60.00	110.00
1909D	4.00	8.00	58.00	74.00	100.00	190.00	390.00
1909O	3.00	4.00	9.00	16.00	29.00	90.00	190.00
1909S	4.00	9.00	79.00	105.00	147.00	310.00	500.00
1910	2.00	3.00	7.00	9.00	19.00	60.00	110.00
1910D	3.00	4.00	9.00	13.00	32.00	90.00	190.00
1910S	3.00	6.00	53.00	63.00	84.00	160.00	370.00
1911	2.00	3.00	7.00	9.00	19.00	60.00	110.00
1911D	2.00	3.00	7.00	9.00	19.00	60.00	110.00
1911S	3.00	4.00	9.00	12.00	27.00	90.00	150.00
1912	2.00	3.00	7.00	9.00	19.00	60.00	110.00
1912D	2.00	3.00	7.00	9.00	19.00	60.00	110.00
1912S	2.00	3.00	6.00	9.00	25.00	80.00	160.00
1913	2.00	3.00	7.00	9.00	19.00	60.00	110.00
1913S	8.00	13.00	63.00	100.00	184.00	270.00	390.00
1914	2.00	3.00	7.00	9.00	19.00	60.00	110.00
1914D	2.00	3.00	7.00	9.00	19.00	60.00	110.00
1914S	3.00	3.00	6.00	12.00	27.00	80.00	150.00
1915	2.00	3.00	7.00	9.00	19.00	60.00	110.00
1915S	3.00	4.00	29.00	40.00	58.00	130.00	250.00
1916	2.00	3.00	7.00	9.00	19.00	60.00	110.00
1916S	2.00	3.00	7.00	9.00	19.00	60.00	110.00

Mercury Head Type
Minted 1916-1945

Mercury Dimes

	Good	VG	Fine	VF	XF	AU	MS60
1916	3.00	4.00	6.00	9.00	11.00	20.00	30.00
1916D	630.00	900.00	1380.00	1956.00	3024.00	3960.00	4800.00
1916S	4.00	4.00	8.00	12.00	20.00	26.00	41.00
1917	2.00	2.00	5.00	6.00	9.00	16.00	33.00
1917D	4.00	5.00	9.00	17.00	45.00	76.00	140.00
1917S	2.00	2.00	5.00	8.00	12.00	29.00	58.00
1918	3.00	3.00	6.00	14.00	29.00	42.00	81.00
1918D	3.00	3.00	6.00	11.00	23.00	45.00	114.00
1918S	3.00	3.00	5.00	8.00	16.00	36.00	95.00
1919	2.00	2.00	5.00	6.00	10.00	23.00	39.00
1919D	3.00	6.00	8.00	16.00	39.00	76.00	159.00
1919S	3.00	3.00	6.00	15.00	33.00	76.00	190.00
1920	2.00	2.00	4.00	6.00	8.00	16.00	33.00
1920D	3.00	3.00	5.00	9.00	17.00	39.00	114.00
1920S	3.00	3.00	5.00	8.00	15.00	35.00	76.00
1921	33.00	56.00	84.00	192.00	540.00	888.00	1140.00
1921D	46.00	84.00	132.00	252.00	564.00	1008.00	1260.00
1923	2.00	2.00	4.00	6.00	10.00	21.00	29.00
1923S	3.00	3.00	5.00	11.00	51.00	89.00	159.00
1924	2.00	2.00	4.00	6.00	10.00	21.00	45.00
1924D	3.00	4.00	5.00	10.00	45.00	92.00	165.00
1924S	3.00	3.00	5.00	10.00	42.00	92.00	165.00
1925	2.00	2.00	4.00	5.00	9.00	20.00	33.00
1925D	4.00	4.00	10.00	33.00	101.00	221.00	328.00
1925S	3.00	3.00	5.00	9.00	46.00	108.00	165.00
1926	2.00	2.00	4.00	5.00	6.00	14.00	33.00
1926D	3.00	4.00	5.00	9.00	17.00	39.00	76.00
1926S	7.00	8.00	17.00	39.00	190.00	467.00	958.00
1927	2.00	2.00	4.00	5.00	8.00	14.00	26.00
1927D	3.00	5.00	6.00	14.00	45.00	101.00	190.00
1927S	2.00	4.00	5.00	8.00	20.00	45.00	140.00
1928	2.00	2.00	4.00	5.00	8.00	14.00	26.00
1928D	3.00	3.00	8.00	17.00	45.00	89.00	152.00
1928S	2.00	2.00	5.00	6.00	12.00	33.00	76.00
1929	2.00	2.00	4.00	5.00	6.00	11.00	23.00
1929D	2.00	3.00	6.00	10.00	14.00	22.00	29.00
1929S	2.00	2.00	4.00	5.00	8.00	17.00	39.00
1930	2.00	2.00	4.00	5.00	8.00	17.00	26.00
1930S	3.00	3.00	6.00	9.00	15.00	45.00	76.00
1931	2.00	3.00	5.00	6.00	11.00	23.00	39.00
1931D	6.00	7.00	12.00	20.00	35.00	56.00	89.00
1931S	3.00	3.00	6.00	9.00	15.00	39.00	76.00
1934	1.00	1.00	1.00	4.00	6.00	11.00	17.00
1934D	1.00	1.00	1.00	4.00	10.00	20.00	36.00
1935	1.00	1.00	1.00	4.00	6.00	9.00	11.00
1935D	1.00	1.00	1.00	4.00	12.00	20.00	36.00
1935S	1.00	1.00	1.00	4.00	8.00	16.00	26.00

Mercury Dimes

	Good	VG	Fine	VF	XF	AU	MS60
1936	1.00	1.00	1.00	4.00	5.00	8.00	10.00
1936D	1.00	1.00	1.00	4.00	9.00	17.00	24.00
1936S	1.00	1.00	1.00	4.00	6.00	8.00	18.00
1937	1.00	1.00	1.00	4.00	5.00	8.00	12.00
1937D	1.00	1.00	1.00	4.00	6.00	11.00	23.00
1937S	1.00	1.00	1.00	4.00	6.00	9.00	21.00
1938	1.00	1.00	1.00	4.00	5.00	6.00	16.00
1938D	1.00	1.00	1.00	4.00	8.00	11.00	17.00
1938S	1.00	1.00	1.00	4.00	5.00	10.00	17.00
1939	1.00	1.00	1.00	4.00	4.00	6.00	11.00
1939D	1.00	1.00	1.00	4.00	5.00	8.00	11.00
1939S	1.00	1.00	1.00	4.00	5.00	10.00	26.00
1940	1.00	1.00	1.00	2.00	3.00	4.00	9.00
1940D	1.00	1.00	1.00	2.00	3.00	4.00	10.00
1940S	1.00	1.00	1.00	2.00	3.00	4.00	10.00
1941	1.00	1.00	1.00	2.00	3.00	4.00	8.00
1941D	1.00	1.00	1.00	2.00	3.00	4.00	10.00
1941S	1.00	1.00	1.00	2.00	3.00	4.00	12.00
1942	1.00	1.00	1.00	2.00	3.00	4.00	8.00
1942/1	360.00	468.00	510.00	582.00	720.00	960.00	1764.00
1942D	1.00	1.00	1.00	2.00	3.00	4.00	10.00
1942D/41D	360.00	420.00	480.00	516.00	600.00	972.00	1644.00
1942S	1.00	1.00	1.00	2.00	3.00	4.00	11.00
1943	1.00	1.00	1.00	2.00	3.00	4.00	9.00
1943D	1.00	1.00	1.00	2.00	3.00	4.00	10.00
1943S	1.00	1.00	1.00	2.00	3.00	4.00	12.00
1944	1.00	1.00	1.00	2.00	3.00	4.00	8.00
1944D	1.00	1.00	1.00	2.00	3.00	4.00	10.00
1944S	1.00	1.00	1.00	2.00	3.00	4.00	11.00
1945	1.00	1.00	1.00	2.00	3.00	4.00	8.00
1945D	1.00	1.00	1.00	2.00	3.00	4.00	10.00
1945S	1.00	1.00	1.00	2.00	3.00	4.00	10.00
1945S Micro S"	3.00	3.00	3.00	4.00	5.00	8.00	18.00

Roosevelt Type
Minted 1946-Date

Roosevelt Dimes

	Good	VG	Fine	VF	XF	AU	MS60
1946	BV	BV	BV	BV	BV	0.60	0.70
1946D	BV	BV	BV	BV	BV	0.80	0.90
1946S	BV	BV	BV	BV	BV	1.00	1.10
1947	BV	BV	BV	BV	BV	0.75	1.00
1947D	BV	BV	BV	BV	BV	1.00	1.70
1947S	BV	BV	BV	BV	BV	0.75	1.00
1948	BV	BV	BV	BV	BV	1.00	2.00
1948D	BV	BV	BV	BV	BV	1.00	2.00
1948S	BV	BV	BV	BV	BV	1.00	1.50

BV = bullion value

Roosevelt Dimes

	Good	VG	Fine	VF	XF	AU	MS60
1949	BV	BV	BV	0.90	1.00	2.00	8.00
1949D	BV	BV	BV	BV	BV	2.00	3.00
1949S	BV	BV	BV	BV	BV	5.00	13.00
1950	BV	BV	BV	BV	BV	1.00	1.50
1950D	BV	BV	BV	BV	BV	1.00	1.50
1950S	BV	BV	BV	BV	1.00	3.00	6.00
1951	BV	BV	BV	BV	BV	BV	0.75
1951D	BV	BV	BV	BV	BV	BV	0.75
1951S	BV	BV	BV	BV	1.00	3.00	4.00
1952	BV	BV	BV	BV	BV	BV	0.75
1952D	BV	BV	BV	BV	BV	BV	0.75
1952S	BV	BV	BV	BV	BV	1.00	3.00
1953	BV	BV	BV	BV	BV	BV	1.00
1953D	BV	BV	BV	BV	BV	BV	0.75
1953S	BV	BV	BV	BV	BV	BV	0.60
1954	BV	BV	BV	BV	BV	BV	BV
1954D	BV	BV	BV	BV	BV	BV	BV
1954S	BV	BV	BV	BV	BV	BV	BV
1955	BV	BV	BV	BV	BV	0.75	1.00
1955D	BV	BV	BV	BV	BV	0.75	1.00
1955S	BV	BV	BV	BV	BV	0.75	1.00
1956	BV	BV	BV	BV	BV	BV	BV
1956D	BV	BV	BV	BV	BV	BV	BV
1957	BV	BV	BV	BV	BV	BV	BV
1957D	BV	BV	BV	BV	BV	BV	BV
1958	BV	BV	BV	BV	BV	BV	BV
1958D	BV	BV	BV	BV	BV	BV	BV
1959	BV	BV	BV	BV	BV	BV	BV
1959D	BV	BV	BV	BV	BV	BV	BV
1960	BV	BV	BV	BV	BV	BV	BV
1960D	BV	BV	BV	BV	BV	BV	BV
1961	BV	BV	BV	BV	BV	BV	BV
1961D	BV	BV	BV	BV	BV	BV	BV
1962	BV	BV	BV	BV	BV	BV	BV
1962D	BV	BV	BV	BV	BV	BV	BV
1963	BV	BV	BV	BV	BV	BV	BV
1963D	BV	BV	BV	BV	BV	BV	BV
1964	BV	BV	BV	BV	BV	BV	BV
1964D	BV	BV	BV	BV	BV	BV	BV

BV = bullion value

Only uncirculated pieces after 1964 have any value over face. And these are generally sold for 20-30 cents each.

Roosevelt 10 Cent - Proof Coins

Proof pieces from Proof sets (1968-2002) are priced below.

Proof Coins	Proof 64	Proof Coins	Proof 64
1968 S	0.50	1992 S Clad	3.00
1969 S	0.50	1992 S Silver	3.00
1970 S	0.50	1993 S Clad	6.00
1971 S	0.50	1993 S Silver	6.00
1972 S	1.00	1994 S Clad	3.00
1973 S	1.00	1994 S Silver	5.00
1974 S	1.00	1995 S Clad	7.00
1975 S	1.00	1995 S Silver	8.00
1976 S	1.00	1996 S Clad	1.00
1977 S	1.00	1996 S Silver	5.00
1978 S	1.00	1997 S Clad	2.00
1979 S	1.00	1997 S Silver	5.00
1980 S	1.00	1998 S Clad	1.00
1981 S	1.00	1998 S Silver	5.00
1982 S	1.00	1999 S Clad	1.00
1983 S	1.00	1999 S Silver	4.00
1984 S	1.00	2000 S Clad	1.00
1985 S	1.00	2000 S Silver	4.00
1986 S	2.00	2001 S Clad	1.00
1987 S	1.00	2001 S Silver	4.00
1988 S	1.00	2002 S Clad	1.00
1989 S	1.00	2002 S Silver	4.00
1990 S	1.00	2003 S Clad	1.00
1991 S	3.00	2003 S Silver	4.00

Twenty-Cent Coins
Minted 1875-1878

Liberty Seated 1875-1978

	Good	VG	Fine	VF	XF	AU	MS60
1875	66.00	72.00	78.00	110.00	170.00	320.00	540.00
1875 CC	66.00	72.00	78.00	140.00	260.00	470.00	660.00
1875 S	66.00	72.00	78.00	100.00	150.00	280.00	450.00
1876	84.00	96.00	160.00	200.00	300.00	440.00	600.00
1876 CC				7800.00	30000.00	36000.00	54000.00
1877	1080.00	1200.00	1440.00	1620.00	1860.00	2160.00	
1878	840.00	960.00	1140.00	1230.00	1350.00	1530.00	

Quarter Dollars
Minted 1796-Date

Twenty-Five Cent Pieces

Draped Bust 1796-1807

	Good	VG	Fine	VF	XF	AU	MS60
1796 Small Eagle	3720.00	5100.00	8580.00	10500.00	15000.00	17400.00	23400.00

74

Heraldic Eagle Type

	Good	VG	Fine	VF	XF	AU	MS60
1804	1800.00	2100.00	3120.00	3600.00	7200.00	15000.00	37200.00
1805	170.00	220.00	380.00	690.00	1470.00	2340.00	4440.00
1806 6 over 5	170.00	260.00	410.00	810.00	2100.00	3120.00	5400.00
1806	170.00	230.00	360.00	660.00	1380.00	1980.00	4200.00
1807	170.00	220.00	380.00	650.00	1410.00	2520.00	4200.00

Capped Bust 1815-1838

	Good	VG	Fine	VF	XF	AU	MS60
1815	50.00	60.00	100.00	240.00	650.00	1050.00	1980.00
1818 8 over 5	50.00	60.00	100.00	240.00	650.00	1050.00	1980.00
1818	50.00	60.00	110.00	330.00	750.00	1080.00	2040.00
1819	50.00	60.00	110.00	260.00	620.00	1050.00	1980.00
1820	50.00	60.00	100.00	240.00	600.00	1050.00	1980.00
1821	50.00	60.00	100.00	230.00	600.00	1050.00	1980.00
1822	50.00	60.00	100.00	260.00	660.00	1020.00	1980.00
1822 25 over 50o	1080.00	2520.00	3720.00	5040.00	9300.00	17400.00	

Capped Bust 1815-1838

	Good	VG	Fine	VF	XF	AU	MS60
1823 3 over 2	6000.00	7800.00	14400.00	22800.00	28800.00	36000.00	
1824 4 over 2	80.00	120.00	200.00	510.00	1440.00	1980.00	4800.00
1825 5 over 2	60.00	80.00	130.00	320.00	690.00	1320.00	2280.00
1825 5 over 3	50.00	60.00	100.00	240.00	620.00	1050.00	1980.00
1825 5 over 4	50.00	60.00	100.00	230.00	600.00	1050.00	1980.00
1827 Original, Proof Only							54000.00
1827 Restrike, Proof Only							42000.00
1828	50.00	60.00	100.00	260.00	600.00	1200.00	2400.00
1828 25 over 50c	90.00	200.00	390.00	800.00	1260.00	2640.00	6000.00

Reduced Size Bust

	Good	VG	Fine	VF	XF	AU	MS60
1831	50.00	50.00	60.00	90.00	220.00	560.00	750.00
1832	50.00	50.00	60.00	90.00	220.00	560.00	750.00
1833	50.00	60.00	60.00	120.00	270.00	690.00	1140.00
1834	50.00	50.00	60.00	90.00	210.00	560.00	750.00
1835	50.00	50.00	60.00	80.00	210.00	560.00	750.00
1836	50.00	50.00	60.00	80.00	210.00	560.00	750.00
1837	50.00	50.00	60.00	80.00	210.00	560.00	750.00
1838	50.00	50.00	60.00	80.00	210.00	560.00	780.00

Liberty Steated Type
Minted 1838-1891

Twenty-Five Cent Pieces

No Drapery -No Motto

	Good	VG	Fine	VF	XF	AU	MS60
1838	20.00	18.00	26.00	56.00	240.00	510.00	1080.00
1839	15.00	18.00	26.00	56.00	240.00	510.00	1080.00
1840 O	15.00	21.00	36.00	90.00	330.00	540.00	1140.00
With Drapery - No Motto							
1840	17.00	26.00	46.00	81.00	140.00	260.00	830.00
1840 O	18.00	28.00	54.00	86.00	150.00	400.00	960.00
1841	41.00	58.00	75.00	108.00	200.00	260.00	720.00
1841 O	15.00	21.00	34.00	58.00	140.00	260.00	650.00
1842 Sm Date /Proof Only							N/A
1842 Large Date	54.00	75.00	120.00	204.00	270.00	600.00	1200.00
1842 O Small Date	234.00	420.00	600.00	1200.00	1980.00	5040.00	6600.00
1842 O Lg Date	15.00	21.00	28.00	42.00	100.00	240.00	840.00

With Drapery - No Motto

	Good	VG	Fine	VF	XF	AU	MS60
1843	15.00	18.00	27.00	36.00	50.00	150.00	390.00
1843 O	15.00	24.00	38.00	84.00	200.00	600.00	1440.00
1844	15.00	18.00	27.00	40.00	60.00	150.00	440.00
1844 O	17.00	21.00	28.00	60.00	110.00	240.00	900.00
1845	15.00	21.00	26.00	30.00	60.00	150.00	450.00
1846	15.00	18.00	26.00	35.00	60.00	150.00	450.00
1847	15.00	18.00	27.00	33.00	60.00	150.00	440.00
1847 O	18.00	32.00	45.00	100.00	170.00	540.00	1740.00
1848	20.00	32.00	66.00	96.00	170.00	270.00	900.00
1849	15.00	18.00	32.00	63.00	110.00	230.00	690.00
1849 O	330.00	432.00	750.00	1320.00	2400.00	4440.00	7500.00
1850	21.00	39.00	54.00	72.00	110.00	200.00	690.00
1850 O	15.00	24.00	42.00	75.00	120.00	380.00	1200.00
1851	30.00	51.00	72.00	96.00	150.00	260.00	720.00
1851 O	114.00	210.00	360.00	552.00	930.00	1830.00	3720.00
1852	36.00	51.00	72.00	108.00	170.00	240.00	450.00
1852 O	126.00	180.00	312.00	588.00	1380.00	3300.00	7200.00
1853 Recut Date	210.00	300.00	450.00	570.00	900.00	1320.00	2160.00

Arrows & Rays

	Good	VG	Fine	VF	XF	AU	MS60
1853	15.00	18.00	26.00	36.00	120.00	260.00	870.00
1853 3 over 4	36.00	66.00	96.00	180.00	270.00	590.00	1680.00
1853 O	15.00	21.00	28.00	54.00	200.00	960.00	2640.00

Arrows at Date

	Good	VG	Fine	VF	XF	AU	MS60
1854	15.00	18.00	26.00	29.00	80.00	210.00	420.00
1854 O	15.00	21.00	27.00	630.00	80.00	210.00	660.00
1854 O Huge O	84.00	102.00	156.00	210.00	420.00	1080.00	2940.00
1855	15.00	18.00	26.00	28.00	70.00	210.00	420.00
1855 O	29.00	46.00	78.00	162.00	290.00	690.00	2160.00
1855 S	27.00	36.00	48.00	108.00	270.00	650.00	1680.00

No Motto

	Good	VG	Fine	VF	XF	AU	MS60
1856	15.00	18.00	27.00	28.00	50.00	150.00	270.00
1856 O	15.00	21.00	28.00	36.00	60.00	200.00	900.00
1856 S	27.00	39.00	66.00	150.00	240.00	660.00	1680.00
1856 S over S	41.00	62.00	114.00	234.00	410.00	750.00	1920.00
1857	15.00	18.00	27.00	28.00	50.00	150.00	270.00
1857 O	15.00	21.00	28.00	29.00	80.00	240.00	840.00
1857 S	36.00	78.00	144.00	300.00	540.00	900.00	2100.00
1858	15.00	18.00	27.00	28.00	50.00	150.00	270.00
1858 O	15.00	21.00	28.00	44.00	80.00	320.00	1200.00
1858 S	30.00	48.00	108.00	222.00	390.00	960.00	5040.00
1859	15.00	18.00	27.00	28.00	50.00	150.00	320.00
1859 O	15.00	22.00	32.00	54.00	100.00	340.00	990.00
1859 S	70.00	96.00	150.00	264.00	660.00	7200.00	12000.00
1860	15.00	18.00	27.00	28.00	50.00	150.00	360.00
1860 O	15.00	21.00	29.00	42.00	70.00	320.00	930.00
1860 S	120.00	186.00	348.00	690.00	1380.00	3600.00	7200.00
1861	15.00	18.00	27.00	28.00	50.00	150.00	270.00
1861 S	39.00	66.00	144.00	264.00	720.00	1560.00	4200.00
1862	15.00	18.00	27.00	28.00	50.00	150.00	270.00
1862 S	42.00	63.00	84.00	192.00	440.00	750.00	1800.00
1863	23.00	30.00	44.00	87.00	120.00	210.00	450.00
1864	48.00	60.00	87.00	120.00	190.00	330.00	530.00
1864 S	222.00	360.00	510.00	744.00	1500.00	3240.00	5400.00
1865	48.00	60.00	84.00	114.00	160.00	270.00	600.00
1865 S	60.00	72.00	120.00	282.00	480.00	960.00	1860.00
1866 Proof Only (1 Known)							

With Motto

	Good	VG	Fine	VF	XF	AU	MS60
1866	270.00	408.00	492.00	702.00	960.00	1140.00	1560.00
1866 S	138.00	222.00	450.00	780.00	1080.00	1620.00	2160.00
1867	138.00	222.00	318.00	420.00	540.00	660.00	720.00
1867 S	90.00	198.00	318.00	420.00	540.00	830.00	1800.00
1868	84.00	102.00	156.00	204.00	270.00	390.00	600.00
1868 S	54.00	66.00	102.00	198.00	450.00	720.00	1740.00
1869	192.00	240.00	342.00	450.00	540.00	720.00	1140.00
1869 S	60.00	96.00	150.00	252.00	470.00	1050.00	1920.00
1870	39.00	50.00	90.00	138.00	200.00	300.00	690.00
1870 CC	1500.00	2760.00	6420.00	9900.00	17400.00	25800.00	33600.00
1871	26.00	34.00	48.00	90.00	120.00	240.00	450.00
1871 CC	1080.00	243.00	3690.00	12000.00	19800.00	27600.00	32400.00
1871 S	210.00	330.00	402.00	600.00	930.00	1500.00	2400.00
1872	21.00	27.00	57.00	84.00	110.00	190.00	410.00
1872 CC	420.00	690.00	1170.00	2160.00	3480.00	5760.00	13200.00
1872 S	600.00	780.00	840.00	1200.00	2100.00	3300.00	5700.00
1873 Closed 3	72.00	144.00	204.00	390.00	480.00	780.00	1650.00
1873 Open 3	24.00	36.00	52.00	75.00	110.00	170.00	330.00
1873 (5 Known)					84000.00	96000.00	108000.00

Arrows at Date

	Good	VG	Fine	VF	XF	AU	MS60
1873	15.00	21.00	26.00	53.00	180.00	390.00	720.00
1873 CC	1200.00	1740.00	4440.00	6840.00	10200.00	18900.00	36000.00
1873 S	15.00	28.00	42.00	78.00	210.00	440.00	1040.00
1874	15.00	18.00	26.00	53.00	180.00	390.00	720.00
1874 S	15.00	18.00	46.00	78.00	200.00	410.00	780.00

With Motto

	Good	VG	Fine	VF	XF	AU	MS60
1875	15.00	18.00	26.00	28.00	50.00	140.00	220.00
1875 CC	48.00	90.00	150.00	240.00	480.00	630.00	1500.00
1875 S	23.00	35.00	58.00	96.00	180.00	270.00	570.00
1876	15.00	18.00	26.00	30.00	50.00	140.00	220.00
1876 CC	15.00	24.00	30.00	39.00	80.00	140.00	310.00
1876 S	15.00	18.00	26.00	28.00	50.00	140.00	220.00
1877	15.00	18.00	26.00	28.00	50.00	140.00	220.00
1877 CC	15.00	24.00	28.00	36.00	70.00	140.00	310.00
1877 S	15.00	18.00	26.00	28.00	50.00	140.00	220.00
1877 S over horizontal S	23.00	39.00	72.00	126.00	210.00	320.00	570.00
1878	15.00	18.00	26.00	28.00	50.00	140.00	220.00
1878 CC	17.00	26.00	44.00	84.00	110.00	140.00	430.00
1878 S	78.00	138.00	204.00	258.00	440.00	600.00	1020.00
1879	102.00	120.00	174.00	198.00	270.00	350.00	450.00
1880	102.00	126.00	174.00	204.00	270.00	350.00	470.00
1881	132.00	150.00	228.00	246.00	290.00	380.00	510.00
1882	114.00	138.00	186.00	246.00	310.00	400.00	510.00
1883	108.00	132.00	204.00	240.00	300.00	370.00	480.00
1884	204.00	240.00	324.00	360.00	420.00	480.00	540.00
1885	108.00	126.00	204.00	234.00	290.00	350.00	500.00
1886	252.00	330.00	444.00	468.00	600.00	660.00	750.00
1887	174.00	222.00	300.00	378.00	440.00	500.00	590.00
1888	168.00	216.00	276.00	360.00	420.00	480.00	570.00
1888 S	15.00	18.00	26.00	28.00	50.00	140.00	220.00
1889	132.00	150.00	186.00	234.00	300.00	380.00	480.00
1890	46.00	51.00	84.00	102.00	160.00	250.00	410.00
1891	15.00	18.00	26.00	28.00	50.00	140.00	220.00
1891 O	96.00	156.00	264.00	360.00	630.00	900.00	2400.00
1891 S	15.00	18.00	26.00	30.00	50.00	140.00	220.00

Liberty Head Type
Minted 1892-1916

Twenty-Five Cent Pieces

Barber Quarters

	Good	VG	Fine	VF	XF	AU	MS60
1892	5.00	5.00	17.00	29.00	74.00	120.00	190.00
1892O	6.00	9.00	21.00	32.00	71.00	150.00	270.00
1892S	13.00	27.00	37.00	53.00	116.00	270.00	400.00
1893	4.00	6.00	21.00	30.00	69.00	120.00	210.00
1893O	5.00	7.00	21.00	37.00	74.00	150.00	270.00
1893S	5.00	9.00	26.00	42.00	95.00	260.00	400.00
1894	4.00	5.00	21.00	32.00	74.00	140.00	210.00
1894O	5.00	7.00	21.00	32.00	69.00	180.00	350.00
1894S	6.00	7.00	21.00	32.00	69.00	150.00	210.00
1895	4.00	5.00	21.00	32.00	69.00	150.00	210.00
1895O	5.00	7.00	21.00	37.00	79.00	210.00	380.00
1895S	5.00	11.00	24.00	42.00	69.00	210.00	370.00
1896	5.00	6.00	21.00	32.00	69.00	140.00	240.00
1896O	6.00	11.00	53.00	184.00	336.00	610.00	870.00
1896S	225.00	325.00	600.00	1000.00	1500.00	3000.00	4600.00
1897	4.00	5.00	17.00	30.00	69.00	130.00	190.00
1897O	8.00	13.00	53.00	158.00	315.00	610.00	790.00
1897S	10.00	26.00	100.00	158.00	258.00	590.00	950.00
1898	4.00	4.00	17.00	30.00	69.00	130.00	190.00
1898O	5.00	10.00	32.00	69.00	153.00	350.00	500.00
1898S	5.00	9.00	24.00	37.00	69.00	190.00	370.00
1899	4.00	4.00	17.00	32.00	69.00	130.00	190.00
1899O	6.00	11.00	21.00	39.00	87.00	270.00	400.00
1899S	8.00	16.00	27.00	37.00	69.00	200.00	390.00
1900	4.00	4.00	17.00	32.00	69.00	130.00	190.00
1900O	5.00	9.00	21.00	42.00	84.00	240.00	420.00
1900S	6.00	8.00	24.00	37.00	71.00	140.00	340.00
1901	5.00	6.00	17.00	32.00	69.00	120.00	190.00
1901O	16.00	32.00	58.00	137.00	273.00	610.00	740.00
1901S	1500.00	2550.00	3450.00	4800.00	7000.00	9000.00	12000.00
1902	4.00	5.00	17.00	32.00	69.00	120.00	190.00
1902O	5.00	6.00	24.00	42.00	100.00	200.00	380.00
1902S	8.00	12.00	25.00	40.00	79.00	200.00	390.00
1903	4.00	5.00	17.00	32.00	69.00	120.00	190.00
1903O	5.00	6.00	21.00	40.00	79.00	190.00	300.00
1903S	7.00	15.00	25.00	48.00	93.00	260.00	380.00
1904	4.00	5.00	17.00	32.00	69.00	120.00	190.00
1904O	6.00	7.00	25.00	53.00	158.00	370.00	700.00
1905	4.00	5.00	17.00	32.00	69.00	120.00	190.00
1905O	6.00	8.00	27.00	58.00	132.00	290.00	380.00
1905S	6.00	9.00	21.00	38.00	84.00	200.00	330.00
1906	4.00	5.00	17.00	32.00	69.00	120.00	190.00

Barber Quarters

	Good	VG	Fine	VF	XF	AU	MS60
1906D	4.00	5.00	24.00	34.00	69.00	150.00	230.00
1906O	4.00	5.00	24.00	34.00	79.00	190.00	270.00
1907	4.00	5.00	17.00	32.00	69.00	120.00	190.00
1907D	4.00	5.00	24.00	32.00	79.00	180.00	290.00
1907O	4.00	5.00	24.00	32.00	69.00	140.00	270.00
1907S	5.00	6.00	24.00	38.00	100.00	230.00	380.00
1908	4.00	5.00	17.00	32.00	69.00	120.00	210.00
1908D	4.00	5.00	17.00	32.00	69.00	120.00	240.00
1908O	4.00	5.00	17.00	32.00	79.00	130.00	210.00
1908S	8.00	13.00	42.00	105.00	252.00	400.00	680.00
1909	4.00	5.00	17.00	32.00	69.00	120.00	190.00
1909D	4.00	5.00	19.00	32.00	69.00	180.00	240.00
1909O	9.00	13.00	42.00	105.00	210.00	370.00	680.00
1909S	4.00	5.00	24.00	36.00	69.00	190.00	290.00
1910	4.00	5.00	17.00	32.00	69.00	120.00	190.00
1910D	4.00	5.00	24.00	37.00	79.00	190.00	320.00
1911	4.00	5.00	17.00	32.00	69.00	120.00	190.00
1911D	4.00	6.00	69.00	168.00	279.00	420.00	610.00
1911S	4.00	5.00	24.00	37.00	116.00	210.00	330.00
1912	4.00	5.00	17.00	32.00	69.00	120.00	190.00
1912S	4.00	5.00	24.00	40.00	90.00	210.00	370.00
1913	9.00	15.00	53.00	132.00	368.00	560.00	950.00
1913D	4.00	5.00	21.00	32.00	69.00	150.00	270.00
1913S	350.00	550.00	1800.00	2600.00	3250.00	3800.00	5000.00
1914	4.00	5.00	17.00	32.00	69.00	120.00	190.00
1914D	4.00	5.00	17.00	32.00	69.00	120.00	190.00
1914S	65.00	100.00	150.00	200.00	400.00	650.00	850.00
1915	4.00	5.00	17.00	32.00	69.00	120.00	190.00
1915D	4.00	5.00	17.00	32.00	69.00	120.00	190.00
1915S	5.00	6.00	21.00	37.00	74.00	190.00	260.00
1916	4.00	5.00	17.00	32.00	69.00	120.00	190.00
1916D	4.00	5.00	17.00	32.00	69.00	120.00	190.00

Liberty Standing Type
Minted 1916-1930

Twenty-Five Cent Pieces

Standing Liberty Quarters

		Good	VG	Fine	VF	XF	AU	MS60
1916	Bare Breast		1540.00	1930.00	2750.00	3300.00	4070.00	4950.00
1917	Bare Breast		13.00	20.00	32.00	70.00	130.00	180.00
1917D	Bare Breast		18.00	27.00	59.00	100.00	150.00	220.00
1917S	Bare Breast		18.00	27.00	70.00	150.00	210.00	240.00
1917	Cov. Breast		16.00	20.00	28.00	60.00	90.00	150.00
1917D	Cov. Breast		27.00	59.00	70.00	110.00	150.00	200.00
1917S	Cov. Breast		21.00	36.00	64.00	90.00	130.00	200.00

79

Standing Liberty Quarters

	Good	VG	Fine	VF	XF	AU	MS60
1918		18.00	27.00	40.00	60.00	100.00	150.00
1918D		30.00	43.00	70.00	90.00	150.00	210.00
1918S		18.00	30.00	36.00	60.00	90.00	200.00
1918/17S		1265.00	1733.00	2310.00	4620.00	8090.00	9900.00
1919		36.00	47.00	53.00	80.00	100.00	160.00
1919D		76.00	116.00	187.00	310.00	470.00	620.00
1919S		70.00	116.00	231.00	400.00	530.00	730.00
1920		18.00	24.00	30.00	60.00	90.00	150.00
1920D		36.00	64.00	93.00	130.00	180.00	220.00
1920S		18.00	28.00	36.00	60.00	100.00	220.00
1921		99.00	132.00	187.00	270.00	380.00	500.00
1923		16.00	29.00	33.00	50.00	80.00	150.00
1923S		176.00	220.00	303.00	410.00	470.00	620.00
1924		18.00	24.00	30.00	50.00	80.00	150.00
1924D		36.00	47.00	70.00	100.00	150.00	170.00
1924S		21.00	27.00	35.00	100.00	200.00	270.00
1925		4.00	7.00	17.00	33.00	70.00	150.00
1926		4.00	6.00	17.00	33.00	70.00	150.00
1926D		9.00	13.00	21.00	55.00	90.00	160.00
1926S		6.00	13.00	24.00	121.00	240.00	360.00
1927		4.00	6.00	17.00	33.00	70.00	150.00
1927D		8.00	15.00	36.00	99.00	150.00	170.00
1927S		13.00	53.00	185.00	1100.00	2530.00	3850.00
1928		4.00	6.00	17.00	33.00	70.00	150.00
1928D		6.00	9.00	18.00	44.00	80.00	150.00
1928S		5.00	7.00	18.00	44.00	80.00	150.00
1929		4.00	6.00	17.00	33.00	70.00	150.00
1929D		6.00	8.00	18.00	44.00	80.00	150.00
1929S		4.00	6.00	18.00	33.00	70.00	150.00
1930		4.00	6.00	18.00	33.00	70.00	150.00
1930S		4.00	6.00	18.00	33.00	70.00	150.00

80

Since one of the high points of the Standing Liberty Quarter is the date, especially for pieces before 1925, items graded good generally have only a partial date and are thus not found desirable by most collectors. As a rule such pieces sell for 25-50% of the "VG" price.

Washington Type
Minted 1932-Date

Washington Quarters

	Good	VG	Fine	VF	XF	AU	MS60
1932	5.00	6.00	7.00	8.00	10.00	15.00	21.00
1932D	80.00	90.00	100.00	110.00	165.00	320.00	700.00
1932S	80.00	90.00	95.00	100.00	120.00	150.00	325.00
1934	3.00	3.00	3.00	4.00	5.00	9.00	21.00
1934D	5.00	6.00	7.00	10.00	14.00	80.00	210.00

Washington Quarters

	Good	VG	Fine	VF	XF	AU	MS6
1935	3.00	3.00	3.00	4.00	5.00	9.00	21.00
1935D	3.00	4.00	5.00	10.00	18.00	81.00	240.00
1935S	3.00	3.00	6.00	7.00	13.00	27.00	63.00
1936	3.00	3.00	3.00	4.00	5.00	9.00	21.00
1936D	4.00	4.00	6.00	15.00	42.00	200.00	400.00
1936S	3.00	3.00	4.00	6.00	11.00	42.00	63.00
1937	3.00	3.00	4.00	4.00	5.00	14.00	21.00
1937D	3.00	3.00	4.00	5.00	12.00	26.00	42.00
1937S	3.00	4.00	5.00	12.00	19.00	74.00	105.00
1938	3.00	5.00	5.00	7.00	13.00	28.00	58.00
1938S	4.00	5.00	6.00	8.00	13.00	32.00	58.00
1939	3.00	3.00	3.00	4.00	5.00	8.00	14.00
1939D	3.00	3.00	4.00	5.00	9.00	14.00	32.00
1939S	4.00	4.00	5.00	6.00	13.00	37.00	63.00
1940	3.00	3.00	3.00	3.00	4.00	6.00	11.00
1940D	3.00	4.00	7.00	9.00	18.00	48.00	70.00
1940S	3.00	3.00	5.00	6.00	7.00	12.00	16.00
1941	BV	BV	BV	2.00	3.00	5.00	6.00
1941D	BV	BV	BV	2.00	3.00	8.00	15.00
1941S	BV	BV	BV	2.00	3.00	7.00	16.00
1942	BV	BV	BV	2.00	3.00	4.00	5.00
1942D	BV	BV	BV	2.00	3.00	5.00	10.00
1942S	BV	BV	BV	2.00	4.00	16.00	51.00
1943	BV	BV	BV	2.00	3.00	4.00	4.00
1943D	BV	BV	BV	2.00	3.00	6.00	19.00
1943S	BV	BV	BV	2.00	3.00	11.00	25.00
1944	BV	BV	BV	2.00	3.00	3.00	4.00
1944D	BV	BV	BV	2.00	3.00	5.00	10.00
1944S	BV	BV	BV	2.00	3.00	6.00	12.00
1945	BV	BV	BV	2.00	3.00	3.00	3.00
1945D	BV	BV	BV	2.00	3.00	4.00	7.00
1945S	BV	BV	BV	2.00	3.00	4.00	6.00
1946	BV	BV	BV	2.00	3.00	3.00	3.00
1946D	BV	BV	BV	2.00	3.00	3.00	3.00
1946S	BV	BV	BV	2.00	3.00	3.00	3.00
1947	BV	BV	BV	2.00	3.00	3.00	5.00
1947D	BV	BV	BV	2.00	3.00	3.00	5.00
1947S	BV	BV	BV	2.00	3.00	3.00	3.00
1948	BV	BV	BV	2.00	3.00	3.00	3.00
1948D	BV	BV	BV	2.00	3.00	3.00	5.00
1948S	BV	BV	BV	2.00	3.00	3.00	5.00
1949	BV	BV	BV	2.00	3.00	6.00	18.00
1949D	BV	BV	BV	2.00	3.00	4.00	10.00
1950	BV	BV	BV	2.00	3.00	3.00	3.00
1950D	BV	BV	BV	2.00	3.00	3.00	3.00
1950S	BV	BV	BV	2.00	3.00	3.00	3.00
1951	BV	BV	BV	2.00	3.00	4.00	4.00
1951D	BV	BV	BV	2.00	3.00	3.00	4.00
1951S	BV	BV	BV	2.00	3.00	4.00	8.00
1952	BV	BV	BV	2.00	3.00	3.00	4.00
1952D	BV	BV	BV	2.00	3.00	3.00	4.00
1952S	BV	BV	BV	2.00	3.00	4.00	6.00
1953	BV	BV	BV	BV	BV	1.50	2.00
1953D	BV	BV	BV	BV	BV	1.50	2.00
1953S	BV	BV	BV	BV	BV	1.50	2.00
1954	BV	BV	BV	BV	BV	1.50	2.00
1954D	BV	BV	BV	BV	BV	1.50	2.00
1954S	BV	BV	BV	BV	BV	1.50	2.00
1955	BV	BV	BV	BV	BV	1.50	2.00
1955D	BV	BV	BV	BV	BV	1.50	2.00
1956	BV	BV	BV	BV	BV	1.50	2.00
1956D	BV	BV	BV	BV	BV	1.50	2.00
1957	BV	BV	BV	BV	BV	1.50	2.00

Washington Quarters

	Good	VG	Fine	VF	XF	AU	MS60
1957D	BV	BV	BV	BV	BV	1.50	2.00
1958	BV	BV	BV	BV	BV	1.50	2.00
1958D	BV	BV	BV	BV	BV	BV	1.50
1959	BV	BV	BV	BV	BV	BV	1.50
1959D	BV	BV	BV	BV	BV	BV	1.50
1960	BV	BV	BV	BV	BV	BV	1.50
1960D	BV	BV	BV	BV	BV	BV	1.50
1961	BV	BV	BV	BV	BV	BV	1.50
1961D	BV	BV	BV	BV	BV	BV	1.50
1962	BV	BV	BV	BV	BV	BV	1.50
1962D	BV	BV	BV	BV	BV	BV	1.50
1963	BV	BV	BV	BV	BV	BV·	1.50
1963D	BV	BV	BV	BV	BV	BV	1.50
1964	BV	BV	BV	BV	BV	BV	1.50
1964D	BV	BV	BV	BV	BV	BV	1.50

BV = bullion value

Pieces minted after 1964 are sold in the 30-50 cents range if uncirculated. The only exceptions to this are the 1982P, 1983P&D, 1984D, 1985P&D, 1986P&D. In MS60 these are generally priced in the $2-$3 range. Also proof issues (1968-1998) are priced below.

Washington 25 Cent - Proof Coins

Proof Coins	Proof 64	Proof Coins	Proof 64
1968S	0.65	1987S	0.65
1969S	0.65	1988S	0.65
1970S	0.65	1989S	0.65
1971S	0.65	1990S	2.00
1972S	0.65	1991S	2.00
1973S	0.65	1992S Clad	2.00
1974S	0.65	1992S Silver	3.00
1975S	0.65	1993S Clad	4.00
1976S	0.65	1993S Silver	6.00
1976S Silver	1.50	1994S Clad	3.00
1977S	0.65	1994S Silver	8.00
1978S	0.65	1995S Clad	15.00
1979S	0.65	1995S Silver	15.00
1980S	0.65	1996S Clad	3.00
1981S	0.65	1996S Silver	7.00
1982S	0.65	1997S Clad	7.00
1983S	1.00	1997S Silver	10.00
1984S	1.00	1998S Clad	7.00
1985S	0.75	1998S Silver	7.00
1986S	2.00		

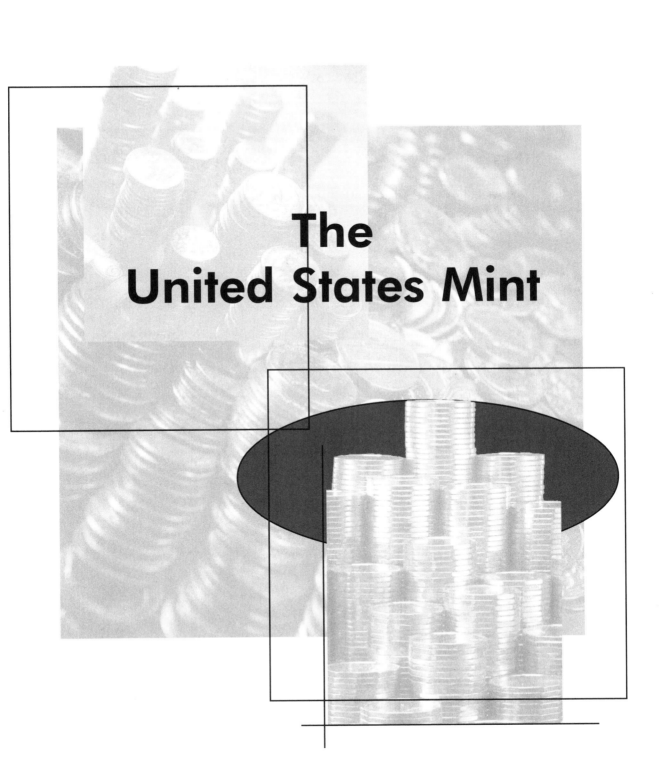

The
United States Mint

50-State Quarters

The United States Mint 50 State Quarters Program				
1999	**2000**	**2001**	**2002**	**2003**
Delaware	Massachusetts	New York	Tennessee	Illinois
Pennsylvania	Maryland	North Carolina	Ohio	Alabama
New Jersey	South Carolina	Rhode Island	Louisiana	Maine
Georgia	New Hampshire	Vermont	Indiana	Missouri
Connecticut	Virginia	Kentucky	Mississippi	Arkansas
2004	**2005**	**2006**	**2007**	**2008**
Michigan	California	Nevada	Montana	Oklahoma
Florida	Minnesota	Nebraska	Washington	New Mexico
Texas	Oregon	Colorado	Idaho	Arizona
Iowa	Kansas	North Dakota	Wyoming	Alaska
Wisconsin	West Virginia	South Dakota	Utah	Hawaii

50 State Quarters
Redesigned Quarter Obverse

Beginning in 1999 the Washington quarter was redesigned with a more detailed portrait of Washington on the obverse and a design on the reverse featuring the unique heritage of each of the fifty states. The Mint projects the issuance of five state quarters per year (about ten weeks apart) for ten years starting in 1999. These are to be sent to the Federal Reserve banks as needed or requested, and will not necessarily be seen first in the particular state commemorated. Both the Philadelphia and Denver mints will mint general circulation coins for each state. Also the program includes the inclusion of San Francisco proof coins in the yearly proof sets. Consequently, a total of 200 different coins will have been minted by the end of the program (50 P-mint, 50 D-mint, 50 S-mint, 50 Silver S-mint). For more information visit www.USMINT.gov or call 1-800-USA-Mint. Special albums to hold all the 50-State quarters are already available. Contact the author, Roderick P. Hughes, Box 3, St. Bonaventure, NY 14778 for styles and prices.

85

This 10–year program will include all 50 states issued in chronological order of entry into the Union. Brief descriptions and photos on the following pages are of the reverses of the coins minted to date.

1999 Reverses

Delaware—Caesar Rodney cast the tiebreaker vote in favor of the Declaration of Independence.

Pennsylvania—The state motto, "Virtue, Liberty, Independence," and the statue atop the Pennsylvania Capitol dome, superimposed over an outline of the state.

New Jersey—George Washington's crossing of the Delaware River to defeat the British at Trenton.

Georgia—A peach, the state motto, "Wisdom, Justice, Moderation", and oak sprigs superimposed upon an outline of the state.

Connecticut—The Charter Oak, hiding place of the colonial government's charter after it was challenged by the government of King George in 1687.

86

	MS60	Proof	Silver Proof
Delaware (P&D mint state, S proof)	1.50	4.00	12.00
Pennsylvania (P&D mint state, S proof)	1.50	4.00	12.00
New Jersey (P&D mint state, S proof)	1.00	4.00	12.00
Georgia (P&D mint state, S proof)	1.00	4.00	12.00
Connecticut (P & D mint state, S proof)	1.00	4.00	12.00

2000 Reverses

Massachusetts—The state map and a minuteman.
Maryland—The Maryland statehouse.
South Carolina—The state map, bird, and flower.
New Hampshire—The Old Man of the Mountain and the state motto.
Virginia—The 400th anniversary of the ships arriving at Jamestown.

	MS60	Proof	Silver Proof
Massachusetts (P & D mint state, S proof)	.50	3.00	6.00
Maryland (P & D mint state, S proof)	.50	3.00	6.00
South Carolina (P & D mint state, S proof)	.50	3.00	6.00
New Hampshire (P & D mint state, S proof)	.50	3.00	6.00
Virginia (P & D mint state, S proof)	.50	3.00	6.00

2001 Reverses

New York—The Statue of Liberty superimposed over an outline of the state.

North Carolina—Kitty Hawk flight with drawing of the Wright Brothers craft, the Flyer.

Rhode Island—A vintage sailboat gliding through Rhode Island's famous Narragansett Bay.

Vermont—Maple sugar production against the background of Vermont's Green Mountains.

Kentucky—The stately mansion, Federal Hill, with thoroughbred racehourse in the foreground.

88

	MS60	Proof	Silver Proof
New York (P & D mint state, S proof)	.50	3.00	8.00
North Carolina (P & D mint state, S proof)	.50	3.00	8.00
Rhode Island (P & D mint state, S proof)	.50	3.00	8.00
Vermont (P & D mint state, S proof)	.50	3.00	8.00
Kentucky (P & D mint state, S proof)	.50	3.00	8.00

2002 Reverses

Tennessee—Various musical instruments.
Ohio—State map and an astronaut.
Louisiana—The Louisiana Purchase and a pelican superimposed on a map of the U.S.
Indiana—State map and Indianapolis 500 race car.
Mississippi—Magnolias.

	MS60	Proof	Silver Proof
Tennessee (P & D mint state, S proof)	.50	3.00	6.00
Ohio (P & D mint state, S proof)	.50	3.00	6.00
Louisiana (P & D mint state, S proof)	.50	3.00	6.00
Indiana (P & D mint state, S proof)	.50	3.00	6.00
Mississippi (P & D mint state, S proof)	.50	3.00	6.00

2003 Reverses

Illinois—Abe Lincoln, Map, Chicago and Farm.
Maine—Lighthouse and Sailing Ship.
Missouri—The Arch and Lewis and Clark
Alabama—Helen Keller.
Arkansas—Diamond and Wildlife Habitat.
Illinois—Abe Lincoln, Map, Chicago and Farm.

.

90

	MS60	Proof	Silver Proof
Illinois (P & D mint state, S proof)	.50	3.00	5.00
Maine (P & D mint state, S proof)	.50	3.00	5.00
Missouri (P & D mint state, S proof)	.50	3.00	5.00
Alabama (P & D mint state, S proof)	.50	3.00	5.00
Arkansas (P & D mint state, S proof)	.50	3.00	5.00

Half Dollars
Minted 1794-Date

Early Types Minted 1794/1839

Flowing Hair 1794 - 1795

92

	Good	VG	Fine	VF	XF	AU	MS60
1794	1620.00	3060.00	4560.00	7680.00	16800.00	34200.00	80400.00
1795	432.00	672.00	1020.00	2400.00	5400.00	8400.00	16500.00
1795 Recut Date	444.00	684.00	1044.00	2580.00	5880.00	9600.00	16800.00
1795 3 Leaves	720.00	1200.00	2400.00	4200.00	7800.00	15000.00	27000.00

Draped Bust Type
(Eagle and Shield Reverse)

Draped Bust 1796-1807

	Good	VG	Fine	VF	XF	AU	MS60
1796 15 stars	14400.00	16800.00	21600.00	29400.00	47400.00	63600.00	93000.00
1796 16 Stars	16200.00	19200.00	25200.00	34200.00	57600.00	72000.00	99000.00
1797 15 Stars	14400.00	16800.00	21600.00	30600.00	51000.00	66000.00	90000.00

Heraldic Eagle

	Good	VG	Fine	VF	XF	AU	MS60
1801	180.00	270.00	462.00	840.00	2400.00	5160.00	20400.00
1802	192.00	270.00	480.00	840.00	2280.00	4920.00	19800.00
1803 Small 3	144.00	162.00	300.00	468.00	1080.00	2640.00	6000.00
1803 Large 3	132.00	144.00	210.00	360.00	720.00	2280.00	5640.00
1805 5 over 4	144.00	240.00	450.00	612.00	1320.00	3360.00	15600.00
1805	132.00	144.00	210.00	324.00	780.00	2280.00	5280.00
1806 6 over 5	132.00	150.00	240.00	318.00	750.00	2250.00	5400.00
1806 6 over inverted 6	144.00	234.00	492.00	810.00	1680.00	2880.00	9000.00
1806 Knob 6, Lg. Stars	132.00	144.00	210.00	312.00	660.00	2220.00	5040.00
1806 Knob 6, Sm. Stars	132.00	144.00	210.00	312.00	660.00	2220.00	5040.00
1806 Knob 6 (stemless claw)		16200.00	23400.00	33000.00	54000.00	66000.00	
1806 Pointed 6	132.00	144.00	210.00	312.00	660.00	2220.00	5040.00
1807	132.00	144.00	210.00	312.00	660.00	2220.00	4800.00

Capped Bust Type

Capped Bust 1807-1839

	Good	VG	Fine	VF	XF	AU	MS60
1807 Small stars	51.00	83.00	162.00	300.00	690.00	1440.00	3360.00
1807 Large stars	47.00	75.00	144.00	270.00	570.00	1440.00	3360.00
1807 50 over 20	41.00	84.00	114.00	204.00	420.00	1920.00	3300.00
1808 8 over 7	40.00	45.00	66.00	120.00	276.00	870.00	1800.00
1808	39.00	48.00	53.00	80.00	216.00	450.00	1260.00
1809	39.00	46.00	52.00	78.00	174.00	420.00	1260.00
1810	39.00	44.00	50.00	66.00	156.00	390.00	1080.00
1811	39.00	46.00	56.00	80.00	126.00	330.00	780.00
1812 2 over 1, Sm 8	39.00	48.00	72.00	138.00	210.00	570.00	2040.00
1812 2 over 1, Lg 8	1200.00	1740.00	3120.00	4680.00	7200.00	15000.00	
1812	39.00	44.00	48.00	64.00	132.00	300.00	660.00
1813	39.00	45.00	50.00	74.00	150.00	384.00	900.00
1813 50c over UNI	39.00	44.00	72.00	114.00	216.00	540.00	1440.00
1814 4 over 3	39.00	50.00	72.00	102.00	222.00	780.00	1800.00
1814 E over A in STATES	42.00	45.00	51.00	74.00	210.00	600.00	1020.00
1814	40.00	46.00	50.00	68.00	150.00	420.00	810.00
1815 5 over 2	720.00	1020.00	1320.00	1620.00	2700.00	4260.00	7200.00
1817 7 over 3	60.00	108.00	138.00	324.00	690.00	1200.00	3000.00
1817 7 over 4	36000.00	54000.00	104400.00	132000.00	174000.00	210000.00	
1817	40.00	46.00	51.00	62.00	144.00	348.00	840.00

Capped Bust 1807-1839

	Good	VG	Fine	VF	XF	AU	MS60
1818 8 over 7	41.00	45.00	50.00	60.00	126.00	678.00	1260.00
1818	41.00	46.00	48.00	58.00	108.00	288.00	762.00
1819 9 over 8	41.00	48.00	57.00	78.00	168.00	378.00	1200.00
1819	39.00	44.00	48.00	56.00	108.00	240.00	768.00
1820 20 over 19	40.00	46.00	59.00	120.00	240.00	690.00	1380.00
1820	39.00	45.00	57.00	84.00	216.00	480.00	990.00
1821	39.00	44.00	50.00	60.00	90.00	468.00	840.00
1822 2 over 1	44.00	51.00	66.00	120.00	204.00	522.00	840.00
1822	39.00	44.00	50.00	66.00	94.00	252.00	480.00
1823 Broken 3	40.00	54.00	72.00	102.00	240.00	540.00	1080.00
1823 Patched 3	40.00	54.00	72.00	90.00	150.00	342.00	900.00
1823	40.00	44.00	48.00	56.00	96.00	276.00	600.00
1824 4 over 1	39.00	45.00	50.00	60.00	126.00	360.00	840.00
1824	39.00	44.00	48.00	54.00	90.00	228.00	414.00
1825	39.00	44.00	48.00	54.00	90.00	228.00	414.00
1826	39.00	44.00	48.00	54.00	90.00	228.00	414.00
1827 7 over 6	39.00	44.00	50.00	66.00	120.00	294.00	930.00
1827	39.00	44.00	48.00	54.00	90.00	228.00	414.00
1828 Curl Base 2	39.00	44.00	48.00	54.00	96.00	228.00	420.00
1828 Square Base 2	39.00	44.00	48.00	54.00	90.00	228.00	420.00
1829 9 over 7	40.00	45.00	54.00	66.00	120.00	300.00	900.00
1829	39.00	44.00	48.00	54.00	90.00	228.00	414.00
1830	39.00	44.00	48.00	54.00	90.00	228.00	414.00
1831	39.00	44.00	48.00	54.00	90.00	228.00	414.00
1832	39.00	44.00	48.00	54.00	90.00	228.00	414.00
1833	39.00	44.00	48.00	54.00	90.00	228.00	414.00
1834	39.00	44.00	48.00	54.00	90.00	228.00	414.00
1835	39.00	44.00	48.00	54.00	90.00	228.00	414.00
1836	39.00	44.00	48.00	54.00	90.00	228.00	414.00
1836 50 over 00	40.00	46.00	57.00	90.00	198.00	630.00	1320.00

Reeded Edge

	Good	VG	Fine	VF	XF	AU	MS60
1836	600.00	798.00	1020.00	1140.00	1920.00	2880.00	5520.00
1837	41.00	47.00	56.00	84.00	132.00	312.00	672.00

"Half Dol." on Rev.

	Good	VG	Fine	VF	XF	AU	MS60
1838	41.00	47.00	56.00	84.00	132.00	312.00	672.00
1838 O					48000.00	72000.00	
1839	41.00	47.00	56.00	84.00	132.00	318.00	900.00
1839 O	108.00	150.00	210.00	300.00	582.00	1020.00	2250.00

Liberty Seated Type
Minted 1839-1891

Liberty Seated Fifty-Cent Piece

No Drapery

	Good	VG	Fine	VF	XF	AU	MS60
1839	36.00	60.00	108.00	312.00	720.00	1620.00	4500.00

No Motto With Drapery

	Good	VG	Fine	VF	XF	AU	MS60
1839	21.00	30.00	50.00	75.00	111.00	186.00	372.00
1840 Sm. Letters Rev. 1839	23.00	32.00	47.00	66.00	108.00	222.00	372.00
1840 Med. Letters Rev. 1838	102.00	150.00	222.00	300.00	540.00	1050.00	2880.00
1840 O	23.00	27.00	45.00	78.00	90.00	192.00	408.00
1841	39.00	48.00	78.00	126.00	198.00	276.00	1080.00
1841 O	18.00	26.00	44.00	72.00	102.00	186.00	540.00
1842 O Sm. Date Sm Letters	480.00	780.00	1170.00	1620.00	3600.00	7200.00	15600.00
1842 Small Date	22.00	40.00	66.00	84.00	102.00	240.00	900.00
1842 Medium Date	18.00	27.00	44.00	62.00	90.00	222.00	630.00
1842 O Med. Date Lg Letters	18.00	24.00	42.00	57.00	90.00	222.00	900.00
1843	18.00	24.00	40.00	50.00	84.00	174.00	396.00
1843 O	18.00	27.00	45.00	53.00	84.00	174.00	396.00
1844	18.00	24.00	40.00	51.00	84.00	174.00	396.00
1844 O	18.00	24.00	40.00	45.00	84.00	174.00	480.00
1844 O Double Date	420.00	600.00	810.00	1050.00	2160.00	5040.00	7800.00
1845	23.00	36.00	53.00	102.00	156.00	270.00	720.00
1845 O	18.00	24.00	40.00	47.00	84.00	174.00	480.00
1845 O No Drapery	24.00	36.00	65.00	94.00	36.00	270.00	1140.00
1846	20.00	27.00	44.00	48.00	90.00	70.00	450.00
1846 Over Horizontal 6	120.00	162.00	210.00	330.00	480.00	1020.00	3000.00
1846 O Medium Date	20.00	27.00	44.00	48.00	96.00	100.00	900.00
1846 O Tall Date	126.00	240.00	318.00	528.00	840.00	1800.00	10800.00
1847 over 46	1320.00	2040.00	2880.00	3600.00	5400.00	8700.00	16800.00
1847	19.00	27.00	44.00	48.00	90.00	190.00	380.00
1847 O	18.00	27.00	44.00	48.00	90.00	200.00	560.00
1848	33.00	53.00	76.00	132.00	204.00	420.00	840.00
1848 O	18.00	27.00	44.00	48.00	90.00	200.00	590.00
1849	27.00	35.00	50.00	68.00	120.00	320.00	810.00
1849 O	20.00	24.00	44.00	48.00	90.00	210.00	660.00
1850	168.00	252.00	378.00	480.00	600.00	780.00	1410.00
1850 O	192.00	264.00	44.00	48.00	90.00	190.00	420.00
1851	252.00	360.00	408.00	510.00	600.00	720.00	1200.00
1851 O	21.00	36.00	50.00	68.00	120.00	200.00	390.00
1852	300.00	444.00	540.00	720.00	930.00	1110.00	1380.00
1852 O	46.00	96.00	138.00	198.00	420.00	750.00	1620.00
1853 O 3 known	162000.00	174000.00	180000.00	192000.00			

Arrows & Rays

	Good	VG	Fine	VF	XF	AU	MS60
1853	24.00	28.00	45.00	78.00	228.00	510.00	1380.00
1853 O	24.00	29.00	48.00	108.00	30.00	660.00	2160.00

Arrows at Date

	Good	VG	Fine	VF	XF	AU	MS60
1854	24.00	28.00	44.00	54.00	108.00	270.00	540.00
1854 O	24.00	28.00	44.00	54.00	108.00	270.00	540.00
1855 over 1854	58.00	78.00	144.00	228.00	330.00	540.00	1980.00
1855	24.00	28.00	44.00	54.00	108.00	270.00	600.00
1855 O	24.00	28.00	44.00	54.00	108.00	270.00	540.00
1855 S	300.00	420.00	630.00	1020.00	2340.00	5880.00	12600.00

No Motto

	Good	VG	Fine	VF	XF	AU	MS60
1856	20.00	27.00	44.00	48.00	90.00	80.00	420.00
1856 O	18.00	27.00	44.00	48.00	90.00	70.00	380.00
1856 S	36.00	54.00	96.00	192.00	36.00	870.00	3420.00
1857	20.00	27.00	44.00	48.00	90.00	190.00	380.00
1857 O	20.00	27.00	44.00	48.00	90.00	190.00	870.00
1857 S	45.00	66.00	108.00	186.00	390.00	960.00	3540.00
1858	18.00	27.00	44.00	48.00	90.00	190.00	380.00
1858 O	18.00	27.00	44.00	48.00	90.00	190.00	380.00
1858 S	20.00	28.00	46.00	90.00	168.00	300.00	690.00
1859	24.00	36.00	48.00	78.00	108.00	200.00	380.00
1859 O	18.00	27.00	44.00	48.00	90.00	190.00	380.00
1859 S	20.00	28.00	45.00	78.00	144.00	270.00	540.00
1860	20.00	27.00	44.00	52.00	90.00	240.00	530.00
1860 O	18.00	27.00	44.00	48.00	90.00	130.00	380.00
1860 S	20.00	27.00	44.00	48.00	90.00	190.00	630.00
1861	20.00	27.00	44.00	48.00	90.00	190.00	440.00
1861 O	20.00	27.00	44.00	48.00	90.00	190.00	420.00
1861 S	20.00	27.00	44.00	48.00	90.00	190.00	450.00
1862	24.00	40.00	56.00	102.00	144.00	260.00	450.00
1862 S	20.00	27.00	44.00	48.00	90.00	200.00	450.00
1863	20.00	29.00	46.00	66.00	96.00	200.00	450.00
1863 S	20.00	27.00	44.00	48.00	90.00	200.00	450.00
1864	23.00	32.00	53.00	81.00	120.00	260.00	450.00
1864 S	20.00	27.00	44.00	50.00	90.00	210.00	600.00
1865	21.00	30.00	48.00	66.00	120.00	240.00	450.00
1865 S	20.00	27.00	44.00	48.00	90.00	210.00	480.00
1866 S	66.00	96.00	156.00	270.00	570.00	1320.00	3300.00

96

With Motto

	Good	VG	Fine	VF	XF	AU	MS60
1866	18.00	27.00	45.00	54.00	90.00	170.00	360.00
1866 S	20.00	27.00	44.00	48.00	82.00	180.00	480.00
1867	23.00	34.00	48.00	102.00	138.00	230.00	360.00
1867 S	18.00	27.00	44.00	48.00	82.00	180.00	420.00
1868	36.00	45.00	75.00	114.00	174.00	230.00	480.00
1868 S	18.00	27.00	44.00	48.00	90.00	180.00	450.00
1869	20.00	28.00	45.00	54.00	94.00	170.00	360.00
1869 S	18.00	27.00	44.00	48.00	108.00	190.00	690.00
1870	21.00	27.00	45.00	58.00	105.00	170.00	450.00
1870 CC	450.00	792.00	1320.00	3300.00	9300.00	18600.00	34200.00
1870 S	20.00	27.00	45.00	52.00	102.00	200.00	780.00
1871	20.00	27.00	44.00	50.00	82.00	170.00	340.00
1871 CC	108.00	192.00	396.00	648.00	1170.00	2100.00	8400.00
1871 S	20.00	27.00	44.00	48.00	82.00	170.00	420.00
1872	20.00	27.00	44.00	48.00	82.00	170.00	400.00
1872 CC	60.00	84.00	162.00	336.00	600.00	1320.00	3180.00
1872 S	24.00	36.00	54.00	96.00	162.00	290.00	900.00
1873 Closed 3	22.00	36.00	57.00	90.00	120.00	2 30.00	480.00
1873 Open 3	2340.00	2760.00	3900.00	4680.00	5520.00	7440.00	12600.00
1873 CC	114.00	174.00	300.00	528.00	990.00	2880.00	7920.00

Arrows at Date

1873	26.00	28.00	44.00	78.00	204.00	380.00	830.00
1873 CC	114.00	216.00	330.00	720.00	1680.00	2280.00	5640.00
1873 S	42.00	60.00	102.00	198.00	360.00	660.00	2160.00
1874	26.00	28.00	44.00	78.00	204.00	380.00	830.00
1874 CC	264.00	432.00	750.00	1188.00	720.00	3360.00	9600.00
1874 S	29.00	36.00	66.00	156.00	312.00	600.00	1560.00

With Motto

	Good	VG	Fine	VF	XF	AU	MS60
1875	20.00	29.00	44.00	48.00	82.00	170.00	390.00
1875 CC	21.00	42.00	52.00	72.00	138.00	230.00	540.00
1875 S	20.00	30.00	44.00	52.00	90.00	170.00	330.00
1876	20.00	27.00	44.00	48.00	82.00	170.00	330.00
1876 CC	20.00	30.00	46.00	66.00	132.00	210.00	550.00
1876 S	20.00	27.00	44.00	48.00	82.00	170.00	330.00
1877	20.00	27.00	44.00	48.00	82.00	170.00	330.00
1877 CC	20.00	27.00	45.00	59.00	120.00	210.00	600.00
1877 S	20.00	27.00	44.00	48.00	82.00	170.00	330.00
1878	22.00	34.00	46.00	72.00	102.00	170.00	390.00
1878 CC	282.00	396.00	552.00	840.00	1740.00	2880.00	4200.00
1878 S	9600.00	12000.00	152400.00	17400.00	21000.00	36000.00	42000.00
1879	210.00	252.00	288.00	324.00	390.00	480.00	600.00
1880	168.00	192.00	228.00	270.00	300.00	410.00	600.00
1881	174.00	198.00	246.00	276.00	300.00	410.00	600.00
1882	252.00	276.00	306.00	330.00	360.00	480.00	600.00
1883	240.00	264.00	288.00	312.00	342.00	420.00	570.00
1884	281.00	294.00	336.00	366.00	384.00	450.00	600.00
1885	288.00	318.00	336.00	348.00	372.00	440.00	600.00
1886	300.00	420.00	450.00	480.00	528.00	600.00	690.00
1887	420.00	480.00	546.00	576.00	660.00	720.00	810.00
1888	180.00	204.00	234.00	264.00	288.00	420.00	570.00
1889	180.00	234.00	264.00	282.00	300.00	420.00	600.00
1890	180.00	204.00	234.00	282.00	312.00	450.00	620.00
1891	36.00	48.00	84.00	102.00	126.00	200.00	390.00

Liberty Head Type
Minted 1892-1915

Liberty Fifty-Cent Piece
(Barber Half)

Barber Half Dollars

	Good	VG	Fine	VF	XF	AU	MS60
1892	22.00	26.00	48.00	89.00	180.00	290.00	410.00
1892O	136.00	167.00	312.00	312.00	400.00	420.00	820.00
1892S	125.00	182.00	229.00	297.00	370.00	590.00	800.00
1893	14.00	23.00	46.00	84.00	170.00	330.00	480.00
1893O	25.00	39.00	73.00	125.00	280.00	370.00	510.00
1893S	89.00	110.00	177.00	312.00	410.00	540.00	1100.00
1894	19.00	35.00	63.00	104.00	230.00	350.00	540.00
1894O	14.00	21.00	63.00	110.00	240.00	310.00	510.00
1894S	16.00	19.00	52.00	73.00	210.00	340.00	460.00

Barber Half Dollars

	Good	VG	Fine	VF	XF	AU	MS60
1895	11.00	16.00	50.00	84.00	210.00	310.00	540.00
1895O	13.00	23.00	52.00	94.00	240.00	370.00	540.00
1895S	21.00	32.00	66.00	115.00	250.00	360.00	510.00
1896	17.00	23.00	52.00	94.00	230.00	340.00	490.00
1896O	28.00	36.00	89.00	156.00	360.00	620.00	1180.00
1896S	63.00	84.00	125.00	208.00	360.00	540.00	1180.00
1897	9.00	11.00	35.00	78.00	140.00	320.00	440.00
1897O	58.00	84.00	354.00	728.00	850.00	1200.00	1480.00
1897S	120.00	136.00	271.00	427.00	690.00	970.00	1280.00
1898	9.00	11.00	32.00	73.00	150.00	330.00	410.00
1898O	21.00	37.00	94.00	172.00	360.00	490.00	870.00
1898S	11.00	17.00	42.00	84.00	210.00	360.00	820.00
1899	11.00	13.00	29.00	73.00	140.00	310.00	410.00
1899O	11.00	15.00	47.00	92.00	240.00	350.00	570.00
1899S	13.00	19.00	52.00	84.00	190.00	350.00	620.00
1900	7.00	9.00	26.00	68.00	140.00	310.00	410.00
1900O	8.00	13.00	39.00	89.00	250.00	330.00	800.00
1900S	9.00	13.00	40.00	94.00	190.00	320.00	590.00
1901	8.00	9.00	26.00	68.00	140.00	310.00	410.00
1901O	10.00	14.00	50.00	115.00	290.00	440.00	1230.00
1901S	16.00	29.00	99.00	219.00	550.00	870.00	1410.00
1902	8.00	9.00	26.00	68.00	140.00	310.00	410.00
1902O	8.00	13.00	39.00	78.00	190.00	350.00	670.00
1902S	8.00	13.00	49.00	89.00	210.00	360.00	600.00
1903	8.00	10.00	37.00	82.00	180.00	320.00	430.00
1903O	8.00	13.00	40.00	78.00	180.00	330.00	690.00
1903S	8.00	13.00	40.00	78.00	230.00	360.00	570.00
1904	8.00	11.00	32.00	68.00	140.00	310.00	410.00
1904O	11.00	15.00	52.00	120.00	310.00	480.00	1020.00
1904S	18.00	30.00	134.00	333.00	640.00	920.00	1840.00
1905	11.00	14.00	52.00	78.00	230.00	330.00	540.00
1905O	13.00	30.00	73.00	136.00	260.00	420.00	720.00
1905S	8.00	10.00	37.00	78.00	200.00	360.00	620.00
1906	8.00	9.00	26.00	73.00	140.00	310.00	410.00
1906D	8.00	9.00	26.00	73.00	140.00	310.00	410.00
1906O	8.00	10.00	37.00	78.00	160.00	310.00	590.00
1906S	8.00	13.00	42.00	78.00	190.00	330.00	570.00
1907	8.00	9.00	26.00	68.00	140.00	290.00	410.00
1907D	8.00	10.00	26.00	68.00	140.00	310.00	410.00
1907O	8.00	10.00	26.00	73.00	160.00	310.00	570.00
1907S	8.00	13.00	60.00	104.00	310.00	490.00	920.00
1908	8.00	9.00	26.00	73.00	140.00	310.00	410.00
1908D	8.00	9.00	26.00	73.00	140.00	310.00	410.00
1908O	8.00	9.00	26.00	73.00	140.00	310.00	510.00
1908S	8.00	12.00	37.00	78.00	190.00	330.00	720.00
1909	8.00	9.00	26.00	68.00	140.00	280.00	410.00
1909O	10.00	12.00	42.00	84.00	260.00	460.00	710.00
1909S	8.00	10.00	32.00	78.00	190.00	330.00	540.00
1910	12.00	17.00	63.00	115.00	270.00	410.00	590.00
1910S	8.00	10.00	32.00	73.00	180.00	330.00	590.00
1911	8.00	9.00	26.00	68.00	140.00	290.00	410.00
1911D	8.00	12.00	39.00	73.00	160.00	280.00	540.00
1911S	8.00	10.00	35.00	78.00	160.00	320.00	540.00
1912	8.00	9.00	26.00	68.00	140.00	310.00	410.00
1912D	8.00	9.00	26.00	73.00	140.00	310.00	410.00
1912S	8.00	9.00	32.00	73.00	160.00	320.00	510.00
1913	21.00	29.00	110.00	182.00	340.00	640.00	890.00
1913D	8.00	10.00	37.00	78.00	180.00	290.00	460.00
1913S	8.00	13.00	42.00	84.00	190.00	360.00	590.00
1914	30.00	52.00	167.00	338.00	460.00	720.00	920.00
1914S	8.00	10.00	35.00	78.00	210.00	350.00	540.00
1915	23.00	30.00	89.00	208.00	360.00	680.00	990.00
1915D	7.00	8.00	26.00	68.00	140.00	260.00	410.00
1915S	7.00	8.00	26.00	68.00	140.00	260.00	410.00

Liberty Walking Type
Minted 1916-1947

Liberty Walking Fifty-Cent Piece

Walking Liberty Half Dollars

	Good	VG	Fine	VF	XF	AU	MS60
1916	26.00	30.00	52.00	110.00	140.00	210.00	260.00
1916DMM On Obverse	21.00	23.00	37.00	80.00	130.00	180.00	250.00
1916SMM On Obverse	90.00	100.00	140.00	320.00	470.00	630.00	810.00
1917	3.75	5.00	8.00	15.00	30.00	56.00	110.00
1917DMM On Obverse	13.00	25.00	37.00	80.00	125.00	200.00	425.00
1917SMM On Obverse	15.00	28.00	45.00	225.00	600.00	1000.00	1770.00
1917D	8.00	13.00	22.00	75.00	180.00	400.00	670.00
1917S	5.00	6.00	11.00	25.00	46.00	120.00	300.00
1918	4.00	7.00	14.00	42.00	115.00	230.00	450.00
1918D	6.00	8.00	18.00	50.00	140.00	320.00	750.00
1918S	4.00	6.00	13.00	26.00	53.00	125.00	350.00
1919	14.00	18.00	35.00	150.00	400.00	540.00	900.00
1919D	11.00	13.00	45.00	135.00	550.00	800.00	2500.00
1919S	12.00	15.00	30.00	140.00	700.00	1370.00	2000.00
1920	4.00	6.00	10.00	23.00	57.00	100.00	300.00
1920D	7.00	9.00	28.00	125.00	360.00	600.00	1050.00
1920S	5.00	7.00	12.00	45.00	200.00	385.00	650.00
1921	90.00	130.00	210.00	560.00	1350.00	2000.00	3000.00
1921D	140.00	180.00	300.00	680.00	2000.00	2500.00	3000.00
1921S	30.00	30.00	100.00	600.00	4000.00	6000.00	8000.00
1923S	8.00	10.00	18.00	54.00	200.00	500.00	1050.00
1927S	4.00	6.00	10.00	28.00	88.00	260.00	700.00
1928S	4.00	6.00	10.00	35.00	92.00	300.00	650.00
1929D	5.00	7.00	9.00	20.00	66.00	150.00	275.00
1929S	4.00	5.00	8.00	18.00	75.00	175.00	300.00
1933S	4.00	6.00	7.00	11.00	42.00	200.00	450.00
1934	3.00	3.25	3.50	4.00	9.00	25.00	48.00
1934D	3.00	3.25	4.00	6.00	22.00	60.00	140.00
1934S	3.00	3.25	4.00	6.00	22.00	85.00	250.00
1935	3.00	3.25	3.50	4.00	5.50	20.00	40.00
1935D	3.00	3.25	4.00	6.00	19.00	50.00	130.00
1935S	3.00	3.25	4.00	6.00	20.00	80.00	185.00
1936	3.00	3.25	3.00	4.00	5.00	20.00	35.00
1936D	3.00	3.25	4.00	6.00	15.00	43.00	70.00
1936S	3.00	3.25	4.00	6.00	17.00	53.00	128.00
1937	3.00	3.25	3.50	4.00	6.00	20.00	35.00
1937D	5.00	3.25	7.00	9.00	23.00	75.00	140.00
1937S	4.00	3.25	6.00	8.00	15.00	65.00	130.00
1938	2.80	3.25	3.50	4.00	9.00	38.00	65.00
1938D	20.00	25.00	27.50	35.00	88.00	255.00	380.00
1939	BV	3.00	3.40	3.50	5.00	20.00	37.00
1939D	BV	3.00	3.40	4.00	9.00	23.00	37.00

Walking Liberty Half Dollars

	Good	VG	Fine	VF	XF	AU	MS60
1939S	BV	4.00	3.40	7.00	12.00	50.00	100.00
1940	BV	3.00	3.40	3.50	4.50	12.00	28.00
1940S	BV	3.00	3.40	4.00	6.00	18.00	28.00
1941	BV	3.00	3.40	3.50	4.00	9.00	26.00
1941D	BV	3.00	3.40	4.00	5.00	14.00	33.00
1941S	BV	3.00	3.40	4.00	7.00	25.00	75.00
1942	BV	3.00	3.40	3.50	4.00	8.00	27.00
1942D	BV	3.00	3.40	4.00	5.00	15.00	33.00
1942S	BV	3.00	3.40	4.00	5.00	18.00	33.00
1943	BV	3.00	3.40	3.50	4.00	8.00	25.00
1943D	BV	3.00	3.40	3.50	5.00	18.00	38.00
1943S	BV	3.00	3.40	3.50	5.00	18.00	33.00
1944	BV	3.00	3.40	3.50	4.00	9.00	27.00
1944D	BV	3.00	3.40	3.50	5.00	16.00	33.00
1944S	BV	3.00	3.40	3.50	5.00	16.00	33.00
1945	BV	3.00	3.40	3.50	4.00	8.00	25.00
1945D	BV	3.00	3.40	3.50	5.00	13.00	29.00
1945S	BV	3.00	3.40	3.50	5.00	14.00	30.00
1946	BV	3.00	3.40	3.50	4.00	10.00	26.00
1946D	BV	3.00	3.40	5.00	8.00	17.00	31.00
1946S	BV	3.00	3.40	3.50	5.00	15.00	31.00
1947	BV	3.00	3.40	3.50	6.00	17.00	32.00
1947D	BV	3.00	3.40	3.50	7.00	17.00	32.00

BV = bullion value

Lower grade coins are bullion sensitive.

100

Franklin Type
Minted 1949-1963

Franklin Fifty-Cent Piece

Franklin Half Dollars

	Good	VG	Fine	VF	XF	AU	MS60
1948	BV	3.30	4.20	4.50	4.80	5.40	14.40
1948D	BV	3.00	3.30	3.80	4.00	4.50	8.00
1949	BV	3.00	4.00	4.30	9.00	10.00	29.00
1949D	BV	3.00	4.00	5.00	10.00	11.00	29.00
1949S	BV	3.00	3.50	5.00	10.00	20.00	45.00
1950	BV	3.00	3.30	3.50	5.00	6.00	16.00
1950D	BV	3.00	3.30	3.50	5.00	7.00	15.00
1951	BV	3.00	3.30	3.50	3.50	4.00	9.00
1951D	BV	3.00	3.30	3.50	4.00	11.00	15.00

Franklin Half Dollars

	Good	VG	Fine	VF	XF	AU	MS60
1951S	BV	3.00	3.30	3.50	4.00	9.00	17.00
1952	BV	3.00	3.30	3.50	4.00	4.00	6.00
1952D	BV	3.00	3.30	3.50	4.00	4.00	6.00
1952S	BV	3.00	3.30	3.50	5.00	20.00	30.00
1953	BV	3.00	4.00	5.00	6.00	9.00	10.00
1953D	BV	3.00	3.30	3.50	3.50	4.00	6.00
1953S	BV	3.00	3.30	3.50	4.00	9.00	10.00
1954	BV	3.00	3.30	3.50	3.50	3.80	4.00
1954D	BV	3.00	3.30	3.50	3.50	3.80	4.00
1954S	BV	3.00	3.30	3.50	4.00	4.00	5.00
1955	6.00	7.00	10.00	11.00	11.50	11.80	12.00
1956	BV	3.00	3.30	3.50	4.00	4.30	4.80
1957	BV	BV	BV	2.80	3.00	3.30	4.00
1957D	BV	BV	BV	2.80	3.00	3.30	4.00
1958	BV	BV	BV	2.80	3.00	3.30	4.00
1958D	BV	BV	BV	2.80	3.00	3.30	4.00
1959	BV	BV	BV	2.80	3.00	3.30	4.00
1959D	BV	BV	BV	2.80	3.00	3.30	4.00
1960	BV	BV	BV	2.80	3.00	3.30	4.00
1960D	BV	BV	BV	2.80	3.00	3.30	4.00
1961	BV	BV	BV	2.80	3.00	3.30	4.00
1961D	BV	BV	BV	2.80	3.00	3.30	4.00
1962	BV	BV	BV	2.80	3.00	3.30	4.00
1962D	BV	BV	BV	2.80	3.00	3.30	4.00
1963	BV	BV	BV	2.80	3.00	3.30	3.80
1963D	BV	BV	BV	2.80	3.00	3.30	3.80

BV = bullion value

Virtually all Franklin Halves survive in better than "good" condition.

101

Kennedy Type
Minted 1964-Date

Kennedy Fifty-Cent Piece

1976 Bicentennial Design

Kennedy Half Dollars

		MS60	Proof
1964	90% Silver	2.50	6.00
1964 D	90% Silver	2.50	
1965	40% Silver	1.25	
1966	40% Silver	1.25	
1967	40% Silver	1.25	
1968 D	40% Silver	1.25	
1968 S	Proof Only	3.00	
1969 D	40% Silver	1.25	
1969 S	Proof Only	3.00	
1970 D			9.00
1970 S	Proof Only		5.00
1971		1.00	
1971 D		1.00	
1971 S	Proof Only		2.00
1972		1.00	
1972 D		1.00	
1972 S	Proof Only		2.00
1973		1.00	
1973 D		1.00	
1973 S	Proof Only		2.00
1974		1.00	
1974 D		1.00	
1974 S	Proof Only		2.00
1976		1.00	
1976 D		1.00	
1976 S	Proof		1.00
1976 S	40% Silver	4.00	5.00

Kennedy Half Dollar

	MS60	Proof
1977	1.00	
1977 D	1.00	
1977 S Proof Only		2.00
1978	1.00	
1978 D	1.00	
1978 S Proof Only		2.00
1979	1.00	
1979 D	1.00	
1979 S Proof Only		2.00
1980 P	0.75	
1980 D	0.75	
1980 S Proof Only		2.00
1981 P	0.75	
1981 D	0.75	
1981 S Proof Only		2.00
1982 P	1.00	
1982 D	1.00	
1982 S Proof Only		2.50
1983 P	1.50	
1983 D	1.00	
1983 S Proof Only		3.00
1984 P	0.75	
1984 D	0.75	
1984 S Proof Only		5.00
1985 P	0.75	
1985 D	0.75	
1985 S Proof Only		4.00
1986 P	3.00	
1986 D	3.00	
1986 S Proof Only		10.00
1987 P	3.00	
1987 D	3.00	
1987 S Proof Only		3.00
1988 P	1.00	
1988 D	1.00	
1988 S Proof Only		5.00
1989 P	1.00	
1989 D	1.00	
1989 S Proof Only		5.00
1990 P	2.00	
1991P	1.00	
1991D	1.00	
1991S Proof Only		10.00
1992P	1.00	
1992D	1.00	
1992S Proof Only		8.00
1992S Silver Proof		10.00
1993P	1.00	
1993D	1.00	
1993S Proof Only		11.00
1993S Silver Proof		20.00
1994P	1.00	
1994D	1.00	
1994S Proof Only		6.00
1994S Silver Proof		26.00
1995P	1.00	
1995D	1.00	
1995S Proof Only		42.00
1995S Silver Proof		80.00

	MS60	Proof
1996P	1.00	
1996D	1.00	
1996S Proof Only		7.00
1996S Silver Proof		40.00
1997P	1.00	
1997D	1.00	
1997S Proof Only		14.00
1997S Silver Proof		70.00
1998P	1.00	
1998D	1.00	
1998S Proof Only		10.00
1998S Silver Proof		24.00
1999P	1.00	
1999D	1.00	
1999S Proof Only		10.00
1999S Silver Proof		12.00
2000P	1.00	
2000D	1.00	
2000S Proof Only		8.00
2000S Silver Proof		12.00
2001P	1.00	
2001D	1.00	
2001S Proof Only		8.00
2001S Silver Proof		10.00
2002P	1.00	
2002D	1.00	
2002S Proof Only		8.00
2002S Silver Proof		10.00
2003P	2.00	
2003D	2.00	
2003S Proof Only		8.00
2003S Silver Proof		10.00

103

Dollars
Minted 1794-1981

Early Types Minted 1794-/1804

Flowing Hair Type

Flowing Hair Type

	Good	VG	Fine	VF	XF	A U	MS60
1794	24000.00	28800.00	36000.00	72000.00	1 26000.00	174000.00	210000.00
1795	840.00	1320.00	2160.00	3720.00	8040.00	9840.00	26400.00

Draped Bust Type

Small Eagle

	Good	VG	Fine	VF	XF	AU	MS60
1795	720.00	840.00	1200.00	1800.00	3600.00	7800.00	20400.00
1796	660.00	810.00	1140.00	1680.00	3600.00	6600.00	20400.00
1797	600.00	780.00	1070.00	1560.00	3600.00	7200.00	19920.00
1798	840.00	1020.00	1380.00	2280.00	4200.00	8760.00	21600.00

Draped Bust Type
(Eagle and Shield Reverse)

Large Eagle

	Good	VG	Fine	VF	XF	AU	MS60
1798	540.00	630.00	990.00	1800.00	2880.00	5160.00	12000.00
1799	540.00	630.00	990.00	1800.00	2880.00	5160.00	11640.00
1800	540.00	630.00	990.00	1800.00	2880.00	5160.00	11400.00
1801	540.00	630.00	990.00	1800.00	2880.00	5160.00	19200.00
1802	560.00	660.00	1050.00	1800.00	2880.00	5160.00	12000.00
1803	570.00	750.00	1110.00	1950.00	2880.00	5160.00	13200.00
1804						Proof 63 $1.35 Million	

Liberty Seated Type
Minted 1840-1873

Liberty Seated Dollar

Liberty Seated Type

	Good	VG	Fine	VF	XF	AU	MS60
1840	150.00	170.00	210.00	270.00	390.00	680.00	1620.00
1841	140.00	150.00	210.00	240.00	360.00	600.00	1440.00
1842	140.00	150.00	200.00	240.00	360.00	600.00	960.00
1843	140.00	150.00	200.00	240.00	330.00	600.00	1200.00

Liberty Seated Type

	Good	VG	Fine	VF	XF	AU	MS60
1844	150.00	220.00	300.00	380.00	510.00	660.00	2160.00
1845	180.00	210.00	240.00	300.00	500.00	660.00	4800.00
1846	140.00	150.00	200.00	260.00	330.00	530.00	1260.00
1846O	140.00	170.00	260.00	300.00	510.00	930.00	2760.00
1847	140.00	150.00	200.00	260.00	330.00	600.00	940.00
1848	190.00	270.00	390.00	450.00	660.00	1080.00	3120.00
1849	140.00	170.00	240.00	270.00	360.00	600.00	1500.00
1850	300.00	390.00	560.00	750.00	1050.00	1920.00	4560.00
1850O	170.00	210.00	320.00	600.00	1200.00	2760.00	6600.00
1851	810.00	1080.00	1500.00	2880.00	7800.00	16800.00	22800.00
1852	780.00	1050.00	1560.00	2400.00	5400.00	15600.00	19200.00
1853	150.00	180.00	240.00	390.00	480.00	840.00	2040.00
1854	840.00	1140.00	1260.00	1980.00	3000.00	4200.00	6480.00
1855	660.00	1020.00	1260.00	1860.00	3000.00	3960.00	6600.00
1856	240.00	360.00	420.00	540.00	960.00	1380.00	2760.00
1857	270.00	360.00	420.00	540.00	1020.00	1380.00	2040.00
1858	2100.00	2400.00	3120.00	3480.00	3960.00	4800.00	12000.00
1859	180.00	220.00	320.00	410.00	480.00	580.00	1080.00
1859O	150.00	160.00	200.00	260.00	330.00	570.00	960.00
1859S	210.00	290.00	360.00	540.00	1320.00	3240.00	7920.00
1860	170.00	210.00	270.00	410.00	480.00	570.00	930.00
1860O	140.00	150.00	210.00	260.00	330.00	570.00	960.00
1861	410.00	630.00	720.00	840.00	1020.00	1650.00	2700.00
1862	300.00	480.00	720.00	840.00	960.00	1560.00	2400.00
1863	200.00	260.00	300.00	480.00	560.00	1020.00	2400.00
1864	180.00	210.00	300.00	420.00	480.00	960.00	2400.00
1865	150.00	210.00	300.00	420.00	480.00	960.00	1920.00
1866	2 Known						

106

Motto Added

	Good	VG	Fine	VF	XF	AU	MS60
1866	150.00	210.00	290.00	410.00	480.00	860.00	1530.00
1867	150.00	200.00	270.00	390.00	420.00	780.00	1200.00
1868	140.00	160.00	240.00	360.00	420.00	810.00	1440.00
1869	140.00	170.00	210.00	270.00	360.00	600.00	1260.00
1870	140.00	150.00	210.00	270.00	360.00	600.00	1260.00
1870CC	210.00	350.00	480.00	810.00	1380.00	3240.00	10200.00
1870S	30000.00	36000.00	42000.00	72000.00	150000.00	240000.00	360000.00
1871	140.00	150.00	210.00	260.00	320.00	580.00	1020.00
1871CC	1020.00	1920.00	3000.00	4440.00	9360.00	18000.00	45000.00
1872	140.00	150.00	210.00	260.00	330.00	600.00	1020.00
1872CC	690.00	1140.00	1500.00	2460.00	3300.00	8400.00	19200.00
1872S	180.00	290.00	390.00	540.00	960.00	2400.00	7680.00
1873	140.00	150.00	210.00	270.00	320.00	570.00	1200.00
1873CC	3000.00	3600.00	5400.00	7800.00	13200.00	24000.00	66000.00

Trade Dollar Type
Minted 1873-1885

Trade Dollar

Trade Dollars

	Good	VG	Fine	VF	XF	AU	MS60
1873	72.00	78.00	110.00	150.00	180.00	260.00	510.00
1873CC	72.00	78.00	170.00	300.00	600.00	1080.00	2400.00
1873S	72.00	78.00	110.00	160.00	210.00	320.00	810.00
1874	72.00	78.00	110.00	140.00	200.00	260.00	500.00
1874CC	72.00	84.00	110.00	170.00	260.00	380.00	1110.00
1874S	72.00	78.00	110.00	100.00	150.00	170.00	450.00
1875	90.00	150.00	320.00	360.00	480.00	780.00	1380.00
1875CC	72.00	84.00	110.00	150.00	240.00	290.00	690.00
1875S	72.00	78.00	110.00	140.00	160.00	260.00	460.00
1875S/CC	120.00	174.00	270.00	390.00	660.00	1200.00	2400.00
1876	72.00	78.00	110.00	140.00	180.00	260.00	460.00
1876CC	72.00	84.00	110.00	180.00	320.00	540.00	2400.00
1876S	72.00	78.00	110.00	140.00	170.00	270.00	460.00
1877	72.00	78.00	110.00	140.00	160.00	290.00	500.00
1877CC	90.00	140.00	210.00	290.00	440.00	570.00	800.00
1877S	72.00	78.00	110.00	140.00	170.00	260.00	460.00
1878 Proof Only	Impaired Proof			900.00	1050.00	Proof60	1320.00
1878CC	240.00	330.00	600.00	900.00	1560.00	3000.00	7920.00
1878S	80.00	80.00	110.00	140.00	160.00	260.00	460.00
1879 Proof Only	Impaired Proof		720.00	780.00	900.00	Proof60	1080.00
1880 Proof Only	Impaired Proof		720.00	780.00	900.00	Proof60	1080.00
1881 Proof Only	Impaired Proof		720.00	840.00	960.00	Proof60	1200.00
1882 Proof Only	Impaired Proof		720.00	840.00	930.00	Proof60	1080.00
1883 Proof Only	Impaired Proof		720.00	840.00	940.00	Proof60	1200.00
1884 Proof Only						Proof60	96000.00
1885 Proof Only						Proof60	300000.00

A Note on Trade Dollars:

As these dollars circulated in the Orient they were stamped with Oriental characters called "chop marks." Collectors generally view such pieces as defaced and their values are considerably less than those listed above.

Liberty Head Type
Minted 1878-1921

Morgan Dollars

	Good	VG	Fine	VF	XF	AU	MS60
1878 8F	10.00	18.00	19.00	19.00	21.00	36.00	104.00
1878 7F	10.00	16.00	17.00	19.00	23.00	43.00	104.00
1878 7/8F	10.00	14.00	16.00	18.00	19.00	29.00	46.00
1878-CC	41.00	74.00	76.00	79.00	81.00	87.00	190.00
1878-S	10.00	14.00	16.00	18.00	19.00	28.00	41.00
1879	9.00	11.00	13.00	13.00	15.00	17.00	23.00
1879-CC	41.00	74.00	76.00	127.00	483.00	903.00	1553.00
1879-O	9.00	11.00	13.00	14.00	15.00	18.00	64.00
1879-S	9.00	13.00	13.00	14.00	16.00	19.00	34.00
1880	9.00	13.00	13.00	13.00	15.00	17.00	23.00
1880-CC	58.00	95.00	127.00	133.00	190.00	253.00	357.00
1880-O	9.00	11.00	13.00	13.00	15.00	18.00	52.00
1880-S	9.00	13.00	13.00	14.00	15.00	19.00	29.00
1881	9.00	13.00	13.00	14.00	15.00	18.00	27.00
1881-CC	58.00	207.00	219.00	230.00	271.00	282.00	357.00
1881-O	9.00	11.00	13.00	13.00	15.00	17.00	23.00
1881S	9.00	11.00	13.00	13.00	15.00	17.00	25.00
1882	9.00	13.00	13.00	13.00	15.00	17.00	23.00
1882-CC	35.00	74.00	76.00	79.00	87.00	83.00	144.00
1882-O	9.00	11.00	13.00	13.00	15.00	17.00	23.00
1882-S	9.00	12.00	13.00	13.00	15.00	22.00	29.00
1883	9.00	11.00	13.00	13.00	15.00	17.00	23.00
1883-CC	35.00	74.00	76.00	79.00	80.00	82.00	133.00
1883-O	9.00	11.00	13.00	13.00	15.00	17.00	23.00
1883-S	9.00	12.00	14.00	15.00	29.00	138.00	432.00
1884	9.00	11.00	13.00	13.00	15.00	18.00	23.00
1884-CC	35.00	74.00	78.00	80.00	82.00	84.00	125.00
1884-O	9.00	11.00	13.00	13.00	15.00	17.00	23.00
1884-S	9.00	12.00	13.00	15.00	36.00	242.00	3105.00
1885	9.00	12.00	13.00	13.00	15.00	17.00	23.00
1885-CC	202.00	276.00	282.00	305.00	317.00	328.00	386.00
1885-O	9.00	12.00	13.00	13.00	15.00	17.00	23.00
1885-S	9.00	13.00	14.00	15.00	19.00	46.00	156.00
1886	9.00	13.00	13.00	13.00	15.00	17.00	23.00
1886-O	9.00	12.00	13.00	13.00	16.00	69.00	443.00
1886-S	9.00	19.00	23.00	41.00	46.00	69.00	202.00
1887	9.00	13.00	13.00	13.00	15.00	18.00	23.00
1887-O	9.00	11.00	13.00	13.00	15.00	18.00	46.00

Morgan Dollars

	Good	VG	Fine	VF	XF	AU	MS60
1887-S	9.00	13.00	14.00	16.00	18.00	34.00	87.00
1888	9.00	11.00	13.00	13.00	15.00	17.00	23.00
1888-O	9.00	11.00	13.00	14.00	15.00	17.00	25.00
1888-S	14.00	38.00	58.00	64.00	81.00	87.00	202.00
1889	9.00	11.00	12.00	13.00	15.00	17.00	23.00
1889-CC	202.00	328.00	414.00	719.00	1553.00	4083.00	8510.00
1889-O	9.00	11.00	13.00	13.00	16.00	27.00	115.00
1889-S	14.00	26.00	29.00	30.00	33.00	55.00	161.00
1890	9.00	11.00	12.00	13.00	15.00	17.00	25.00
1890-CC	38.00	74.00	76.00	79.00	87.00	107.00	288.00
1890-O	9.00	11.00	13.00	13.00	16.00	21.00	43.00
1890-S	9.00	11.00	13.00	13.00	15.00	17.00	49.00
1891	9.00	11.00	13.00	13.00	15.00	19.00	46.00
1891-CC	38.00	74.00	76.00	79.00	87.00	115.00	299.00
1891-O	9.00	12.00	13.00	13.00	16.00	30.00	115.00
1891-S	9.00	11.00	13.00	14.00	17.00	21.00	52.00
1892	11.00	15.00	16.00	17.00	27.00	64.00	127.00
1892-CC	38.00	75.00	82.00	92.00	102.00	288.00	598.00
1892-O	11.00	13.00	15.00	15.00	27.00	53.00	115.00
1892-S	11.00	15.00	18.00	37.00	144.00	1438.00	18745.00
1893	41.00	81.00	84.00	92.00	150.00	196.00	420.00
1893-CC	69.00	133.00	173.00	288.00	834.00	1150.00	2300.00
1893-O	42.00	64.00	92.00	127.00	202.00	547.00	1208.00
1893-S	920.00	1352.00	1697.00	2530.00	5865.00	16100.00	46000.00
1894	202.00	432.00	518.00	547.00	564.00	690.00	1122.00
1894-O	18.00	20.00	26.00	29.00	46.00	138.00	443.00
1894-S	18.00	26.00	35.00	52.00	87.00	265.00	440.00
1895 Proof	13110.00	13800.00	14950.00	16100.00	18400.00	20125.00	23575.00
1895-O	58.00	81.00	104.00	150.00	242.00	771.00	10350.00
1895S	92.00	138.00	202.00	213.00	374.00	690.00	1495.00
1896	9.00	13.00	13.00	13.00	15.00	17.00	26.00
1896-O	9.00	13.00	13.00	14.00	16.00	161.00	748.00
1896-S	11.00	15.00	23.00	41.00	127.00	397.00	771.00
1897	9.00	13.00	13.00	14.00	15.00	17.00	26.00
1897-O	9.00	13.00	13.00	15.00	20.00	95.00	547.00
1897-S	9.00	13.00	13.00	15.00	16.00	21.00	49.00
1898	9.00	14.00	15.00	15.00	16.00	17.00	25.00
1898-O	9.00	13.00	15.00	15.00	15.00	17.00	26.00
1898-S	11.00	13.00	15.00	15.00	23.00	59.00	213.00
1899	14.00	21.00	35.00	37.00	48.00	63.00	87.00
1899-O	9.00	12.00	13.00	13.00	15.00	18.00	25.00
1899-S	11.00	13.00	15.00	20.00	32.00	78.00	265.00
1900	9.00	12.00	14.00	14.00	16.00	17.00	26.00
1900-O	9.00	12.00	14.00	14.00	18.00	21.00	27.00
1900-S	11.00	14.00	15.00	18.00	32.00	72.00	213.00
1901	11.00	17.00	19.00	27.00	52.00	305.00	2013.00
1901-O	9.00	12.00	13.00	14.00	17.00	18.00	28.00
1901-S	11.00	13.00	18.00	26.00	37.00	150.00	294.00
1902	10.00	14.00	16.00	16.00	17.00	20.00	37.00
1902-O	9.00	13.00	16.00	16.00	18.00	19.00	26.00
1902-S	12.00	23.00	37.00	79.00	92.00	138.00	259.00
1903	12.00	25.00	32.00	33.00	35.00	41.00	46.00
1903-O	125.00	167.00	179.00	207.00	242.00	282.00	328.00
1903-S	12.00	25.00	32.00	81.00	207.00	920.00	2530.00
1904	10.00	14.00	16.00	16.00	19.00	29.00	69.00
1904-O	10.00	13.00	16.00	16.00	19.00	21.00	29.00
1904-S	11.00	15.00	21.00	44.00	161.00	460.00	909.00
1921	9.00	10.00	10.00	10.00	10.00	12.00	18.00
1921-D	9.00	10.00	10.00	10.00	10.00	13.00	35.00
1921-S	9.00	10.00	10.00	10.00	11.00	13.00	23.00

109

Lower grade coins are bullion sensitive.

Peace Type
Minted 1921-1935

Peace Dollar

Peace Dollars

110

	Good	VG	Fine	VF	XF	AU	MS60
1921	21.00	43.00	44.00	45.00	49.00	84.00	144.00
1922	7.00	9.00	9.00	9.00	9.00	11.00	14.00
1922-D	7.00	9.00	9.00	9.00	10.00	11.00	21.00
1922-S	7.00	9.00	9.00	9.00	11.00	12.00	20.00
1923	7.00	9.00	9.00	9.00	9.00	11.00	14.00
1923-D	7.00	9.00	10.00	10.00	10.00	15.00	46.00
1923-S	7.00	9.00	10.00	10.00	10.00	12.00	25.00
1924	7.00	9.00	9.00	9.00	10.00	11.00	14.00
1924-S	7.00	9.00	10.00	13.00	21.00	42.00	161.00
1925	7.00	9.00	9.00	9.00	9.00	11.00	14.00
1925-S	7.00	9.00	9.00	10.00	12.00	26.00	56.00
1926	7.00	11.00	11.00	12.00	13.00	13.00	28.00
1926-D	7.00	10.00	11.00	11.00	14.00	22.00	51.00
1926-S	7.00	10.00	11.00	11.00	11.00	13.00	33.00
1927	7.00	14.00	18.00	19.00	23.00	40.00	58.00
1927-D	7.00	14.00	15.00	18.00	21.00	64.00	127.00
1927-S	7.00	14.00	15.00	18.00	21.00	58.00	115.00
1928	75.00	156.00	207.00	225.00	242.00	248.00	253.00
1928-S	7.00	15.00	16.00	17.00	21.00	38.00	121.00
1934	7.00	13.00	14.00	15.00	18.00	32.00	87.00
1934-D	7.00	13.00	14.00	15.00	18.00	35.00	81.00
1934-S	7.00	14.00	15.00	44.00	115.00	420.00	1380.00
1935	7.00	14.00	14.00	14.00	15.00	26.00	52.00
1935-S	7.00	13.00	14.00	14.00	21.00	60.00	207.00

Lower grade coins are bullion sensitive.

Eisenhower Type
Minted 1971-1978

Eisenhower Dollar

1976 Bicentennial Design

Eisenhower Dollars

	MS60	Proof		MS60	Proof
1971	3.00		1974 S 40% Silver	6.00	6.00
1971 D	2.00		1976		2.00
1971 S 40% Silver	6.00	6.00	1976 D		2.50
1972	2.00		1976 S Clad		6.00
1972 D	2.00		1976 S 40% Silver	12.00	14.00
1972 S 40% Silver	6.00	6.00	1977		3.50
1973	10.00		1977 D		3.00
1973 D	10.00		1977 S Clad		6.00
1973 S Clad		7.00	1978		2.00
1973 S 40% Silver	7.00	25.00	1978 D		2.50
1974		2.50	1978 S Clad		7.00
1974 D		2.50			
1974 S Clad		6.00			

Although this coin is rarely seen in circulation, it, nevertheless, carries only a very modest premium in circulated condition.
A special Liberty Bell and moon reverse is found on the Bicentennial coins dated 1776-1976

Anthony Type
Minted 1979-1981, 1999

Anthony Dollar

Anthony Dollars

	MS60	Proof
1979P	1.50	
1979D	1.50	
1979S	1.50	5.50
1980P	1.50	
1980D	1.50	
1980S	1.50	4.50
1981P	3.50	
1981D	3.50	
1981S	3.50	5.50
1999P	2.00	
1999D	2.00	
1999S		7.00

112

A Note on Anthony Dollars:
Received very poorly by the public for circulation purposes. Due to forced usage by the Postal Service and others the coin was minted again in 1999.

Sacagawea Type
Minted Beginning 2000

Sacagawea Dollar

Sacagawea Dollars

	MS60	Proof		MS60	Proof
2000P	1.00		2002P	1.00	
2000D	1.00		2002D	1.00	
2000S		7.00	2002S		7.00
2001P	1.00		2003P	1.00	
2001D	1.00		2003D	1.00	
2001S		7.00	2003S		7.00

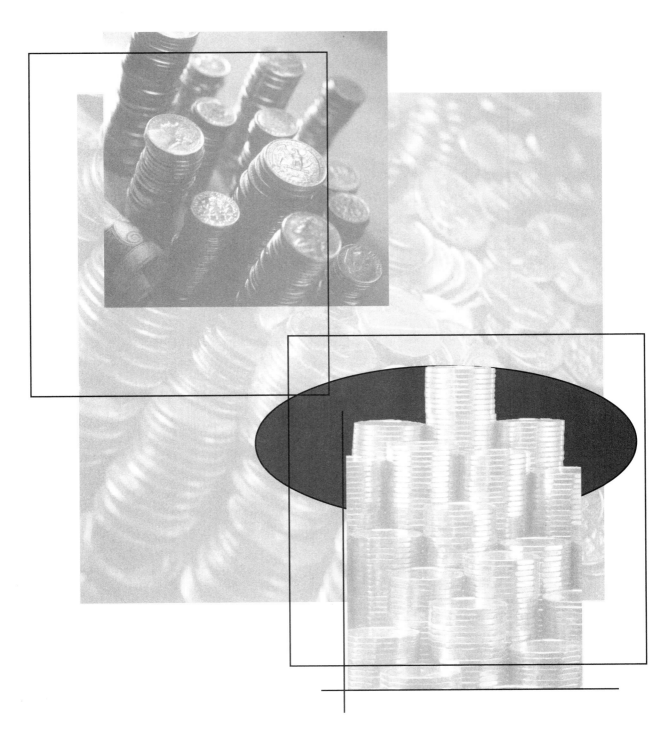

Chapter 5

GOLD COINS

What About Gold Coins?

114

The U.S. government has minted coins in gold since 1792 (some pattern pieces) when the first authorizing act was passed permitting the mintage of gold coins with the values of $2.50, $5 and $10. Until 1933, when gold coins were discontinued for general circulation, over four and one-half billion dollars' worth of gold coins had been made. Pursuant to the gold law, many of these were melted down and were for a time in bars at Fort Knox.

Naturally, people were quick to ask whether they could still collect gold coins and keep those they already owned. The law made provision for keeping coins of recognized value to collectors which involved dates and mint marks, as well as recognized conditions, like those coins of metals other than gold. Many coins of marginal collector value found their way overseas. With the rise in price of the metal and the loosening of restrictions for Americans who wanted to hold gold, many of these coins have, since 1974, found their way back into the United States.

However, no provision was made for the expanded interest in coin collecting that was due to come. The best way to understand the ramifications of the gold act is to read the following copy of the law relating to "Hoarding of Gold."

Values of the various dates are covered later in this chapter.

The following is a copy of the law relating to gold coins:

HOARDING OF GOLD

EXECUTIVE ORDER NO. 6260

Section 4, Acquisition of gold coin and gold bullion.

"No person other than a Federal Reserve bank shall after the date of this order acquire in the United States any gold coin, gold bullion, or gold certificates except under license therefore issued pursuant to this Executive Order, provided that member banks of the Federal Reserve System may accept delivery of such coin, bullion, and certificates, for surrender promptly to a Federal Reserve bank and provided further that persons requiring gold for use in industry, profession or art in which they are regularly engaged may replenish their stocks of gold up to an aggregate amount of $100, by acquisitions of gold bullion held under licenses issued under Section 5 (b), without necessity of obtaining a license for such acquisitions; and provided further that collectors of rare and unusual coin may acquire from one another and hold without necessity of obtaining a license therefore gold coin having a recognized special value to collectors of rare and unusual coin may acquire from one another and hold without necessity of obtaining a license thereof gold coin having a recognized special value to collectors of rare and unusual gold (but not including quarter eagles, otherwise known as $2.50 pieces, unless held, together with rare and unusual coin, as part of a collection for historical, scientific or numismatic purposes, containing not more than four quarter eagles of the same date and design and struck by the same mint)."

On December 31, 1974, the gold law was rescinded after being in effect for a full 40 years. Since that period, the price of gold has soared to many times what it was in 1933, reaching a high of $900/ oz. in early 1980. In a sense, this means that all gold coins could be regarded as collector's items, regardless of rarity or condition. Of course, the fluctuations of the gold market figure in such calculations. Gold would have to sell at about $205 an ounce for U.S. coins to be worth ten times their face value. At the time the above law was written, gold had only approached that figure. A week after the law was rescinded, the U.S. Treasury was accepting all bids of $153 to $185 an ounce, which meant specifically that a $5 gold piece would be worth about $37.50 to $44.75; a $10 gold piece from about $75 to $89.50; and a $20 gold piece from $150 to $179. That, however, applied only to the value of the metal; anyone acquiring gold U.S. coins at those prices could sell them at whatever profit the demand by collectors would bring.

Today a $20 gold piece can be purchased for just a nominal amount above its gold content value. Also, more recently, the U.S. government has decided to get back into the gold coin business. It currently has sold a variety of commemorative and bullion gold pieces.

VALUES OF GOLD COINS

Gold Dollars
Minted 1849-1889

Liberty Head Type
Gold Dollar

Liberty Head Type Minted 1849-1854

	Fine	VF	XF	AU	MS60
1849 Open wreath	100.00	140.00	200.00	230.00	380.00
1849 Closed wreath	100.00	140.00	190.00	210.00	350.00
1849 C Closed wreath	600.00	780.00	1140.00	1620.00	7980.00
1849 C Open wreath	120000.00	210000.00	294000.00	432000.00	
1849 O Open wreath	600.00	780.00	1140.00	1380.00	3900.00
1849 O Open wreath	120.00	150.00	230.00	310.00	660.00
1850	100.00	140.00	190.00	210.00	340.00
1850 C	600.00	780.00	1140.00	1980.00	7560.00
1850 D	600.00	780.00	1170.00	2220.00	7800.00
1850 O	180.00	240.00	350.00	720.00	2640.00
1851	100.00	140.00	190.00	210.00	240.00
1851 C	600.00	780.00	1140.00	1380.00	2280.00
1851 D	600.00	780.00	1140.00	1680.00	4440.00
1851 O	140.00	160.00	210.00	230.00	720.00
1852	100.00	140.00	190.00	210.00	240.00
1852 C	600.00	780.00	1140.00	1380.00	3720.00
1852 D	600.00	780.00	1140.00	1770.00	7680.00
1852 O	120.00	140.00	230.00	320.00	1050.00
1853	100.00	140.00	190.00	210.00	240.00
1853 C	600.00	780.00	1140.00	1560.00	4920.00
1853 D	600.00	780.00	1140.00	2040.00	7920.00
1853 O	130.00	150.00	210.00	230.00	580.00
1854	100.00	140.00	190.00	210.00	250.00
1854 D	600.00	830.00	1710.00	4800.00	10800.00
1854 S	240.00	290.00	410.00	650.00	1980.00

Indian Head (Small) Gold Dollar

Small Indian Head Type Minted 1854-1846

	Fine	VF	XF	AU	MS60
1854	200.00	280.00	410.00	540.00	3270.00
1855	200.00	280.00	410.00	540.00	3270.00
1855 C	600.00	1020.00	2700.00	5520.00	18000.00
1855 D	3000.00	4200.00	7500.00	19200.00	45000.00
1855 O	330.00	390.00	530.00	1050.00	5640.00
1856 S	440.00	720.00	1200.00	2160.00	7500.00

Indian Head (Large) Gold Dollar

Large Indian Head Minted 1856-1889

	Fine	VF	XF	AU	MS60
1856 Upright 5	120.00	150.00	200.00	230.00	450.00
1856 Slanted 5	130.00	140.00	190.00	210.00	260.00
1856 D	2160.00	3360.00	5280.00	6900.00	26400.00
1857	110.00	140.00	190.00	210.00	260.00
1857 C	600.00	780.00	1260.00	2580.00	10500.00
1857 D	600.00	780.00	1620.00	3360.00	9000.00
1857 S	240.00	490.00	580.00	1050.00	5520.00
1858	110.00	140.00	190.00	210.00	260.00
1858 D	600.00	780.00	1170.00	2040.00	9000.00
1858 S	270.00	360.00	480.00	1080.00	5040.00
1859	110.00	140.00	190.00	210.00	260.00
1859 C	600.00	780.00	1170.00	2880.00	9000.00
1859 D	600.00	780.00	1140.00	2370.00	9000.00
1859 S	180.00	230.00	480.00	1010.00	4800.00
1860	110.00	140.00	190.00	210.00	340.00
1860 D	1980.00	2280.00	3600.00	6000.00	14400.00
1860 S	280.00	320.00	460.00	680.00	2220.00
1861	110.00	140.00	190.00	210.00	260.00
1861 D	4500.00	6300.00	9000.00	16200.00	27600.00
1862	110.00	140.00	190.00	210.00	260.00
1863	330.00	420.00	810.00	1560.00	3600.00
1864	270.00	350.00	440.00	750.00	900.00
1865	270.00	350.00	540.00	690.00	1440.00
1866	270.00	350.00	420.00	630.00	900.00
1867	300.00	390.00	480.00	600.00	1070.00
1868	240.00	270.00	390.00	460.00	900.00
1869	300.00	330.00	480.00	600.00	1020.00
1870	240.00	270.00	380.00	460.00	770.00
1870 S	280.00	440.00	720.00	1080.00	2100.00
1871	240.00	270.00	360.00	450.00	690.00
1872	240.00	270.00	350.00	430.00	840.00
1873 Closed 3	300.00	390.00	750.00	870.00	1500.00
1873 Open 3	110.00	140.00	190.00	210.00	260.00
1874	110.00	140.00	190.00	210.00	260.00
1875	1530.00	1800.00	3600.00	4620.00	5760.00
1876	220.00	270.00	330.00	440.00	600.00
1877	140.00	170.00	320.00	440.00	590.00
1878	170.00	200.00	340.00	440.00	600.00
1879	150.00	180.00	260.00	300.00	480.00
1880	140.00	150.00	200.00	220.00	390.00
1881	140.00	150.00	200.00	220.00	390.00
1882	150.00	170.00	200.00	220.00	390.00
1883	140.00	150.00	200.00	220.00	390.00
1884	130.00	150.00	200.00	220.00	390.00
1885	140.00	150.00	200.00	220.00	390.00
1886	140.00	150.00	200.00	220.00	390.00
1887	140.00	150.00	200.00	220.00	390.00
1888	140.00	150.00	200.00	220.00	390.00
1889	140.00	150.00	200.00	220.00	320.00

$2.50 Gold Pieces
Minted 1796-1929

Early Types Minted 1796-1839

Capped Bust Type
(Facing Right)

Capped Bust to Right Minted 1796-1807

	Fine	VF	XF	AU	MS60
1796 No Stars	15000.00	26400.00	54000.00	66000.00	138000.00
1796 Stars	13800.00	21600.00	30000.00	48000.00	102000.00
1797	13800.00	16200.00	21000.00	39000.00	78000.00
1798	4200.00	6000.00	7440.00	19800.00	46200.00
1802 2 over 1	4200.00	6000.00	7200.00	9060.00	18000.00
1804 13 Stars	22800.00	30000.00	66000.00	132000.00	
1804 14 Stars	4200.00	6000.00	7200.00	9600.00	19320.00
1805	4200.00	6000.00	7200.00	9180.00	18900.00
1806 6 over 4	4320.00	6120.00	7320.00	9300.00	20400.00
1806 6 over 5	5400.00	7500.00	11400.00	25200.00	66000.00
1807	4200.00	6000.00	7200.00	9000.00	18000.00

Capped Bust Type
(Facing Left)

Capped Bust to Left Minted 1808-1834

	Fine	VF	XF	AU	MS60
1808	22200.00	27600.00	34800.00	46800.00	66000.00
Large Size					
1821	4800.00	6000.00	7320.00	9360.00	19200.00
1824 4over 1	4800.00	6000.00	7200.00	9240.00	16800.00
1825	4800.00	6000.00	7200.00	9000.00	15000.00
1826 6 over 5	5040.00	6240.00	7800.00	9600.00	28800.00
1827	5160.00	6600.00	8400.00	9960.00	17400.00
Small Size					
1829	4500.00	5400.00	6300.00	8400.00	11400.00
1830	4500.00	5400.00	6300.00	8400.00	11400.00
1831	4500.00	5400.00	6300.00	8400.00	11400.00
1832	4500.00	5400.00	6300.00	8580.00	11400.00
1833	4500.00	5400.00	6360.00	8580.00	11700.00
1834 Motto	6600.00	9360.00	15000.00	20400.00	32400.00

Classic Head Type

Classic Head Minted 1834-1839

	Fine	VF	XF	AU	MS60
1834 No Motto	240.00	280.00	410.00	600.00	1680.00
1835	240.00	280.00	410.00	600.00	2160.00
1836	240.00	280.00	410.00	600.00	1680.00
1837	240.00	280.00	450.00	990.00	2640.00
1838	240.00	280.00	410.00	750.00	1680.00
1838 C	660.00	930.00	1800.00	5520.00	22800.00
1839/8	240.00	290.00	600.00	1380.00	4080.00
1839 C	660.00	840.00	1860.00	3360.00	21600.00
1839/8 D	660.00	870.00	2580.00	5700.00	20400.00
1839 O	360.00	480.00	870.00	1320.00	5400.00

Liberty $2.50 Gold Piece

Liberty Minted 1840-1907

	VF	XF	AU	MS60
1840	180.00	840.00	2400.00	5880.00
1840 C	840.00	1320.00	3960.00	11040.00
1840 D	2040.00	7200.00	12930.00	34800.00
1840 O	240.00	780.00	1770.00	9900.00
1841 Proof Only	48000.00	90000.00	96000.00	126000.00
1841 C	840.00	1320.00	3240.00	16800.00
1841 D	1320.00	3300.00	9300.00	25200.00
1842	820.00	2400.00	6000.00	19800.00
1842 C	1080.00	2520.00	6900.00	25200.00
1842 D	1350.00	2820.00	10200.00	36000.00
1842 O	340.00	1080.00	1980.00	10800.00
1843	170.00	220.00	300.00	1140.00
1843 C Small Date	1980.00	4980.00	8040.00	21600.00
1843 C Large Date	840.00	1320.00	2940.00	7980.00
1843 D Small Date	840.00	1320.00	2280.00	9240.00
1843 O Small Date	180.00	230.00	300.00	1500.00
1843 O Large Date	230.00	420.00	1500.00	6000.00
1844	360.00	750.00	1860.00	6540.00
1844 C	840.00	1560.00	5820.00	16200.00
1844 D	840.00	1320.00	2160.00	6420.00
1844	360.00	750.00	1860.00	6540.00
1844 C	840.00	1560.00	5820.00	16200.00
1844 D	840.00	1320.00	2160.00	6420.00
1845	240.00	290.00	350.00	1110.00

Liberty Minted 1840-1907

	VF	XF	AU	MS60
1845 D	90.00	1320.00	2280.00	13200.00
1845 O	930.00	1860.00	5760.00	14400.00
1846	260.00	480.00	840.00	5160.00
1846 C	960.00	2040.00	8400.00	16800.00
1846 D	840.00	1320.00	1980.00	10080.00
1846 O	280.00	390.00	1020.00	5880.00
1847	220.00	350.00	780.00	3360.00
1847 C	840.00	1320.00	1920.00	6000.00
1847 D	840.00	1320.00	1950.00	8700.00
1847 O	220.00	360.00	940.00	3120.00
1848	480.00	810.00	1680.00	5700.00
1848 "CAL"	8400.00	15600.00	22800.00	34800.00
1848 C	840.00	1320.00	2640.00	13200.00
1848 D	840.00	1320.00	2040.00	10080.00
1849	270.00	460.00	780.00	2400.00
1849 C	840.00	1440.00	4620.00	22200.00
1849 D	840.00	1320.00	3000.00	15000.00
1850	170.00	210.00	350.00	990.00
1850 C	840.00	1320.00	3120.00	15600.00
1850 D	840.00	1320.00	2520.00	10800.00
1850 O	210.00	440.00	1140.00	4500.00
1851	170.00	200.00	230.00	310.00
1851 C	840.00	1320.00	4200.00	11580.00
1851 D	840.00	1320.00	3300.00	11400.00
1851 O	180.00	210.00	840.00	4500.00
1852	170.00	200.00	230.00	320.00
1852 C	840.00	1440.00	3960.00	16800.00
1852 D	870.00	1980.00	6720.00	16200.00
1852 O	180.00	290.00	900.00	4800.00
1853	170.00	200.00	230.00	350.00
1853 D	1440.00	2640.00	4320.00	16200.00
1854	170.00	200.00	230.00	350.00
1854 C	840.00	1680.00	4680.00	14400.00
1854 D	2520.00	4740.00	10500.00	27000.00
1854 O	170.00	210.00	410.00	1500.00
1854 S	36000.00	60000.00	132000.00	
1855	170.00	200.00	230.00	360.00
1855 C	840.00	1680.00	4680.00	14400.00
1855 D	3000.00	6840.00	15000.00	43800.00
1856	170.00	200.00	230.00	380.00
1856 C	870.00	1920.00	3600.00	14400.00
1856 D	6180.00	9000.00	22800.00	48000.00
1856 O	210.00	690.00	1200.00	7500.00
1856 S	200.00	360.00	870.00	4200.00
1857	170.00	200.00	230.00	380.00
1857 D	840.00	1920.00	3600.00	12000.00
1857 O	200.00	350.00	960.00	4200.00
1857 S	200.00	330.00	840.00	5280.00
1858	170.00	240.00	330.00	1200.00
1858 C	840.00	1320.00	2400.00	9000.00
1859	170.00	240.00	380.00	1200.00
1859 D	1320.00	2400.00	4320.00	1800.00
1859 S	300.00	900.00	2400.00	6180.00
1860	170.00	240.00	440.00	1080.00
1860 C	840.00	1560.00	3120.00	20400.00
1860 S	190.00	630.00	1080.00	3780.00
1861	170.00	200.00	230.00	320.00
1861 S	330.00	870.00	2880.00	7200.00
1862 2 over 1	840.00	1800.00	3240.00	7680.00
1862	200.00	300.00	480.00	1200.00
1862 S	840.00	2040.00	4080.00	16800.00
1863 Proof Only			Proof 63	30000.00
1861	170.00	200.00	230.00	320.00
1861 S	330.00	870.00	2880.00	7200.00

Liberty Minted 1840-1907

	VF	XF	AU	MS60
1862 2 over 1	840.00	1800.00	3240.00	7680.00
1862	200.00	300.00	480.00	1200.00
1862 S	840.00	2040.00	4080.00	16800.00
1863 Proof Only			Proof 63	30000.00
1863 S	470.00	1410.00	3000.00	14400.00
1864	5400.00	10800.00	21600.00	36000.00
1865	3960.00	7200.00	18000.00	36000.00
1865 S	210.00	590.00	1200.00	4200.00
1866	1170.00	3360.00	4800.00	11400.00
1866 S	270.00	630.00	1380.00	5880.00
1867	360.00	780.00	1110.00	4680.00
1867 S	230.00	590.00	1560.00	3960.00
1868	220.00	390.00	630.00	1500.00
1868 S	180.00	290.00	960.00	3840.00
1869	230.00	440.00	690.00	2940.00
1869 S	210.00	450.00	780.00	4200.00
1870	220.00	400.00	720.00	3600.00
1870 S	180.00	410.00	720.00	4800.00
1871	230.00	320.00	570.00	2160.00
1871 S	180.00	270.00	510.00	2160.00
1872	360.00	780.00	1080.00	4500.00
1872 S	180.00	360.00	870.00	4320.00
1873 Closed 3	170.00	210.00	260.00	500.00
1873 Open 3	170.00	200.00	240.00	280.00
1873 S	210.00	360.00	830.00	2700.00
1874	240.00	360.00	690.00	1980.00
1875	3300.00	4800.00	8040.00	10800.00
1875 S	170.00	290.00	720.00	4200.00
1876	270.00	620.00	870.00	3240.00
1876 S	230.00	510.00	920.00	3180.00
1877	360.00	750.00	1010.00	2940.00
1877 S	160.00	200.00	230.00	600.00
1878	160.00	200.00	230.00	270.00
1878 S	160.00	200.00	230.00	330.00
1879	160.00	200.00	230.00	270.00
1879 S	200.00	270.00	480.00	2100.00
1880	180.00	330.00	590.00	1260.00
1881	1800.00	2760.00	4080.00	8280.00
1882	190.00	290.00	390.00	650.00
1883	190.00	380.00	950.00	2160.00
1884	180.00	380.00	570.00	1500.00
1885	600.00	1680.00	2340.00	4080.00
1886	180.00	260.00	420.00	1050.00
1887	170.00	240.00	320.00	660.00
1888	170.00	220.00	270.00	300.00
1889	170.00	210.00	250.00	320.00
1890	180.00	220.00	280.00	480.00
1891	170.00	200.00	230.00	400.00
1892	170.00	230.00	320.00	720.00
1893	170.00	200.00	230.00	280.00
1894	170.00	220.00	310.00	750.00
1895	160.00	210.00	270.00	380.00
1896	160.00	200.00	230.00	280.00
1897	160.00	200.00	230.00	280.00
1898	160.00	200.00	230.00	280.00
1899	160.00	200.00	230.00	280.00
1900	160.00	240.00	360.00	450.00
1901	160.00	200.00	220.00	270.00
1902	160.00	200.00	220.00	270.00
1903	160.00	200.00	220.00	270.00
1904	160.00	200.00	220.00	270.00
1905	160.00	200.00	220.00	270.00
1906	160.00	200.00	220.00	270.00
1907	160.00	200.00	220.00	270.00
1907	160.00	200.00	210.00	270.00

Lower grade coins are bullion sensitive.

Indian Head $2.50 Gold Piece

Indian Head Type Minted 1908-1929

	XF	AU	MS60
1908	180.00	200.00	240.00
1909	180.00	200.00	240.00
1910	180.00	200.00	240.00
1911	180.00	200.00	240.00
1911D	1200.00	1380.00	3120.00
1912	180.00	200.00	240.00
1913	180.00	200.00	240.00
1914	180.00	270.00	600.00
1914D	180.00	200.00	360.00
1915	180.00	200.00	240.00
1925D	180.00	200.00	240.00
1926	180.00	200.00	240.00
1927	180.00	200.00	240.00
1928	180.00	200.00	240.00
1929	180.00	200.00	240.00

122

Lower grade coins are bullion sensitive.

$3.00 Gold Pieces
Minted 1854-1889

Indian Head $3.00 Gold Piece

Indian Head Type Minted 1854-1889

	VF	XF	AU	MS60
1854	590.00	840.00	1190.00	1760.00
1854 D	7560.00	11400.00	21600.00	58800.00
1854 O	840.00	1620.00	2760.00	16200.00
1855	590.00	840.00	1200.00	1920.00
1855 S	900.00	1800.00	4800.00	21000.00
1856	590.00	840.00	1200.00	2130.00
1856 S	600.00	1020.00	1800.00	8640.00

Indian Head Type Minted 1854-1889

	VF	XF	AU	MS60
1857	590.00	840.00	1200.00	2760.00
1857 S	690.00	1560.00	4200.00	15000.00
1858	720.00	1260.00	2400.00	6840.00
1859	590.00	840.00	1200.00	2340.00
1860	600.00	860.00	1230.00	2520.00
1860 S	740.00	1380.00	5280.00	13800.00
1861	650.00	870.00	1290.00	2940.00
1862	650.00	870.00	1380.00	2940.00
1863	660.00	900.00	1350.00	2940.00
1864	690.00	900.00	1350.00	2940.00
1865	960.00	1920.00	4200.00	7200.00
1866	690.00	900.00	1320.00	2940.00
1867	690.00	900.00	1590.00	2760.00
1868	640.00	860.00	1290.00	2520.00
1869	740.00	900.00	1440.00	3300.00
1870	600.00	900.00	1440.00	3600.00
1870 S	480000.00	960000.00		
1871	710.00	960.00	1470.00	3240.00
1872	660.00	900.00	1290.00	2940.00
1873 Closed 3	2760.00	4200.00	7800.00	22200.00
1873 Open 3 Proof only			7800.00	
1874	590.00	830.00	1160.00	1760.00
1875 Proof only			45000.00	
1876 Proof only			12600.00	
1877	1050.00	2400.00	4800.00	11040.00
1878	590.00	830.00	1160.00	1760.00
1879	600.00	840.00	1260.00	2190.00
1880	650.00	1380.00	1920.00	2520.00
1881	1080.00	1980.00	3600.00	5040.00
1882	720.00	900.00	1470.00	2640.00
1883	660.00	1080.00	1740.00	2760.00
1884	1020.00	1320.00	1920.00	2640.00
1885	1020.00	1380.00	2040.00	3120.00
1886	960.00	1440.00	1860.00	3480.00
1887	600.00	840.00	1380.00	1770.00
1888	600.00	840.00	1230.00	1760.00
1889	600.00	840.00	1200.00	1770.00

123

$4.00 Gold Pieces
Minted 1879-1880

$4.00 Gold Stellas

1879	Flowing Hair Proof Only	Proof60	52800.00
1879	Coiled Hair Proof Only	Proof60	114000.00
1880	Flowing Hair Proof Only	Proof60	87600.00
1880	Coiled Hair Proof Only	Proof64	210000.00

$5.00 Gold Pieces
Minted 1795-1929

Capped Bust Type
(Eagle & Shield Reverse)

Capped Bust to Right Minted 1795-1807
Small Eagle

	F	VF	XF	AU	MS60
1795	9000.00	12600.00	16200.00	21600.00	33600.00
1796 6 over 5	9240.00	12900.00	18000.00	24600.00	58800.00
1797 15 Stars	10800.00	14400.00	28800.00	57000.00	132000.00
1797 16 Stars	9600.00	13200.00	24000.00	44400.00	120000.00
1798	84000.00	144000.00	264000.00	348000.00	

Heraldic Eagle

	F	VF	XF	AU	MS60
1795	7680.00	11700.00	17700.00	37800.00	78000.00
1797 7 over 5	7560.00	11100.00	18600.00	51000.00	144000.00
1797 16 Star Obverse					
1798 Small 8	2100.00	2640.00	3840.00	9600.00	19200.00
1798 Large 8, 13 Stars	2040.00	2520.00	3360.00	7080.00	14100.00
1798 Large 8, 14 Stars		2220.00	2880.00	5760.00	15000.00
1799	2130.00	2520.00	3510.00	6720.00	13200.00
1800	2040.00	2400.00	2820.00	5250.00	6960.00
1802 2 over 1	2040.00	2400.00	2820.00	5220.00	6960.00
1803 3 over 2	2040.00	2400.00	2820.00	5220.00	6960.00
1804 Small 8	2040.00	2400.00	2820.00	5220.00	6960.00
1804 Sm 8 over Lg 8	2040.00	2400.00	2820.00	5220.00	7800.00
1805	2040.00	2400.00	2820.00	5220.00	6840.00
1806 Pointed Top 6	2070.00	2460.00	2850.00	5250.00	7020.00
1806 Round Top 6	2040.00	2400.00	2820.00	5220.00	6840.00
1807	2040.00	2400.00	2820.00	5220.00	6960.00

Capped Head Type

Capped Bust to Left Minted 1807-1812

	F	VF	XF	AU	MS60
1807	1800.00	2100.00	2760.00	4320.00	5760.00
1808 8 over 7	1860.00	2880.00	3300.00	4920.00	9900.00
1808	1800.00	2100.00	2760.00	4320.00	5880.00
1809 9 over 8	1800.00	2100.00	2760.00	4320.00	5880.00
1810 Sm. Date, Sm. 5	8400.00	19800.00	30600.00	43200.00	90000.00
1810 Sm. Date, Tall 5	1830.00	2130.00	2790.00	4350.00	5940.00
1810 Large Date, Small 5	12000.00	22200.00	32400.00	54000.00	108000.00
1810 Lg. Date, Lg. 6	1800.00	2100.00	2760.00	4320.00	5760.00
1811	1800.00	2100.00	2760.00	4320.00	5760.00
1812	1800.00	2100.00	2760.00	4320.00	5760.00

Capped Bust Minted 1813-1834
Large Size Bust

	F	VF	XF	AU	MS60
1813	2100.00	2400.00	2940.00	4320.00	6420.00
1814 4 over 3	2160.00	2490.00	3120.00	4680.00	8160.00
1815	33000.00	46200.00	69000.00	96000.00	114000.00
1818	2130.00	2430.00	3000.00	4440.00	6600.00
1818 5D over 50				9600.00	18000.00
1819	8400.00	14400.00	24000.00	33600.00	54000.00
1819 5D over 50				32400.00	60000.00
1820	2160.00	2460.00	3180.00	4680.00	8700.00
1821	5040.00	12000.00	18000.00	26400.00	62400.00
1822	480000.00				
1823	2160.00	2940.00	4080.00	6000.00	13800.00
1824	4320.00	9000.00	13800.00	19200.00	26400.00
1825 5 over 1	4500.00	7200.00	10200.00	16800.00	33000.00
1825 5 over 4					
1826	3180.00	6600.00	8100.00	12600.00	21600.00
1827	4920.00	8400.00	10800.00	16800.00	30000.00
1828 8 over 7					
1828	4800.00	10800.00	16800.00	26400.00	57000.00
1829 Large Date					

Capped Bust Minted 1813-1834
Small Size Bust

	F	VF	XF	AU	MS60
1829 Small Date		32100.00	45000.00	72000.00	
1830	8400.00	11100.00	13800.00	16200.00	25200.00
1831	8400.00	11100.00	13800.00	16500.00	26400.00
1832 12 Stars		36000.00	54000.00	78000.00	102000.00
1832 13 stars	8400.00	11100.00	13800.00	16200.00	25200.00
1833 Large Date	8400.00	11100.00	13800.00	16200.00	25200.00
1833 Small Date		8760.00	11700.00	14400.00	17400.00
1834 Plain 4	8400.00	11100.00	13800.00	16200.00	25200.00
1834 Crosslet 4	8400.00	11100.00	13800.00	16500.00	26400.00

125

Classic Head Type

Classic Head Minted 1834-1838

	F	VF	XF	AU	MS60
1834 Plain 4	240.00	290.00	470.00	660.00	2220.00
1834 Crosslet 4	840.00	1440.00	2400.00	4800.00	15000.00
1835	240.00	290.00	480.00	750.00	2760.00
1836	240.00	290.00	470.00	660.00	2240.00
1837	240.00	290.00	490.00	990.00	3090.00
1838	240.00	290.00	480.00	660.00	3210.00
1838 C	960.00	1680.00	3360.00	9360.00	33600.00
1838 D	780.00	1350.00	3000.00	6000.00	19200.00

126

Liberty Head 1839-1908

No Motto

	VF	XF	AU	MS60
1839	240.00	410.00	1020.00	3480.00
1839 C	1020.00	2340.00	5100.00	17400.00
1839 D	1020.00	1920.00	4500.00	16200.00
1840	210.00	320.00	1110.00	3240.00
1840 C	960.00	2160.00	6000.00	21600.00
1840 D	960.00	1440.00	5880.00	12600.00
1840 O	280.00	750.00	1590.00	9600.00
1841	340.00	810.00	1560.00	4380.00
1841 C	960.00	1320.00	2640.00	14400.00
1841 D	960.00	1320.00	2700.00	12600.00
1842 Small Letters	300.00	960.00	2640.00	12000.00
1842 Large Letters	600.00	1800.00	2520.00	9600.00
1842 C Small Date	7800.00	19800.00	38400.00	126000.00
1842 C Large Date	960.00	1410.00	2940.00	15000.00
1842 D Small Date	960.00	1320.00	2400.00	13200.00
1842 D Large Date	1920.00	5040.00	11400.00	42000.00
1842 O	900.00	2610.00	8400.00	19200.00

No Motto

	VF	XF	AU	MS60
1843	200.00	230.00	310.00	1650.00
1843 C	960.00	1320.00	3360.00	10200.00
1843 D	960.00	1320.00	2160.00	10200.00
1843 O Small Letters	450.00	1200.00	1860.00	19200.00
1843 O Large Letters	230.00	990.00	1740.00	10500.00
1844	200.00	210.00	330.00	1740.00
1844 C	960.00	2640.00	5640.00	19200.00
1844 D	960.00	1320.00	2160.00	9600.00
1844 O	230.00	330.00	530.00	3480.00
1845	200.00	210.00	320.00	1800.00
1845 D	960.00	1320.00	2160.00	10320.00
1845 O	360.00	630.00	2400.00	8640.00
1846	200.00	210.00	320.00	2220.00
1846 C	960.00	2520.00	5520.00	19800.00
1846 D	960.00	1320.00	3120.00	11100.00
1846 O	330.00	840.00	2760.00	10200.00
1847	200.00	220.00	290.00	1320.00
1847 C	960.00	1320.00	3000.00	11400.00
1847 D	960.00	1320.00	2280.00	7200.00
1847 O	1680.00	6600.00	8400.00	22800.00
1848	200.00	240.00	360.00	1320.00
1848 C	960.00	1320.00	2400.00	16800.00
1848 D	960.00	1320.00	2340.00	12600.00
1849	200.00	240.00	660.00	2400.00
1849 C	960.00	1320.00	2160.00	11700.00
1849 D	960.00	1320.00	2880.00	12000.00
1850	240.00	530.00	930.00	3240.00
1850 C	960.00	1320.00	2400.00	10080.00
1850 D	960.00	1320.00	3480.00	25200.00
1851	200.00	210.00	320.00	2520.00
1851 C	960.00	1320.00	2700.00	14400.00
1851 D	960.00	1440.00	2640.00	12600.00
1851 O	500.00	1320.00	3480.00	10500.00
1852	200.00	220.00	290.00	1080.00
1852 C	960.00	1320.00	2340.00	5880.00
1852 D	960.00	1320.00	2160.00	11040.00
1853	200.00	220.00	320.00	1260.00
1853 C	960.00	1320.00	2160.00	7380.00
1853 D	960.00	1320.00	2160.00	5820.00
1854	200.00	230.00	450.00	1920.00
1854 C	960.00	1320.00	3360.00	12360.00
1854 D	960.00	1320.00	2160.00	6900.00
1854 O	270.00	460.00	1230.00	7200.00
1854 S			240000.00	
1855	200.00	210.00	330.00	1500.00
1855 C	960.00	1500.00	2820.00	13200.00
1855 D	960.00	1320.00	2700.00	15300.00
1855 O	540.00	1860.00	4080.00	18000.00
1855 S	350.00	840.00	1860.00	13800.00
1856	200.00	220.00	290.00	2010.00
1856 C	960.00	1320.00	2880.00	18000.00
1856 D	960.00	1320.00	3240.00	9120.00
1856 O	570.00	1080.00	4080.00	10800.00
1856 S	270.00	540.00	1080.00	6000.00
1857	200.00	220.00	360.00	1410.00
1857 C	960.00	1320.00	2850.00	7800.00
1857 D	960.00	1320.00	3060.00	11400.00
1857 O	560.00	1230.00	4080.00	14400.00
1857 S	270.00	470.00	990.00	11700.00

Liberty Head Minted 1839-1908
No Motto

	VF	XF	AU	MS60
1858	220.00	480.00	630.00	3360.00
1858 C	960.00	1320.00	2760.00	9000.00
1858 D	960.00	1320.00	2700.00	10800.00
1858 S	620.00	2040.00	4740.00	27000.00
1859	290.00	540.00	720.00	6360.00
1859 C	960.00	1320.00	3300.00	13200.00
1859 D	960.00	1560.00	2700.00	12600.00
1859 S	1080.00	3120.00	4680.00	25200.00
1860	240.00	510.00	960.00	3540.00
1860 C	960.00	1920.00	2880.00	11100.00
1860 D	960.00	1800.00	3120.00	15000.00
1860 S	960.00	1860.00	5040.00	22200.00
1861	200.00	230.00	320.00	1050.00
1861 C	1470.00	3360.00	6120.00	20400.00
1861 D	3840.00	6120.00	14400.00	46800.00
1861 S	900.00	3960.00	5700.00	31800.00
1862	600.00	1470.00	2730.00	18000.00
1862 S	2700.00	5520.00	9300.00	54000.00
1863	1050.00	3300.00	5400.00	24000.00
1863 S	1260.00	3600.00	8820.00	31200.00
1864	560.00	1620.00	3600.00	12900.00
1864 S	4260.00	13800.00	26400.00	48000.00
1865	1160.00	3600.00	7620.00	17400.00
1865 S	1140.00	2400.00	4440.00	15000.00
1866 S	1440.00	3480.00	10920.00	35400.00

With Motto

	VF	XF	AU	MS60
1866	690.00	1320.00	3000.00	13200.00
1866 S	840.00	2400.00	6960.00	22200.00
1867	440.00	1380.00	3240.00	9300.00
1867 S	1110.00	2280.00	6720.00	24000.00
1868	600.00	900.00	3000.00	9000.00
1868 S	360.00	1320.00	3240.00	17400.00
1869	810.00	2100.00	3240.00	14400.00
1869 S	440.00	1530.00	3420.00	24000.00
1870	690.00	1800.00	2460.00	15600.00
1870 CC	4440.00	11280.00	22800.00	96000.00
1870 S	690.00	2040.00	6720.00	25200.00
1871	810.00	1620.00	2760.00	10200.00
1871 CC	980.00	2880.00	9600.00	54000.00
1871 S	450.00	870.00	2760.00	10800.00
1872	750.00	1680.00	2460.00	11400.00
1872 CC	980.00	3720.00	15600.00	54000.00
1872 S	390.00	690.00	3000.00	9600.00
1873 Closed 3	160.00	200.00	360.00	1040.00
1873 Open 3	160.00	200.00	330.00	750.00
1873 CC	1680.00	8880.00	24000.00	48000.00
1873 S	470.00	1260.00	3000.00	19200.00
1874	580.00	1470.00	2220.00	11400.00
1874 CC	720.00	1500.00	7800.00	33000.00
1874 S	560.00	1860.00	3720.00	19800.00
1875	30000.00	36000.00	51600.00	168000.00
1875 CC	1200.00	3840.00	10080.00	45000.00
1875 S	590.00	2280.00	4200.00	14400.00

With Motto

	VF	XF	AU	MS60
1876	960.00	2190.00	3480.00	9600.00
1876 CC	1040.00	4080.00	11040.00	40800.00
1876 S	1440.00	3120.00	7620.00	27000.00
1877	780.00	2400.00	3480.00	9600.00
1877 CC	890.00	2520.00	9600.00	45600.00
1877 S	350.00	570.00	1240.00	8040.00
1878	140.00	170.00	220.00	380.00
1878 CC	2640.00	6300.00	17400.00	54000.00
1878 S	140.00	190.00	270.00	600.00
1879	140.00	170.00	210.00	350.00
1879 CC	470.00	1160.00	2640.00	19200.00
1879 S	160.00	200.00	220.00	720.00
1880	140.00	150.00	150.00	200.00
1880 CC	380.00	680.00	1200.00	8640.00
1880 S	140.00	150.00	150.00	200.00
1881 1 over 0	300.00	480.00	570.00	1320.00
1881	140.00	150.00	150.00	200.00
1881 CC	450.00	1190.00	6000.00	19800.00
1881 S	140.00	150.00	150.00	200.00
1882	140.00	150.00	150.00	200.00
1882 CC	350.00	480.00	710.00	6600.00
1882 S	140.00	150.00	150.00	200.00
1883	140.00	150.00	170.00	230.00
1883 CC	410.00	920.00	2640.00	15000.00
1883 S	180.00	220.00	270.00	900.00
1884	150.00	170.00	200.00	570.00
1884 CC	490.00	860.00	2520.00	15000.00
1884 S	150.00	170.00	190.00	320.00
1885	140.00	150.00	150.00	200.00
1885 S	140.00	150.00	150.00	200.00
1886	140.00	150.00	160.00	210.00
1886 S	140.00	150.00	150.00	200.00
1887 Proof Only				
1887 S	140.00	150.00	150.00	200.00
1888	160.00	210.00	270.00	520.00
1888 S	160.00	180.00	290.00	1080.00
1889	260.00	390.00	450.00	960.00
1890	360.00	440.00	480.00	1920.00
1890 CC	290.00	360.00	500.00	1040.00
1891	150.00	180.00	200.00	410.00
1891 CC	280.00	370.00	470.00	650.00
1892	140.00	150.00	150.00	200.00
1892 CC	280.00	370.00	510.00	1350.00
1892 O	450.00	870.00	1200.00	2880.00
1892 S	150.00	170.00	200.00	480.00
1893	140.00	150.00	150.00	200.00
1893 CC	280.00	400.00	680.00	1200.00
1893 O	200.00	280.00	420.00	830.00
1893 S	150.00	180.00	190.00	210.00
1894	140.00	150.00	150.00	200.00
1894 O	180.00	320.00	500.00	1160.00
1894 S	220.00	330.00	510.00	2520.00
1895	140.00	150.00	150.00	200.00
1895 S	180.00	240.00	350.00	2760.00

Liberty Head Type Minted1839-1908
With Motto

	VF	XF	AU	MS60
1896	140.00	150.00	160.00	210.00
1896 S	180.00	220.00	270.00	1170.00
1897	140.00	150.00	150.00	200.00
1897 S	170.00	190.00	210.00	750.00
1898	140.00	150.00	150.00	200.00
1898 S	160.00	180.00	190.00	210.00
1899	140.00	150.00	150.00	200.00
1899 S	150.00	170.00	170.00	210.00
1900	140.00	150.00	150.00	200.00
1900 S	150.00	170.00	180.00	210.00
1901	140.00	150.00	150.00	200.00
1901 S, 1 over 0	170.00	200.00	210.00	330.00
1901 S	140.00	150.00	150.00	200.00
1902	140.00	150.00	150.00	200.00
1902 S	140.00	150.00	150.00	200.00
1903	140.00	150.00	150.00	200.00
1903 S	140.00	150.00	150.00	200.00
1904	140.00	150.00	150.00	200.00
1904 S	160.00	210.00	260.00	870.00
1905	140.00	150.00	150.00	200.00
1905 S	160.00	180.00	210.00	480.00
1906	140.00	150.00	150.00	200.00
1906 D	140.00	150.00	150.00	200.00
1906 S	150.00	170.00	180.00	210.00
1907	140.00	150.00	150.00	200.00
1907 D	140.00	150.00	150.00	200.00
1908	140.00	150.00	150.00	200.00

Lower grade coins are bullion sensitive

Indian Head $5.00 Gold Piece

Indian Head Type Minted 1908-1929

	VF	XF	AU	MS60
1908	170.00	200.00	210.00	300.00
1908D	170.00	200.00	210.00	300.00
1908S	480.00	510.00	600.00	1130.00
1909	170.00	200.00	210.00	310.00
1909D	170.00	200.00	210.00	290.00

Indian Head Type Minted 1908-1929

	VF	XF	AU	MS60
1909O	960.00	1200.00	1200.00	5640.00
1909S	170.00	200.00	210.00	1440.00
1910	170.00	200.00	210.00	330.00
1910D	170.00	200.00	210.00	330.00
1910S	170.00	200.00	300.00	780.00
1911	170.00	200.00	210.00	300.00
1911D	360.00	410.00	460.00	2940.00
1911S	170.00	200.00	210.00	500.00
1912	170.00	200.00	210.00	300.00
1912S	170.00	200.00	210.00	1500.00
1913	170.00	200.00	210.00	300.00
1913S	240.00	260.00	290.00	1230.00
1914	170.00	200.00	210.00	300.00
1914D	170.00	200.00	210.00	300.00
1914S	170.00	200.00	300.00	1080.00
1915	170.00	200.00	270.00	300.00
1915S	340.00	360.00	400.00	1790.00
1916S	210.00	280.00	320.00	530.00
1929	4080.00	4800.00	5280.00	5760.00

Lower grade coins are bullion sensitive.

$10.00 Gold Pieces
Minted 1795-1933

Capped Bust Type

Capped Bust to Right Minted 1795-1804

	F	VF	XF	AU	MS60
1795 9 Leaves	18000.00	30000.00	48000.00	66000.00	138000.00
1795 13 Leaves	10800.00	14400.00	21000.00	31200.00	48000.00
1796	10800.00	14700.00	21600.00	31800.00	54000.00
1797 Small Eagle	12000.00	15600.00	25200.00	48000.00	174000.00

Heraldic Eagle Reverse

	F	VF	XF	AU	MS60
1797	3600.00	5460.00	7080.00	11040.00	20700.00
1798 over 7, 9 stars left	6300.00	10800.00	20100.00	28800.00	69000.00
1798 over 7, 7 stars left	12600.00	21000.00	48000.00	106800.00	180000.00
1799	3600.00	5400.00	6900.00	9000.00	13200.00
1800	3600.00	5400.00	6900.00	9180.00	17100.00
1801	3600.00	5400.00	6900.00	9000.00	13200.00
1803	3600.00	5460.00	7020.00	9240.00	14100.00
1804 Crosslet 4	4080.00	5760.00	7800.00	14160.00	22800.00
1804 Plain 4 Proof only					

Liberty $10.00 Gold Piece

Liberty Head Type Minted 1838-1907
No Motto

	VF	XF	AU	MS60
1838	960.00	2520.00	5160.00	27600.00
1839 Large Letters Type of 1838	960.00	1710.00	4500.00	22200.00
1839 Small Letters Type of 1840	1320.00	3120.00	57600.00	25800.00
1840	350.00	570.00	1230.00	9240.00
1841	320.00	440.00	990.00	6720.00
1841 O	1920.00	4320.00	10680.00	30000.00
1842	310.00	470.00	1070.00	14400.00
1842 O	310.00	420.00	2100.00	15600.00
1843	310.00	440.00	1380.00	16500.00
1843 O	310.00	410.00	980.00	9840.00
1844	1010.00	2640.00	4860.00	14400.00
1844 O	310.00	450.00	1440.00	13200.00
1845	590.00	690.00	1860.00	16200.00
1845 O	410.00	660.00	1680.00	12600.00
1846	630.00	920.00	4320.00	21000.00
1846 O	450.00	720.00	3000.00	14400.00
1847	310.00	360.00	490.00	2760.00
1847 O	310.00	360.00	510.00	5040.00
1848	330.00	390.00	750.00	4560.00
1848 O	540.00	1020.00	3000.00	12600.00
1849	310.00	360.00	520.00	3120.00
1849 O	360.00	1920.00	4740.00	21000.00
1850 Large Date	310.00	360.00	520.00	3540.00
1850 Small Date	490.00	750.00	1560.00	11400.00
1850 O	380.00	710.00	2700.00	15000.00
1851	320.00	400.00	540.00	4920.00
1851 O	330.00	380.00	840.00	5520.00

Liberty Head Type Minted 1838-1907
No Motto

	VF	XF	AU	MS60
1852	320.00	360.00	510.00	4200.00
1852 O	530.00	960.00	3420.00	22800.00
1853 3 over 2	480.00	690.00	1620.00	13800.00
1853	310.00	360.00	510.00	3540.00
1853 O	330.00	380.00	900.00	12000.00
1854	330.00	440.00	660.00	5760.00
1854 O	320.00	640.00	1440.00	8400.00
1854 S	310.00	360.00	750.00	9600.00
1855	310.00	360.00	510.00	3480.00
1855 O	600.00	1200.00	4800.00	20400.00
1855 S	1200.00	1920.00	6600.00	30000.00
1856	310.00	360.00	530.00	3480.00
1856 O	600.00	1200.00	3600.00	14400.00
1856 S	310.00	500.00	990.00	9000.00
1857	380.00	810.00	1740.00	12300.00
1857 O	840.00	1680.00	2880.00	18000.00
1857 S	380.00	780.00	1920.00	10440.00
1858	4500.00	6240.00	9840.00	32400.00
1858 O	320.00	720.00	1560.00	8400.00
1858 S	1320.00	2820.00	4680.00	30000.00
1859	350.00	600.00	1140.00	9000.00
1859 O	3840.00	6600.00	13200.00	46800.00
1859 S	1800.00	4440.00	11400.00	42000.00
1860	390.00	660.00	1140.00	7800.00
1860 O	510.00	1080.00	2160.00	13200.00
1860 S	2220.00	4560.00	13800.00	42000.00
1861	310.00	360.00	480.00	2820.00
1861 S	1320.00	2760.00	5520.00	33000.00
1862	480.00	930.00	2160.00	12600.00
1862 S	1560.00	2880.00	4920.00	36000.00
1863	3720.00	7620.00	14400.00	48000.00
1863 S	1260.00	3060.00	8100.00	23400.00
1864	1590.00	3600.00	6600.00	13800.00
1864 S	4320.00	10680.00	25200.00	54000.00
1865	1680.00	3480.00	6120.00	33000.00
1865 S	3120.00	8040.00	14400.00	46800.00
1865 S Over Inverted 186	3000.00	5820.00	9000.00	47400.00
1866 S	2220.00	3000.00	10800.00	45600.00

Liberty Head Type Minted 1838-1907
With Motto

	VF	XF	AU	MS60
1866	720.00	1590.00	3360.00	15000.00
1866 S	1320.00	3240.00	6120.00	23520.00
1867	1380.00	2340.00	3840.00	27000.00
1867 S	2160.00	5580.00	7680.00	42000.00
1868	530.00	720.00	1410.00	12900.00
1868 S	1200.00	2040.00	3360.00	24000.00
1869	1380.00	2400.00	4320.00	33000.00
1869 S	1200.00	2280.00	4800.00	22800.00

133

Liberty Head Type Minted 1838-1907
With Motto

	VF	XF	AU	MS60
1870	780.00	1050.00	1890.00	16200.00
1870 CC	7680.00	21600.00	42000.00	96000.00
1870 S	900.00	2160.00	5520.00	33000.00
1871	1320.00	2520.00	3720.00	18000.00
1871 CC	1800.00	4680.00	12600.00	57600.00
1871 S	990.00	1380.00	5220.00	26400.00
1872	2220.00	3060.00	9000.00	15600.00
1872 CC	1980.00	7320.00	19200.00	57600.00
1872 S	530.00	780.00	1620.00	21600.00
1873	3840.00	9000.00	14400.00	45000.00
1873 CC	1920.00	7320.00	19200.00	60000.00
1873 S	900.00	1560.00	4290.00	24000.00
1874	210.00	220.00	270.00	1680.00
1874 CC	770.00	2040.00	7620.00	42000.00
18745	960.00	2760.00	5700.00	42000.00
1875	36000.00	45000.00	58800.00	
1875 CC	3000.00	8040.00	20400.00	66000.00
1876	2640.00	5760.00	11400.00	54000.00
1876 CC	2760.00	6600.00	13200.00	54000.00
1876 S	1170.00	1440.00	4860.00	38400.00
1877	2160.00	4680.00	6600.00	28800.00
1877 CC	1920.00	4680.00	12000.00	48000.00
1877 S	480.00	680.00	1740.00	23400.00
1878	210.00	230.00	290.00	740.00
1878 CC	2940.00	8040.00	18600.00	48000.00
1878 S	420.00	510.00	1440.00	15000.00
1879	210.00	220.00	260.00	480.00
1879 CC	5040.00	9900.00	19200.00	66000.00
1879 O	1680.00	3660.00	7680.00	30600.00
1879 S	210.00	220.00	260.00	950.00
1880	210.00	220.00	230.00	270.00
1880 CC	450.00	720.00	1380.00	12600.00
1880 O	350.00	630.00	1260.00	7200.00
1880 S	210.00	220.00	260.00	320.00
1881	210.00	220.00	230.00	260.00
1881 CC	430.00	600.00	890.00	5220.00
1881 O	370.00	750.00	1040.00	6300.00
1881 S	210.00	220.00	230.00	260.00
1882	210.00	220.00	230.00	260.00
1882 CC	600.00	1040.00	2640.00	13200.00
1882 O	360.00	470.00	1080.00	5220.00
1882 S	210.00	230.00	290.00	400.00
1883	210.00	220.00	230.00	260.00
1883 CC	480.00	720.00	1920.00	12000.00
1883 O	2160.00	6900.00	9300.00	31800.00
1883 S	210.00	230.00	300.00	870.00
1884	210.00	220.00	260.00	570.00
1884 CC	480.00	840.00	1920.00	10800.00
1884 S	210.00	230.00	300.00	390.00
1885	210.00	230.00	280.00	310.00
1885 S	210.00	230.00	280.00	310.00

Liberty Head Type Minted 1838-1907
With Motto

	VF	XF	AU	MS60
1886	210.00	230.00	270.00	330.00
1886 S	210.00	220.00	230.00	270.00
1887	230.00	260.00	300.00	600.00
1887 S	210.00	220.00	230.00	260.00
1888	210.00	230.00	270.00	520.00
1888 O	210.00	230.00	280.00	500.00
1888 S	210.00	220.00	230.00	280.00
1889	380.00	470.00	900.00	2160.00
1889 S	210.00	220.00	230.00	260.00
1890	210.00	220.00	260.00	600.00
1890 CC	410.00	440.00	600.00	1650.00
1891	210.00	220.00	230.00	290.00
1891 CC	410.00	440.00	510.00	680.00
1892	210.00	220.00	230.00	260.00
1892 CC	410.00	450.00	590.00	2880.00
1892 O	210.00	220.00	230.00	310.00
1892 S	210.00	220.00	270.00	390.00
1893	210.00	220.00	230.00	260.00
1893 CC	410.00	650.00	1350.00	6300.00
1893 O	270.00	300.00	360.00	580.00
1893 S	210.00	220.00	230.00	300.00
1894	210.00	220.00	230.00	260.00
1894 O	210.00	230.00	290.00	810.00
1894 S	230.00	370.00	690.00	3300.00
1895	210.00	220.00	230.00	260.00
1895 O	210.00	220.00	290.00	470.00
1895 S	210.00	230.00	480.00	2160.00
1896	210.00	230.00	270.00	290.00
1896 S	210.00	220.00	420.00	2100.00
1897	210.00	220.00	230.00	260.00
1897 O	230.00	240.00	290.00	630.00
1897 S	210.00	230.00	260.00	720.00
1898	210.00	220.00	230.00	260.00
1898 S	210.00	220.00	230.00	320.00
1899	210.00	220.00	230.00	260.00
1899 O	230.00	230.00	330.00	500.00
1899 S	210.00	220.00	270.00	290.00
1900	210.00	220.00	270.00	290.00
1900 S	230.00	270.00	340.00	750.00
1901	210.00	220.00	230.00	260.00
1901 O	210.00	230.00	290.00	330.00
1901 S	210.00	220.00	230.00	260.00
1902	210.00	220.00	230.00	270.00
1902 S	210.00	220.00	230.00	260.00
1903	210.00	230.00	270.00	290.00
1903 O	210.00	230.00	290.00	340.00
1903 S	210.00	220.00	230.00	260.00
1904	210.00	220.00	230.00	270.00
1904 O	210.00	230.00	270.00	300.00
1905	210.00	220.00	230.00	260.00
1905 S	210.00	220.00	240.00	990.00
1906	210.00	220.00	230.00	260.00
1906 D	210.00	220.00	230.00	260.00
1906 O	210.00	230.00	300.00	380.00
1906 S	210.00	230.00	300.00	450.00
1907	210.00	220.00	230.00	260.00
1907 D	210.00	220.00	230.00	260.00
1907 S	210.00	230.00	260.00	510.00

135

Indian Head $10.00 Gold Piece

Indian Head Type Minted 1907-1933

		XF	AU	MS60
1907	Wire EdgeWith Periods	11000.00	12100.00	13200.00
1907	W/O Stars		Unique—1 exists.	
1907	Rolled EdgeWith Periods	22000.00	24200.00	26400.00
1907	W/O Periods	350.00	390.00	690.00
1908	W/O Motto	500.00	550.00	770.00
1908D	W/O Motto	340.00	370.00	610.00

Motto Added

	XF	AU	MS60
1908	320.00	330.00	410.00
1908D	330.00	340.00	600.00
1908S	350.00	370.00	1270.00
1909	310.00	340.00	420.00
1909D	310.00	340.00	460.00
1909S	310.00	340.00	520.00
1910	310.00	340.00	350.00
1910D	310.00	340.00	390.00
1910S	310.00	340.00	500.00
1911	310.00	330.00	360.00
1911D	690.00	720.00	3080.00
1911S	500.00	580.00	910.00
1912	310.00	340.00	380.00
1912S	310.00	330.00	610.00
1913	310.00	340.00	360.00
1913S	580.00	720.00	2970.00
1914	310.00	340.00	440.00
1914D	310.00	340.00	460.00
1914S	310.00	330.00	550.00
1915	310.00	330.00	460.00
1915S	640.00	720.00	2480.00
1916S	310.00	330.00	600.00
1920S	6600.00	7260.00	13970.00
1926	310.00	330.00	340.00
1930S	550.00	7150.00	7590.00
1932	310.00	340.00	340.00
1933			49500.00

136

$20.00 Gold Pieces
Minted 1849-1907

Liberty $20.00 Gold Piece

Liberty Type Minted 1849-1907

No Motto Ty 1

	VF	XF	AU	MS60
1849 (1 Minted)	NA	NA	NA	NA
1850	600.00	960.00	2160.00	5400.00
1850 O	720.00	1200.00	6000.00	28800.00
1851	570.00	620.00	810.00	2640.00
1851 O	640.00	750.00	1440.00	14400.00
1852	570.00	630.00	780.00	2880.00
1852 O	660.00	750.00	1620.00	12600.00
1853 3 over 2	670.00	1140.00	2880.00	34200.00
1853	570.00	630.00	810.00	3840.00
1853 O	640.00	990.00	2250.00	20400.00
1854	570.00	630.00	810.00	5112.00
1854 O	25200.00	50400.00	96000.00	168000.00
1854 S	600.00	720.00	1140.00	3312.00
1855	570.00	650.00	1020.00	7200.00
1855 O	2040.00	5040.00	15300.00	66000.00
1855 S	570.00	620.00	960.00	5040.00
1856	590.00	650.00	990.00	7800.00
1856 O	36000.00	66000.00	103800.00	192000.00
1856 S	570.00	630.00	990.00	3360.00
1857	570.00	620.00	800.00	3000.00
1857 O	930.00	1530.00	3540.00	19200.00
1857 S	570.00	620.00	820.00	3000.00
1858	650.00	810.00	1080.00	4320.00
1858 O	1200.00	1800.00	4200.00	24000.00
1858 S	570.00	630.00	890.00	6900.00
1859	810.00	1860.00	3600.00	27600.00
1859 O	3000.00	6000.00	13200.00	72000.00
1859 S	570.00	620.00	810.00	4320.00

Liberty Type Minted 1849-1907
No Motto Ty 1

	VF	XF	AU	MS60
1860	570.00	620.00	780.00	3420.00
1860 O	2820.00	5280.00	13500.00	78000.00
1860 S	570.00	620.00	840.00	5100.00
1861	560.00	600.00	780.00	2172.00
1861 O	1560.00	2880.00	7200.00	42000.00
1861 S	570.00	630.00	1410.00	7320.00
1861 Paquet Rev.	NA	NA	NA	NA
1861 S Paquet Rev.	6600.00	14400.00	22800.00	56400.00
1862	750.00	1200.00	2280.00	13800.00
1862 S	560.00	690.00	1410.00	9240.00
1863	570.00	710.00	1560.00	15000.00
1863 S	570.00	690.00	1200.00	5760.00
1864	630.00	830.00	1440.00	12000.00
1864 S	560.00	600.00	1500.00	5760.00
1865	570.00	630.00	870.00	5280.00
1865 S	570.00	600.00	840.00	3480.00
1866 S	1440.00	2520.00	9600.00	24000.00

No Motto Ty 2

	VF	XF	AU	MS60
1866	560.00	680.00	1070.00	4320.00
1866 S	500.00	570.00	1050.00	13800.00
1867	500.00	530.00	750.00	1920.00
1867 S	500.00	600.00	1290.00	11400.00
1868	750.00	960.00	1620.00	8700.00
1868 S	500.00	620.00	1040.00	7500.00
1869	570.00	780.00	1020.00	5280.00
1869 S	500.00	510.00	900.00	4500.00
1870	580.00	790.00	1380.00	7920.00
1870 CC	78000.00	102000.00	150000.00	210000.00
1870 S	500.00	550.00	740.00	4560.00
1871	570.00	810.00	1380.00	3480.00
1871 CC	3000.00	5400.00	12000.00	36000.00
1871 S	500.00	510.00	600.00	3060.00
1872	500.00	560.00	590.00	2370.00
1872 CC	1560.00	2040.00	4620.00	21600.00
1872 S	500.00	500.00	560.00	2580.00
1873 Closed 3	510.00	620.00	870.00	2160.00
1873 Open 3	500.00	500.00	510.00	840.00
1873 CC Closed 3	1530.00	2400.00	4800.00	20400.00
1873 S Closed 3	500.00	500.00	510.00	1380.00
1874	500.00	500.00	510.00	1010.00
1874 CC	950.00	1160.00	2040.00	6600.00
1874 S	500.00	500.00	510.00	1200.00
1875	500.00	500.00	510.00	860.00
1875 CC	950.00	1100.00	1320.00	2020.00
1875 S	500.00	500.00	510.00	860.00
1876	500.00	500.00	510.00	840.00
1876 CC	950.00	1100.00	1320.00	3360.00
1876 S	500.00	500.00	510.00	840.00

138

Liberty Type Minted 1849-1907

Dollars on Rev. Type 3

	VF	XF	AU	MS60
1877	1070.00	1260.00	1740.00	14400.00
1877 CC	450.00	460.00	470.00	540.00
1877 S	450.00	460.00	470.00	540.00
1878	1560.00	2400.00	3600.00	18000.00
1878 CC	450.00	460.00	470.00	600.00
1878 S	450.00	460.00	470.00	900.00
1879	1680.00	2400.00	4800.00	21600.00
1879 CC	3840.00	6000.00	13200.00	53400.00
1879 O	450.00	460.00	470.00	1200.00
1879 S	450.00	460.00	470.00	2640.00
1880	450.00	460.00	470.00	870.00
1880 S	4080.00	6000.00	12000.00	38400.00
1881	450.00	460.00	470.00	780.00
1881 S	6300.00	13200.00	24600.00	54000.00
1882	1010.00	1160.00	1560.00	5520.00
1882 CC	450.00	460.00	470.00	530.00
1882 S				
1883 Proof Only	N/A	N/A	N/A	N/A
1883 CC	450.00	460.00	470.00	520.00
1883 S				
1884 Proof Only	N/A	N/A	N/A	N/A
1884 CC	450.00	460.00	470.00	520.00
1884 S	6000.00	7500.00	9780.00	27000.00
1885	1740.00	2520.00	4680.00	9840.00
1885 CC	450.00	460.00	470.00	520.00
1885 S	7200.00	10080.00	20400.00	38400.00
1886				
1887 Proof Only	N/A	N/A	N/A	N/A
1887 S	450.00	460.00	470.00	530.00
1888	450.00	460.00	470.00	530.00
1888 S	450.00	460.00	480.00	580.00
1889	1100.00	1230.00	1740.00	2760.00
1889 CC	450.00	460.00	470.00	540.00
1889 S	450.00	460.00	470.00	530.00
1890	950.00	1040.00	1200.00	2040.00
1890 CC	450.00	460.00	470.00	530.00
1890 S	2940.00	4500.00	7800.00	26400.00
1891	2880.00	4440.00	6720.00	12000.00
1891 CC	450.00	460.00	470.00	500.00
1891 S	1020.00	1440.00	2280.00	4800.00
1892	1040.00	1200.00	1620.00	2760.00
1892 CC	450.00	460.00	470.00	500.00
1892 S	450.00	460.00	470.00	500.00
1893	1200.00	1440.00	1680.00	2160.00
1893 CC	450.00	460.00	470.00	500.00
1893 S	450.00	460.00	470.00	500.00

Liberty Type Minted 1849-1907
Dollars on Rev. Type 3

	VF	XF	AU	MS60
1894	450.00	460.00	470.00	500.00
1894 S	450.00	460.00	470.00	500.00
1895	450.00	460.00	470.00	500.00
1895 S	450.00	460.00	470.00	500.00
1896	450.00	460.00	470.00	500.00
1896 S	450.00	460.00	470.00	500.00
1897	450.00	460.00	470.00	500.00
1897 S	450.00	460.00	480.00	530.00
1898	450.00	460.00	470.00	500.00
1898 S	450.00	460.00	470.00	500.00
1899	450.00	460.00	470.00	500.00
1899 S	450.00	460.00	470.00	500.00
1900	450.00	460.00	470.00	500.00
1900 S	450.00	460.00	470.00	500.00
1901	450.00	460.00	470.00	500.00
1901 S	450.00	460.00	510.00	810.00
1902	450.00	460.00	470.00	500.00
1902 S	450.00	460.00	470.00	500.00
1903	450.00	460.00	470.00	500.00
1903 S	450.00	460.00	470.00	500.00
1904	450.00	460.00	470.00	500.00
1904 S	450.00	460.00	510.00	870.00
1905	450.00	460.00	470.00	500.00
1905 S	450.00	460.00	470.00	500.00
1906	450.00	460.00	470.00	500.00
1906 D	450.00	460.00	470.00	500.00
1906 S	450.00	460.00	470.00	500.00
1907	450.00	460.00	470.00	500.00
1907 D	450.00	460.00	470.00	500.00
1907 S				

Lower grade coins are bullion sensitive.

Saint-Gaudents $20.00 Gold Piece

Saint-Gaudens Type Minted 1907-1933

	XF	AU	MS60
1907 Ex. High Relief Plain Edge		Unique—1 exists.	
1907 Ex. High Relief Lettered Edge		$ 1,000,000+	
1907 High Relief Roman Numerals Plain Edge		150,000.00	
1907 High Relief Roman Numerals Wire Rim	11000.00	12100.00	13420.00
1907 High Relief Roman Numerals Flat Rim	22000.00	24200.00	26400.00
1907 Large Letters On Edge		Unique-1 exists.	
1907 Small Letters On Edge	440.00	460.00	470.00
1908	440.00	460.00	470.00
1908 D	440.00	460.00	470.00

Saint-Gaudens Type Minted 1907-1933

Motto Added

	XF	AU	MS60
1908	440.00	460.00	470.00
1908D	440.00	460.00	470.00
1908S	440.00	460.00	470.00
1909	540.00	570.00	580.00
1909D	680.00	710.00	990.00
1909S	640.00	690.00	1320.00
1910	440.00	460.00	470.00
1910D	440.00	460.00	470.00
1910S	440.00	460.00	470.00
1911	440.00	460.00	470.00
1911D	440.00	460.00	470.00
1911S	440.00	460.00	470.00
1912	440.00	460.00	470.00
1913	440.00	460.00	470.00
1913D	440.00	460.00	470.00
1913S	440.00	460.00	470.00
1914	440.00	470.00	480.00
1914D	440.00	460.00	470.00
1914S	440.00	460.00	470.00
1915	470.00	490.00	540.00
1915S	440.00	460.00	470.00
1916S	440.00	460.00	530.00
1920	440.00	460.00	470.00
1920S	9350.00	10450.00	20900.00
1921	12100.00	17600.00	31350.00
1922	440.00	460.00	470.00
1922S	610.00	660.00	720.00
1923	440.00	470.00	480.00
1923D	440.00	470.00	480.00
1924	440.00	470.00	480.00
1924D	990.00	1080.00	1600.00
1924S	910.00	1020.00	2090.00
1925	440.00	470.00	480.00
1925D	1520.00	1740.00	2750.00
1925S	1100.00	1430.00	4730.00
1926	440.00	470.00	480.00
1926D	2530.00	2860.00	7150.00
1926S	990.00	1100.00	1540.00
1927	440.00	470.00	480.00
1927D	121000.00	220000.00	225500.00
1927S	3470.00	4070.00	10120.00
1928	440.00	470.00	480.00
1929	6050.00	7150.00	8250.00
1930S	11000.00	12100.00	20900.00
1931	7370.00	8250.00	12930.00
1931D	6820.00	7700.00	14300.00
1932	9130.00	10450.00	14300.00
1933		MS65	$8 Million

Chapter 6

COMMEMORATIVE COINS

142

By Act of Congress, the mint over the years has been authorized to issue commemorative coins, each celebrating a current or historic event or honoring an outstanding citizen. Such coins show a great variety of design and inscription. Most would not be recognizable to the public as legal tender, although some issues were placed in general circulation.

Usually, these coins are offered to the public at a premium over their face value. For example, the Columbian Exposition half dollar was sold for $1 at the World's Columbian Exposition in Chicago during 1893. The fact that the mintage of commemorative coins is usually quite small also is a factor that puts them at a premium with collectors.

Since commemoratives were generally not issued to circulate, most pieces are well preserved and grade toward the high end of the scale that we have used for previous coins. Consequently, in what follows, pricing for two grades has been used, XF-AU which can even apply to an uncirculated coin that has been knocking around in a desk drawer for a few decades, and MS60, the lowest of the uncirculated grades. As with other coins, high-end uncirculated specimens can easily command prices in excess of five to ten times that of MS60.

Quarter Dollars

Isabella Quarter

Minted in 1893, this was the first U.S. coin portraying a foreign monarch. The obverse shows Queen Isabella of Spain who helped Columbus finance his voyage of discovery. The reverse displays a kneeling female who represents women's industry.

XF-AU	**MS60**
350.00	600.00

143

Half Dollars

Columbian Exposition

Issued in 1892 and 1893 in celebration of the 400th anniversary of the discovery of America by Columbus, and the Chicago World's Fair of 1893. The obverse shows a portrait of Columbus; the reverse the ship, Santa Maria, spanning the two hemispheres.

	XF-AU	**MS60**
1892	13.00	25.00
1893	10.00	25.00

Panama-Pacific

Issued by the Panama-Pacific International Exposition in 1915 to commemorate the completion of the Panama Canal. The obverse shows Columbia. The reverse displays the eagle and shield.

XF-AU	**MS60**
200.00	300.00

144

Illinois Centennial

Issued in 1918 to commemorate the 100th anniversary of the admission of Illinois into the Union. The obverse shows a bust of Lincoln. The reverse depicts portions of the Illinois state seal.

XF-AU	**MS60**
75.00	95.00

Maine Centennial

Issued in 1920 to commemorate the 100th anniversary of the admission of Maine into the Union. The obverse reproduces the Great Seal of the state. The reverse places the inscription "Maine Centennial, 1820-1920" within a wreath.

XF-AU	MS60
75.00	95.00

145

Pilgrim Tercentenary

Issued in 1920 and 1921 to commemorate the 300th anniversary of the landing of the Pilgrims. The obverse is a portrait of Governor Bradford. The reverse shows the *Mayflower*.

	XF-AU	MS60
1920 (No Date on Obverse)	50.00	65.00
1921 (Date on Obverse)	85.00	110.00

Alabama

Issued in 1921 two years late for the 100th anniversary of the admission of Alabama into the Union. The obverse shows the busts of the first (W.W. Bibb) and the then current (T.E. Kilby) governors of the State. Two varieties of the coin exist. The first has the St. Andrews cross between the number "22" (Alabama was the 22nd state) in the field of the obverse behind the governors' heads. The reverse shows an eagle.

	XF-AU	MS60
1921 with 22	135.00	275.00
1921 without 22	80.00	200.00

146

Missouri Centennial

Issued in 1921 to commemorate the 100th anniversary of Missouri's admission into the Union. The obverse displays the bust of a frontiersman. The reverse shows a standing frontiersman and an Indian. One variety has a small "2 x 4" on the obverse below the chin of the frontiersman, as Missouri was the 24th state.

	XF-AU	MS60
1921 with 24	300.00	450.00
1921 without 24	225.00	425.00

Grant Memorial

Issued in 1922 to commemorate the 100th anniversary of Grant's birth, the obverse is a bust of Grant. The reverse is a portrait of Grant's log cabin boyhood home. One variety has a star on the obverse above Grant's last name.

	XF/AU	**MS60**
1922 with star	475.00	1100.00
1922 without star	65.00	80.00

Monroe Doctrine Centennial

Issued in 1923 to mark the 100th anniversary of the proclamation of the Monroe Doctrine. The obverse shows the busts of Monroe and John Quincy Adams. The reverse shows the Western Hemisphere, the portion of the world the European powers were warned against interfering in.

XF-AU	**MS60**
25.00	40.00

Huguenot-Walloon Tercentenary

Issued in 1924 to commemorate the 300th anniversary of the arrival of the Huguenots and Walloons, Protestant refugees from Belgium. The obverse shows the busts of Admiral Coligny and William the Silent. The reverse depicts the ship, *New Netherland*.

XF-AU	MS60
65.00	100.00

148

California Jubilee

Issued in 1925 to commemorate the 75th anniversary of the admission of California into the Union. The obverse shows a kneeling gold miner. The reverse displays the emblem of the state, a California grizzly bear.

XF-AU	MS60
85.00	105.00

Lexington-Concord Sesquicentennial

Issued in 1925 to mark the 150th anniversary of these two famous Revolutionary War battles. The obverse bears a portrait of a standing Minute Man. The reverse depicts the Old Belfry in Lexington.

XF-AU	**MS60**
55.00	70.00

149

Stone Mountain Memorial

Issued in 1925 to raise funds for sculpturing figures of Confederate heroes on Stone Mountain in Georgia. The obverse shows Lee and Jackson on horseback. The reverse has an eagle perched on the mountain.

XF-AU	**MS60**
35.00	58.00

Vancouver Centennial

Issued in 1925 to mark the 100th anniversary of the building of Fort Vancouver. The obverse shows a bust of the builder, Dr. John McLaughlin. The reverse has a frontiersman standing with a rifle. In the background is the old fort and mountains.

XF-AU	MS60
200.00	270.00

150

Sesquicentennial of American Independence

Issued in 1926 to commemorate the 150th anniversary of the signing of the Declaration of Independence. The obverse has busts of Washington and Coolidge facing right. The reverse shows the Liberty Bell.

XF-AU	MS60
50.00	70.00

Oregon Trail Memorial

Issued first in 1926, and subsequently in 1928, 1933, 1934, 1936-1939, to commemorate the memory of the pioneers who died along the Oregon Trail. The obverse depicts a covered wagon moving west. The reverse shows an American Indian superimposed on a map of the U.S.

	XF-AU	**MS60**
1926	80.00	90.00
1926 S	80.00	90.00
1928	100.00	160.00
1933 D	200.00	240.00
1934 D	100.00	130.00
1936	80.00	110.00
1936 S	100.00	130.00
1937 D	100.00	125.00
1938 P,D,S (Set)	430.00	520.00
1939 P,D,S (Set)	1000.00	1100.00

Vermont Sesquicentennial

Issued in 1927 to mark the 150th anniversary of the independence of Vermont. The bverse shows the bust of Ira Allen, founder of Vermont. The reverse captures a stalking mountain lion.

XF-AU	**MS60**
125.00	155.00

Hawaiian Sesquicentennial

Issued in 1928 to mark the 150th anniversary of the landing of Captain Cook in the Hawaiian Islands. The obverse carries a bust of Captain Cook. The reverse displays a full-length statue of a native chief.

XF-AU	**MS60**
900.00	1250.00

152

Boone Bicentennial

Issued first in 1934 and subsequently through 1938, these coins mark the 100th anniversary of Daniel Boone's birth. The obverse has Boone facing left. The reverse has standing figures of Boone and Chief Black Fish.

	XF-AU	**MS60**
1934	65.00	75.00
1934 P,D,S (Set)		600.00
(Actually issued in 1935. Small "1934" on reverse.)		
1935 P,D,S		225.00
1936 P,D,S		225.00
1937 P,D,S		600.00
1938 P,D,S		800.00

Maryland Tercentenary

Issued in 1934 to commemorate the 300th anniversary of the granting of the original charter of Maryland to Lord Baltimore. The reverse displays Maryland's coat of arms.

XF-AU	**MS60**
100.00	115.00

153

Texas Centennial

Issued from 1934 through 1938 to commemorate the revolt of Texas from Mexico in 1836. The obverse has an eagle superimposed on the "Lone Star." The reverse contains small portraits of Sam Houston and Stephen Austin flanking a figure of winged Victory.

	XF-AU	**MS60**
1934	80.00	100.00
1935 P,D,S (Set)		300.00
1936 P,D,S (Set)		300.00
1937 P,D,S (Set)		325.00
1938 P,D,S (Set)		625.00

Arkansas Centennial

First issued in 1935, a year before the actual centennial, and then through 1939, these coins commemorate the 100th anniversary of the admission of Arkansas into the Union. The obverse shows a soaring eagle; reverse, the heads of an Indian chief and a then contemporary American girl.

154

	XF-AU	MS60
Type coin (any year)	60.00	70.00
1935 P,D,S (Set)		200.00
1936 P,D,S (Set)		200.00
1937 P,D,S (Set)		220.00
1938 P,D,S (Set)		340.00
1939 P,D,S (Set)		600.00

Connecticut Tercentenary

Issued in 1935 to commemorate the 300th anniversary of the founding of the colony of Connecticut. The obverse bears a standing eagle reminiscent of the Peace Dollar. The reverse bears a representation of the oak tree in Hartford where, according to tradition, the state's charter was hidden from the British governor in 1687.

XF-AU	MS60
150.00	175.00

Hudson Sesquicentennial

Issued in 1935 to mark the 150th anniversary of the founding of Hudson, New York. The obverse shows Henry Hudson's ship, the *Half Moon*. The seal of the city of Hudson, depicting a mythical sea scene, is found on the reverse.

XF-AU	MS60
390.00	475.00

San Diego Exposition

Issued with the dates 1935 and 1936 for the opening of the exposition, the obverse shows a seated female warrior with a bear in the background. The reverse displays the State of California building at the exposition.

	XF-AU	MS60
1935 S	55.00	80.00
1936 D	55.00	95.00

Spanish Trail

Issued in 1935 to commemorate the 400th anniversary of the blazing of the "Old Spanish Trail" by de Vaca in 1535. The obverse portrays a longhorn cow from the explorer's name. The reverse maps the trail from Florida to Texas on which is superimposed a yucca tree.

XF-AU	MS60
700.00	775.00

Albany Charter

Issued in 1936 to mark the 250th anniversary of the charter of the City of Albany, New York. The obverse depicts a beaver at work. The reverse shows Peter Schuyler and Robert Livingston with Governor Dongan of New York after receiving the city's charter.

XF-AU	MS60
175.00	200.00

Bridgeport Centennial

Issued in 1936 to commemorate the 100th anniversary of the incorporation of the city of Bridgeport, Connecticut. The obverse shows the portrait of P.T. Barnum, once mayor and Bridgeport's most famous citizen. The reverse shows an eagle about to soar.

XF-AU	MS60
80.00	125.00

Cincinnati Music Center

Issued in 1936 to commemorate the 50th anniversary of Cincinnati as a music center. The obverse carries a portrait of Stephen Foster. The reverse shows an allegorical figure representing music.

	XF-AU	MS60
1936 Type single	185.00	215.00
1936 P,D,S (Set)	550.00	700.00

Cleveland Exposition

Issued in 1936 to mark the 100th anniversary of the founding of Cleveland as part of the Great Lakes Exposition held in Cleveland during that year. The obverse portrays General Moses Cleaveland (old spelling), and ancestor of President Grover Cleveland. The reverse shows a map of nine large cities on the Great Lakes.

XF-AU	MS60
60.00	70.00

158

Columbia Sesquicentennial

Issued in 1936 on the 150th anniversary of the founding of the city of Columbia, South Carolina. The obverse shows justice with sword and scales. The reverse shows a palmetto tree, emblem of the state of South Carolina.

	XF-AU	MS60
1936 type single	140.00	165.00
1936 P,D,S (Set)	450.00	500.00

Delaware Tercentenary

Issued in 1936 on the 300th anniversary of the landing of Swedish immigrants in Delaware. The obverse shows the Old Swedes Church in Wilmington. The reverse displays the vessel, *Kalmor Nyckel*, used for the journey.

XF-AU	**MS60**
160.00	200.00

159

Elgin Centennial

Issued in 1936 to mark the 100th anniversary of the founding of Elgin, Illinois. The obverse shows a pioneer's portrait. The reverse depicts a Pioneer Memorial Statue to be fashioned from the monies received by the commemorative coin.

XF-AU	**MS60**
140.00	155.00

Gettysburg

Issued in 1936 to commemorate the Battle of Gettysburg. The obverse shows a Union and Confederate soldier. The reverse displays the shields of the Union and Confederacy.

XF-AU	**MS60**
225.00	300 .00

160

Long Island Tercentenary

Issued in 1936 to commemorate the 300th anniversary of the Dutch Settlement of Jamaica Bay, Long Island, New York. The obverse shows a Dutch settler and a native American. A Dutch sailing vessel is depicted on the reverse.

XF-AU	**MS60**
55.00	60.00

Lynchburg Sesquicentennial

Issued in 1936 to mark the 150th anniversary of the charter for Lynchburg, Virginia. The obverse portrays Carter Glass, long-time U.S. Senator from Virginia and Secretary of the Treasury under Woodrow Wilson. The reverse shows Liberty standing before the city courthouse.

XF-AU	**MS60**
135.00	170.00

161

Norfolk Bicentennial

Issued in 1936 to commemorate the 200th anniversary of the borough of Norfolk. The obverse is a representation of the city's Great Seal. On the reverse is found the Royal Mace of Norfolk.

XF-AU	**MS60**
325.00	350.00

Rhode Island Tercentenary

Issued in 1936 to commemorate the 300th anniversary of the founding of Providence. The obverse shows the founder, Roger Williams, welcomed by a native American. Rhode Island's state motto, "Hope," and an anchor are found on the reverse.

	XF-AU	MS60
1936 Type single	65.00	70.00
1936 P,D,S (Set)	175.00	200.00

162

Robinson-Arkansas Centennial

Issued in 1936 to commemorate the 100th anniversary of Arkansas statehood. (See the previous commemoration.) The obverse again shows a soaring eagle. The reverse (even though it contains a portrait, usually considered the mark of the obverse of a coin) depicts then Senator Joseph T. Robinson.

XF-AU	MS60
100.00	110.00

San Francisco Bay Bridge

Issued in 1936 to celebrate the opening of the bridge connecting San Francisco to Oakland. The obverse has a California grizzly bear facing front. The reverse shows the bridge—then the world's largest.

XF-AU	**MS60**
80.00	100.00

163

Wisconsin Centennial

Issued in 1936 to commemorate the 100th anniversary of the Wisconsin Territorial government. The obverse has a badger superimposed over the state emblem. The Territorial Seal, depicting the mining industry, is found on the reverse.

XF-AU	**MS60**
135.00	150.00

York County Tercentenary

Issued in 1936 to commemorate the 300th anniversary of the founding of York County, the first county in Maine. The obverse is of the old fort on the Saco River. The reverse depicts the York County Seal.

XF-AU	MS60
125.00	150.00

164

Antietam

Issued in 1937 for the 75th anniversary of the Battle of Antietam. The obverse shows the opposing commanders of the Civil War battle, Lee and McClellan. The reverse shows a critical objective of the battle, the Burnside Bridge.

XF-AU	MS60
350.00	410.00

Roanoke Island

Issued in 1937 to mark the 350th anniversary of the attempt to colonize Roanoke Island, North Carolina. The obverse shows Sir Walter Raleigh who was active in the early attempts to colonize Virginia. The reverse commemorates the birth of Virginia Dare, supposedly the first white person born in the American colonies.

XF-AU	MS60
150.00	210.00

165

New Rochelle

Issued in 1938 to mark the 250th anniversary of the founding of New Rochelle, New York. The obverse shows a calf which was to be given away every year as part of the terms of gaining title to the land. The reverse depicts the fleur-de-lys, the national symbol of France, since it was the French Huguenots who purchased the land.

XF-AU	MS60
225.00	250.00

Iowa Centennial

Issued in 1946 to commemorate the 100th anniversary of Iowa's entrance into the Union. The obverse shows the first capitol building in Iowa City. The reverse depicts the state seal.

XF-AU	MS60
60.00	75.00

Booker T. Washington Memorial

Issued from 1946 to 1951 to further the views and ideals of this great black American educator. The obverse is the bust of Washington. The reverse has at its center the legend, "From Slave Cabin to Hall of Fame."

	XF-AU	MS60
Single Type Coin	10.00	14.00
1946 P,D,S (Set)		40.00
1947 P,D,S (Set)		70.00
1948 P,D,S (Set)		130.00
1949 P,D,S (Set)		200.00
1950 P,D,S (Set)		110.00
1951 P,D,S (Set)		110.00

Washington-Carver

Issued from 1951 to 1954 to honor the memories of two distinguished black Americans, Booker T. Washington and George Washington Carver. The obverse shows the busts of the two men. The reverse is a map of the United States.

	XF-AU	MS60
Single Type Coin	10.00	14.00
1951 P,D,S (Set)		80.00
1952 P,D,S (Set)		75.00
1953 P,D,S (Set)		75.00
1954 P,D,S (Set)		75.00

Silver Dollar
Commemorative

Lafayette Dollar

168

Issued in 1900 in memory of Lafayette's contributions to the United States during the revolution. The obverse has Washington's profile superimposed over Lafayette's. The reverse is a reproduction of a monument in Paris showing LaFayette astride his horse.

XF-AU	MS60
300.00	530.00

Early Commemorative
Gold Coins

Louisiana Purchase Centennial

Dated 1903 and issued for the Louisiana Purchase Exposition held in St. Louis in 1904. Two obverses exist: One with the bust of Jefferson, the other with that of McKinley. The reverse is the same on both, showing the denomination and dates.

	XF-AU	**MS60**
$1.00 Gold (Both varieties)	320.00	420.00

Lewis & Clark Centennial

Issued in 1904 and 1905 to mark the 100th anniversary of the exploration by these two famous men. Their portraits appear on the obverse and reverse.

	XF-AU	**MS60**
$1.00 Gold 1904	440.00	700.00
$1.00 Gold 1905	440.00	825.00

Panama-Pacific Exposition

$1.00 Gold $2.50 Gold

$50.00 Gold
(Round)

$50.00 Gold
(Octagonal)

Issued in three denominations to commemorate the opening of the Panama Canal in 1915. The obverse of the $1 coin shows the bust of a canal laborer. The reverse has two dolphins surrounding the denomination. The obverse of the $2.50 coin shows Columbia astride a hippocampus. On the reverse is an eagle facing left. The $50 coin was issued in both a round and octagonal variety. The obverse of both shows a bust of Minerva. The reverse displays an owl.

Panama-Pacific Exposition

	XF-AU	MS60
$1.00 Gold 1915 S	325.00	360.00
$2.50 Gold 1915 S	1100.00	1350.00
$50.00 Gold 1915 S (Round)	23000.00	27000.00
$50.00 Gold 1915 S (Octagonal)	20000.00	25000.00

McKinley MemoriaL

Dated 1916 and 1917 and issued to mark the death of President McKinley and to raise funds for a memorial building at his birthplace, the obverse is a bust of the slain president. The reverse is a replica of the structure to be built in his honor.

	XF-AU	MS60
$1.00 Gold 1916	275.00	350.00
$1.00 Gold 1917	325.00	475.00

Grant Memorial

Issued in 1922 to commemorate the 100th anniversary of Grant's birth. The obverse and reverse designs are the same as the half dollar.

	XF-AU	MS60
$1.00 Gold 1922 w/star	1000.00	1200.00
$1.00 Gold 1922 w/o star	1000.00	1200.00

Sesquicentennial of American Independence

Issued in 1926 to commemorate the 150th anniversary of the signing of the Declaration of Independence. The obverse has Liberty holding a scroll of the Declaration of Independence. The reverse shows Independence Hall.

	XF-AU	**MS60**
$2.50 Gold 1926	240.00	300.00

172

Modern
Commemoratives

George Washington Memorial

Dated 1982 to commemorate the 150th anniversary of the birth of Georg Washington, the obverse shows Washington in full uniform mounted on a horse. While the reverse depicts his home at Mt. Vernon, Virginia.

	MS60	**Proof**
1982 D	6.00	
1982 S		6.00

Los Angeles Olympic

1984 PDS $10.00 Gold Olympic Coins
Issued to commemorate the 23rd Olympiad.

	MS60	Proof
1983 P Silver Dollar (Discus Thrower/Eagle)	11.00	
1983 D Silver Dollar (Discus Thrower/Eagle)	11.00	
1983 S Silver Dollar (Discus Thrower/Eagle)	11.00	11.00
1984 P Silver Dollar (Coliseum/Eagle)	14.00	
1984 D Silver Dollar (Coliseum/Eagle)	20.00	
1984 S Silver Dollar (Coliseum/Eagle)	20.00	11.00
1984 P $10.00 Gold (Runners/Eagle)		240.00
1984 D $10.00 Gold (Runners/Eagle)		230.00
1984 S $10.00 Gold (Runners/Eagle)		215.00
1984 W $10.00 Gold (Runners/Eagle)	210.00	205.00

Statue of Liberty

1986 Dollar, Half Dollar and $5.00 Statue of Liberty Coins

Issued in 1986 on the 100th anniversary of the giving of the statue by France to the United States. The half dollar is clad with the obverse showing the statue welcoming a boatload of immigrants. The reverse shows an immigrant family on Ellis Island facing New York City. The dollar is stuck in .900 fine silver and shows the statue on the obverse. The reverse displays Liberty's torch. The gold $5 coin has Liberty's face on the obverse. The reverse shows a landing eagle.

	MS60	Proof
1986 D Clad Half	7.00	
1986 S " "		7.00
1986 P Silver Dollar	14.00	
1986 S " "		14.00
1986 W $5.00 Gold	105.00	105.00

Constitutional

Issued in 1987 to commemorate the 200th anniversary of the signing of the Constitution. The obverse of the $1 coin features the inscription,"We the People, " superimposed on a sheaf of parchment and a quill pen. The reverse shows a cross-section of Americans from the past and present representing our country's political heritage. The obverse of the $5 gold coin shows an American eagle holding a quill pen. The reverse also displays the pen with a "We the People" inscription.

	MS60	**Proof**
1987 P Silver Dollar	11.00	
1987 S Silver Dollar		12.00
1987 W $5.00 Gold	110.00	110.00

1988 Olympic

176

Two U.S. coins were minted to commemorate the 1988 Olympics in Seoul, South Korea. The silver $1 coin depicts the passing of the Olympic flame to the Statue of Liberty torch. The reverse shows the Olympic rings. The obverse of the $5 gold coin portrays the Greek goddess of victory and the reverse displays the five Olympic rings above the Olympic flame.

	MS60	Proof
1988D Silver Dollar	12.00	
1988S Silver Dollar		12.00
1988W $5.00 Gold	110.00	110.00

Congressional

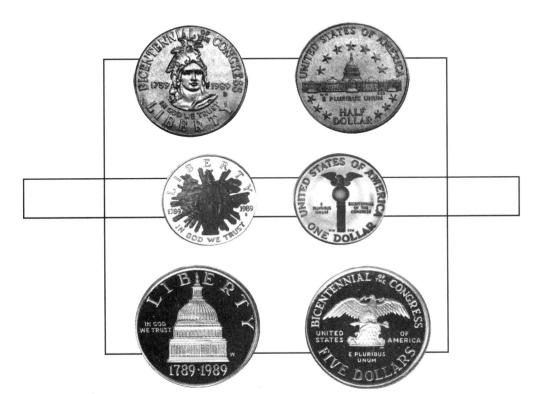

177

Three coins were issued to celebrate the bicentennial of Congress. The obverse of the half dollar displays the bust of the statue atop the Capitol Building; the reverse shows the entire building. The dollar coin shows the entire statue, while on the reverse is found the mace of Congress. On the obverse of the $5 coin is the dome of the Capitol Building with a perched eagle on the reverse.

	MS60	Proof
1989D Half Dollar	8.00	
1989S Half Dollar		8.00
1989D Silver Dollar	15.00	
1989S Silver Dollar		17.00
1989W $5.00 Gold	120.00	115.00

Eisenhower

178

Issued to commemorate the 100th anniversary of Dwight Eisenhower's birth. The obverse is a doubled portrait of Eisenhower as Commander of the Allied Forces and as President. The reverse shows the Eisenhower home.

	MS60	Proof
1990W Silver Dollar	15.00	
1990P Silver Dollar		17.50

Mount Rushmore

Issued to commemorate the golden anniversary of Mount Rushmore. The half dollar shows the memorial on the obverse. On the reverse is a standing bison. The dollar coin again has a full-faced view of the mountain's carvings on the obverse; the reverse has the Presidential Seal superimposed on a map of the United States. The $5 coin's obverse shows an eagle over the memorial. On the reverse is found the inscription, "Mount Rushmore National Memorial."

	MS60	Proof
1991D Half Dollar	14.00	
1991S Half Dollar		14.00
1991P Silver Dollar	28.00	
1991S Silver Dollar		35.00
1991W $5.00 Gold	150.00	125.00

Korean War

Issued to commemorate the 50th anniversary of the Korean War. The obverse shows a soldier fighting up a hill; the reverse displays a map of Korea.

	MS60	Proof
1991D Silver Dollar	15.00	
1990S Silver Dollar		16.00

180

USO Commemorative

Commemorating the 50th anniversary of the USO, the obverse of this coin shows the flag of the USO; the reverse displays an eagle perched on the globe.

	MS60	Proof
1991D Silver Dollar	15.00	
1991S Silver Dollar		15.00

1992 Olympic

Three U.S. coins were minted to commemorate the 1992 Olympics. The half dollar displays a gymnast on the obverse, and torch and olive branch on the reverse. The silver $1 coin's obverse depicts a baseball pitcher, while an original flag of the U.S. topped by the Olympic rings is found on the reverse. The obverse of the $5 gold coin portrays a track athlete and the reverse displays the five Olympic rings above an eagle.

	MS60	Proof
1992P Half Dollar	8.00	
1992S Half Dollar		8.00
1992D Silver Dollar	20.00	
1992S Silver Dollar		24.00
1992W $5.00 Gold	140.00	125.00

White House

Issued to commemorate the 200th anniversary of the White House, the obverse of this silver dollar shows a frontal view of the building; the reverse portrays a bust of James Hoban, its architect.

	MS60	Proof
1992D Silver Dollar	24.00	
1992W Silver Dollar		24.00

Columbus Quincentenary

182

Issued to commemorate the 500th anniversary of Columbus' first voyage. The obverse of the half dollar shows Columbus coming ashore; the reverse is a portrait of his ship. The one dollar coin shows Columbus standing with the flag of Spain on the obverse. The reverse again shows his sailing vessel. The five-dollar coin has a portrait of Columbus facing the New World on the obverse. The reverse shows an early map.

	MS60	Proof
1992D Half Dollar	11.00	
1992S Half Dollar		11.00
1992D Silver Dollar	25.00	
1992P Silver Dollar		35.00
1992W $5.00 Gold	165.00	140.00

Bill of Rights/Madison

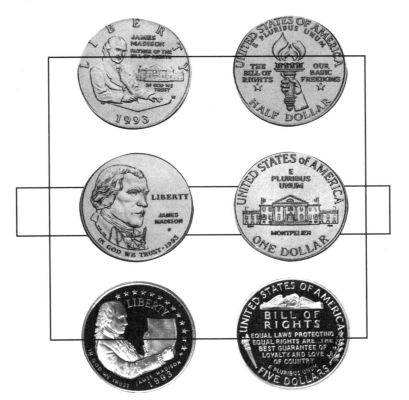

Issued to commemorate the 200th anniversary of the Bill of Rights. The half dollar shows James Madison on the obverse; a torch on the reverse. The dollar coin shows a bust of Madison on the obverse; his Montpelier home on the reverse. The $5 gold piece has Madison reading over the Rights on the obverse; the reverse is inscribed "Equal Laws Protecting Equal Rights Are The Best Guarantee Of Loyalty And Love Of Country."

	MS60	Proof
1993W Half Dollar	15.00	
1993S Half Dollar		14.00
1993D Silver Dollar	18.00	
1993S Silver Dollar		19.00
1993W $5.00 Gold	175.00	150.00

World War II

184

Issued to honor America's contribution to the Allied victory in World War II. The half dollar shows soldiers of three service branches superimposed over the victory "V." The reverse shows a soldier ashore on a Pacific island. The dollar coin displays the Normandy Invasion of June 6th, 1944 on the obverse. The reverse displays a quotation by Dwight D. Eisenhower. On the $5 gold coin's obverse is a triumphant soldier. The reverse again depicts the "V" of the allied victory. Surcharges from the sale of these commemoratives helped fund two World War II memorials—one in Washington, D.C.; the other in Normandy, France.

	MS60	**Proof**
1993P Half Dollar	25.00	
1993P Half Dollar		25.00
1993D Silver Dollar	25.00	
1993W Silver Dollar		35.00
1993W $5.00 Gold	175.00	145.00

World Cup Soccer

Issued to honor the hosting by the United States of the World Cup Soccer matches during the summer of 1994.

	MS60	Proof
1994D Half Dollar	9.00	
1994P Half Dollar		9.00
1994D Silver Dollar	23.00	
1994S Silver Dollar		26.00
1993W $5.00 Gold	160.00	130.00

Jefferson 200th Anniversary

Issued on the 200th anniversary of Jefferson's presidency.

	MS60	Proof
1994P Silver Dollar	24.00	
1994S Silver Dollar		25.00

Prisoners of War Museum

Issued to commemorate the opening of the Prisoners of War Museum.

	MS60	Proof
1994W Silver Dollar	70.00	
1994P Silver Dollar		50.00

186

Vietnam Veterans Memorial

Issued to commemorate the Vietnam Veterans. The obverse shows the Memorial Wall placed between the Lincoln and Washington monuments. The reverse shows various medals awarded to veterans during the Vietnam era.

	MS60	Proof
1994W Silver Dollar	60.00	
1994P Silver Dollar		75.00

Women in the Military

Issued to commemorate the women who have served in each of the military branches.

	MS60	Proof
1994W Silver Dollar	33.00	
1994P Silver Dollar		30.00

Capitol Bicentennial Dollar

Issued for the 200th anniversary of the Capitol building.

	MS60	Proof
1994D Silver Dollar	20.00	
1994S Silver Dollar		20.00

Civil War Battlefields

188

A portion of the monies raised for this issue was used to refurbish various Civil War battlefields.

	MS60	Proof
1995D Half Dollar	30.00	
1995S Half Dollar		30.00
1995P Silver Dollar	40.00	
1995S Silver Dollar		60.00
1995W $5 Gold	360.00	280.00

Special Olympics

Issued to commemorate the Special Olympics World Games.

	MS60	**Proof**
1995D Dollar	20.00	
1995S Dollar		25.00

1996 Olympics (Issued in 1995 and 1996)

Issued to commemorate the 1996 Summer Olympics. The XXVI Olympiad was held in Atlanta.

	MS60	Proof
1995S Basketball Half Dollar	20.00	16.00
1995S Baseball Half Dollar	20.00	15.00
1995D Gymnastics Silver Dollar	59.00	
1995P Gymnastics Silver Dollar		30.00
1995D Cycling Silver Dollar	90.00	
1995P Cycling Silver Dollar		36.00
1995D Track & Field Silver Dollar	70.00	
1995P Track & Field Silver Dollar		33.00
1995D Blind Runner Silver Dollar	70.00	
1995P Blind Runner Silver Dollar		30.00
1995W Torch Runner $5 Gold	180.00	150.00
1995W Atlanta Stadium $5 Gold	240.00	175.00
1996S Swimming Half Dollar	100.00	27.00
1996S Soccer Half Dollar	50.00	80.00
1996D Tennis Silver Dollar	180.00	
1996P Tennis Silver Dollar		55.00
1996D Rowing Silver Dollar	210.00	
1996P Rowing Silver Dollar		50.00
1996D High Jump Silver Dollar	250.00	
1996P High Jump Silver Dollar		40.00
1996D Wheelchair Athlete Silver Dollar	250.00	
1996P Wheelchair Athlete Silver Dollar		55.00
1996W Olympic Flame $5 Gold	250.00	200.00
1996W Flagbearer $5 Gold	280.00	220.00

150th Anniversary of the Smithsonian Institution

Issued to commemorate the Institution founded in 1846 for the "increase and question of knowledge."

	MS60	Proof
1996D and P Dollar	95.00	50.00
1996W $5 Gold	425.00	275.00

National Community Service

Issued to commemorate community service in the United States.

	MS60	Proof
1997D and S Dollar	200.00	75.00

Botanical Gardens

Issued to commemorate the U.S. Botanical Gardens pavilion.

	MS60	**Proof**
1997P Dollar	40.00	38.00

A Botanical Gardens Coin and Currency set was also issued. This set includes a matte proof Jefferson nickel, the $1 coin above and a 1997 Federal Reserve note.

The issue price for the set was $36. It is currently being sold for $225-$250 due to the limited mintage of only 25,000. In 1994 a similar set was issued with the Jefferson dollar. It included a 1994 matte proof Jefferson nickel and a 1976 $2 bill which portrays Thomas Jefferson on the obverse. This set currently sells for $120.

Jackie Robinson

Issued to commemorate the 50th anniversary of Robinson's debut in the major leagues.

	MS60	**Proof**
1997S Dollar	55.00	45.00
1997W $5 Gold	1250.00	400.00

Franklin Delano Roosevelt

Issued to commemorate the 100th anniversary of the birth of FDR. The irony of course is that it was Roosevelt who took us off the gold standard.

	MS60	**Proof**
1997 $5 Gold	250.00	250.00

Law Enforcement Officers

Issued to commemorate the memorial of those who "serve and protect."

	MS60	**Proof**
1997P Dollar	125.00	120.00

Robert F. Kennedy

Issued on the 30th anniversary of RFK's death.

	MS60	**Proof**
1998S Dollar	30.00	40.00

194

In addition, a set of two coins were issued containing a matte finished RFK dollar and a JFK half dollar. This set currently trades at around $125.

Black Patriots

Minted to commemorate Black Revolutionary patriots. The obverse is a portrait of Crispus Attucks, the first patriot killed in the Boston Massacre of 1770.

	MS60	**Proof**
1998S Dollar	90.00	90.00

Dolley Madison

Minted to commemorate the important contributions of James Madison's wife in saving governmental artifacts as British troops were about to burn the White House.

	MS60	**Proof**
1999P Dollar	36.00	36.00

195

George Washington

Minted to celebrate the life and legacy of the "Father of his country."

	MS60	**Proof**
1999W $5 Gold	250.00	250.00

Yellowstone National Park

Issued to commemorate our most famous National Park.

	MS60	**Proof**
2000 Dollar	45.00	45.00

196

Library of Congress

Issued to commemorate the 200th anniversary of the Library of Congress.

	MS60	**Proof**
2000 Dollar	32.00	34.00
2000 $10 Bimetallic (Gold and Platinum)	1000.00	525.00

Leif Ericson Millennium

Issued to commemorate the "Founder of the New World."

	MS60	Proof
2000 Dollar	65.00	45.00

U.S. Capitol Visitor Center

Issued to celebrate the first meeting of Congress in the U.S. Capitol and to help build the first ever Visitor Center for the U.S. Capitol.

	MS60	Proof
2001 Half Dollar	11.00	15.00
2001 Dollar	40.00	40.00
2001 $5 Gold	550.00	250.00

American Buffalo

198

A reproduction of one of this country's favorite coin designs—the Buffalo nickel.

	MS60	**Proof**
2001 Dollar	120.00	110.00
Coin & Currency Set	130.00	

2002 Olympic Winter Games

	MS60	**Proof**
2002 Silver Dollar	37.00	37.00

	MS60	**Proof**
2002 $5 Gold Coin	225.00	235.00

West Point

Issued for the 200th anniversary of West Point.

	MS60	Proof
2002 Dollar (W)	33.00	35.00

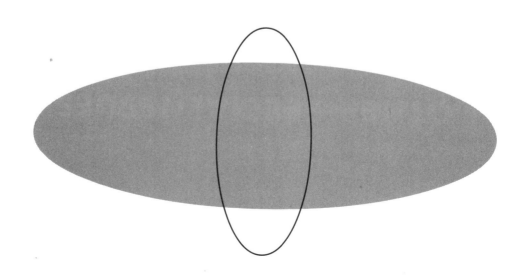

Chapter 7

OTHER SPECIAL ISSUES

Throughout the history of the U.S. coinage, the Mint has seen fit to issue, for a variety of special purposes, coins that exhibit the highest achievement of the minting process. Until 1936 these "proof"coins, as they were called, were issued sporadically, and usually for the purposes of souvenir presentations and the like. Since 1936, proof sets have been made available for the general public with the exceptions of the years 1943-1949 and 1965-1967. Until 1964 these sets were issued by the Philadelphia Mint. Since 1968 they bear the San Francisco Mint mark. These recent sets have generally contained only regular issue coins. Special "prestige" sets in 1983-1984 and 1986-1997 have included appropriate commemorative coins. Each year from 1992-1998, four separate kinds of sets have been issued—the regular set, the prestige, the silver and the silver premier.

Proof coins are stuck under a process whereby a great deal of care is taken so that each coin is sharply struck with virtually no imperfections or flaws. Each planchet is struck and restruck by highly polished dies so as to guarantee a sharp impression. Proof coins, unless mishandled, often evidence a mirror-like field with frosty surfaces. However, as is the case with regularly issued coins, differences in condition can be found depending on die wear, care in packaging, etc.

Proof Sets

Prices for early proof coins are considerable, most often in excess of even the highest uncirculated grades. The sets issued since 1936 undergo periodic large price fluctuations. Currently, they are priced as follows:

202

Year		Price	Year		Price
1936		$5,500.00	1973S		$12.00
1937		$3,000.00	1974S		$11.00
1938		$1,200.00	1975S		$15.00
1939		$1,200.00	1976S		$9.00
1940		$1,000.00	1976S	3 pc. Silver	$22.00
1941		$880.00	1977S		$9.00
1942		$900.00	1978S		$10.00
1942	w/type 2 5c	$1,050.00	1979S		$10.00
1950		$550.00	1980S		$11.00
1951		$550.00	1981S		$10.00
1952		$275.00	1982S		$6.00
1953		$275.00	1983S		$7.00
1954		$155.00	1983S	Prestige	$75.00
1955		$125.00	1984S		$12.00
1955	flat	$125.00	1984S	Prestige	$22.00
1956		$60.00	1985S		$7.00
1957		$23.00	1986S		$23.00
1958		$50.00	1986S	Prestige	$33.00
1959		$26.00	1987S		$6.00
1960		$20.00	1987S	Prestige	$22.00
1960	Small date	$35.00	1988S		$12.00
1961		$10.00	1988S	Prestige	$28.00
1962		$10.00	1989S		$10.00
1963		$12.00	1989S	Prestige	$34.00
1964		$11.00	1990S		$15.00
1968S		$8.00	1990S	Prestige	$28.00
1969S		$8.00	1991S		$19.00
1970S		$13.00	1991S	Prestige	$70.00
1970S	Small Date	$85.00	1992S		$11.00
1971S		$7.00	1992S	Prestige	$40.00
1972S		$6.00	1992S	Silver	$16.00
			1992S	Premier Silver	$16.00

Other Special Issues

Year		Price	Year		Price
1993S		$15.00	1998S		$33.00
1993S	Prestige	$44.00	1998S	Silver	$35.00
1993S	Silver	$35.00	1998S	Premier Silver	$35.00
1993S	Premier Silver	$35.00	1999S	9-pc. Set	$90.00
1994S		$23.00	1999S	5-quarter set	$45.00
1994S	Prestige	$50.00	1999S	Sil. 9-pc. Set	$180.00
1994S	Silver	$35.00	2000S	9-pc. set	$20.00
1994S	Premier Silver	$45.00	2000S	5-quarter set	$16.00
1995S		$60.00	2000S	Sil. 9-pc. Set	$32.00
1995S	Prestige	$120.00	2001S	9-pc. set	$60.00
1995S	Silver	$90.00	2001S	5-quarter set	$30.00
1995S	Premier Silver	$95.00	2001S	Sil. 9-pc. Set	$33.00
1996S		$15.00	2002S	9-pc. set	$22.00
1996S	Prestige	$260.00	2002S	5-quarter set	$16.00
1996S	Silver	$50.00	2002S	Sil. 9-pc. Set	$60.00
1996S	Premier Silver	$50.00	2003S	9-pc. set	$22.00
1997S		$55.00	2003S	5-quarter set	$16.00
1997S	Prestige	$150.00	2003S	Sil. 9-pc. Set	$35.00
1997S	Silver	$90.00			
1997S	Premier Silver	$90.00			

Mint Sets

Since 1947 official uncirculated sets of coins from each mint have been packaged for sale to collectors. Until 1959 each set contained two examples of each regularly issued coin, placed in small cardboard holders. This original packaging is important since the "official" mint sets sell for a bit more than privately assembled sets.

Beginning in 1959 uncirculated coin sets come sealed in plastic envelopes and contain only one example of each date and mint mark.

Only in the years 1965 through 1967 has any special care been taken by the mint to insure that better quality coins were used to make up the sets. This was likely done in lieu of proof sets which were not produced in those years.

204

Year		Price	Year		Price
1947		$1250.00	1964		$9.00
1948		$550.00	1965		$11.00
1949		$825.00	1966		$12.00
1951		$800.00	1967		$17.00
1952		$650.00	1968		$5.00
1953		$500.00	1969		$7.00
1954		$300.00	1970		$17.00
1955		$160.00	1970	Small Date	$45.00
1956		$150.00	1971		$5.00
1957		$230.00	1972		$5.00
1958		$160.00	1973		$23.00
1959		$35.00	1974		$8.00
1960		$22.00	1975		$10.00
1961		$40.00	1976		$12.00
1962		$18.00	1976	3pc. Silver	$16.00
1963		$14.00			

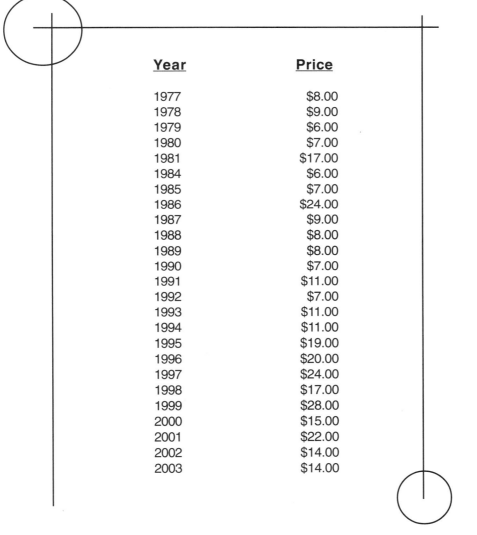

Year	Price
1977	$8.00
1978	$9.00
1979	$6.00
1980	$7.00
1981	$17.00
1984	$6.00
1985	$7.00
1986	$24.00
1987	$9.00
1988	$8.00
1989	$8.00
1990	$7.00
1991	$11.00
1992	$7.00
1993	$11.00
1994	$11.00
1995	$19.00
1996	$20.00
1997	$24.00
1998	$17.00
1999	$28.00
2000	$15.00
2001	$22.00
2002	$14.00
2003	$14.00

205

Official order forms for the purchase of Proof and Uncirculated Mint Sets can be had by writing Customer Care Center, United States Mint, Lanham, MD 20706-4331.

U.S. Bullion Coins

Silver Eagles

The one-ounce silver bullion coin is denominated "One Dollar." The obverse is a design virtually identical to the Liberty Walking half dollar last issued in 1947. The reverse displays the eagle with shield. Thus the coin is nicknamed the "silver eagle."

206

Year	Denomination	MS65	Proof
1986	$1	$14.00	$25.00
1987	$1	$7.00	$25.00
1988	$1	$9.00	$50.00
1989	$1	$9.00	$25.00
1990	$1	$9.00	$25.00
1991	$1	$7.00	$40.00
1992	$1	$8.00	$32.00
1993	$1	$8.00	$110.00 ·
1994	$1	$9.00	$105.00
1995	$1	$9.00	$80.00
1995W	$1	N/A	$2200.00
1996	$1	$22.00	$45.00
1997	$1	$9.00	$75.00
1998	$1	$8.00	$30.00
1999	$1	$8.00	$60.00
2000	$1	$7.00	$28.00
2001	$1	$7.00	$25.00
2002	$1	$7.00	$23.00
2003	$1	$7.00	$23.00

Gold Coins

Since 1986 the United States has minted gold pieces in various denominations called Eagles to compete with similar bullion coins issued by other countries such as South Africa (Krugerrand) and Canada (Maple Leaf). These pieces have not been minted in order to circulate but rather to provide convenient units of value for the possession of the precious metal. However, the coins are denominated and, presumably, are legal tender. The obverse of all four denominations is reminiscent of the $20 Saint-Gaudens gold piece issued until 1933. The reverse shows an eagle landing on a nest.

(Gold at $350/ounce)

Year	Denomination	Size	MS65	Proof
1986	$5.00	1/10 oz.	$45.00	None made
1986	$10.00	1/4 oz.	$105.00	None made
1986	$25.00	1/2 oz.	$210.00	None made
1986	$50.00	1 oz.	$400.00	$540.00
1987	$5.00	1/10 oz.	$45.00	None made
1987	$10.00	1/4 oz.	$105.00	None made
1987	$25.00	1/2 oz.	$230.00	$280.00
1987	$50.00	1 oz.	$400.00	$540.00
1988	$5.00	1/10 oz.	$160.00	$55.00
1988	$10.00	1/4 oz.	$130.00	$140.00
1988	$25.00	1/2 oz.	$275.00	$280.00
1988	$50.00	1 oz.	$540.00	$550.00

Gold Coins - (Gold at $350/ounce)

Year	Denomination	Size	MS65	Proof
1989	$5.00	1/10 oz.	$70.00	$70.00
1989	$10.00	1/4 oz.	$120.00	$150.00
1989	$25.00	1/2 oz.	$350.00	$280.00
1989	$50.00	1 oz.	$400.00	$550.00
1990	$5.00	1/10 oz.	$55.00	$60.00
1990	$10.00	1/4 oz.	$120.00	$150.00
1990	$25.00	1/2 oz.	$300.00	$160.00
1990	$50.00	1 oz.	$400.00	$550.00
1991	$5.00	1/10 oz.,	$100.00	$60.00
1991	$10.00	1/4 oz.	$200.00	$140.00
1991	$25.00	1/2 oz.	$600.00	$300.00
1991	$50.00	1 oz.	$400.00	$540.00
1992	$5.00	1/10 oz.,	$50.00	$70.00
1992	$10.00	1/4 oz.	$110.00	$140.00
1992	$25.00	1/2 oz.	$220.00	$275.00
1992	$50.00	1 oz.	$400.00	$550.00
1993	$5.00	1/10 oz.,	$55.00	$60.00
1993	$10.00	1/4 oz.	$125.00	$145.00
1993	$25.00	1/2 oz.	$210.00	$280.00
1993	$50.00	1 oz.	$400.00	$550.00
1994	$5.00	1/10 oz.,	$50.00	$60.00
1994	$10.00	1/4 oz.	$110.00	$145.00
1994	$25.00	1/2 oz.	$210.00	$280.00
1994	$50.00	1 oz.	$400.00	$550.00
1995	$5.00	1/10 oz.,	$50.00	$60.00
1995	$10.00	1/4 oz.	$110.00	$145.00
1995	$25.00	1/2 oz.	$210.00	$280.00
1995	$50.00	1 oz.	$400.00	$550.00

208

1995 10th Anniversary Set with Westpoint Silver Eagle $2900.00

Gold Coins - (Gold at $350/ounce)

Year	Denomination	Size	MS65	Proof
1996	$5.00	1/10 oz.,	$45.00	$70.00
1996	$10.00	1/4 oz.	$110.00	$145.00
1996	$25.00	1/2 oz.	$210.00	$280.00
1996	$50.00	1 oz.	$400.00	$550.00
1997	$5.00	1/10 oz.,	$45.00	$80.00
1997	$10.00	1/4 oz.	$110.00	$145.00
1997	$25.00	1/2 oz.	$210.00	$280.00
1997	$50.00	1 oz.	$400.00	$550.00
1998	$5.00	1/10 oz.,	$45.00	$60.00
1998	$10.00	1/4 oz.	$110.00	$145.00
1998	$25.00	1/2 oz.	$210.00	$280.00
1998	$50.00	1 oz.	$400.00	$550.00
1999	$5.00	1/10 oz.,	$45.00	$60.00
1999	$10.00	1/4 oz.	$110.00	$145.00
1999	$25.00	1/2 oz.	$210.00	$280.00
1999	$50.00	1 oz.	$400.00	$550.00
2000	$5.00	1/10 oz.,	$45.00	$60.00
2000	$10.00	1/4 oz.	$110.00	$145.00
2000	$25.00	1/2 oz.	$210.00	$280.00
2000	$50.00	1 oz.	$400.00	$550.00
2001	$5.00	1/10 oz.,	$45.00	$60.00
2001	$10.00	1/4 oz.	$110.00	$145.00
2001	$25.00	1/2 oz.	$210.00	$280.00
2001	$50.00	1 oz.	$400.00	$550.00
2002	$5.00	1/10 oz.,	$45.00	$60.00
2002	$10.00	1/4 oz.	$110.00	$145.00
2002	$25.00	1/2 oz.	$210.00	$280.00
2002	$50.00	1 oz.	$400.00	$550.00
2003	$5.00	1/10 oz.,	$45.00	$60.00
2003	$10.00	1/4 oz.	$110.00	$145.00
2003	$25.00	1/2 oz.	$210.00	$280.00
2003	$50.00	1 oz.	$400.00	$550.00

Platinum Coins

The year 1997 marked the inaugural issue of the American Eagle Platinum coins. Issues are mint and proof.

210

Year	Denomination	MS65	Proof
1997	$10.00	$80.00	$100.00
1997	$25.00	$230.00	$200.00
1997	$50.00	$350.00	$375.00
1997	$100.00	$700.00	$725.00
1998	$10.00	$80.00	$100.00
1998	$25.00	$230.00	$200.00
1998	$50.00	$350.00	$375.00
1998	$100.00	$700.00	$725.00
1999	$10.00	$80.00	$100.00
1999	$25.00	$230.00	$200.00
1999	$50.00	$350.00	$375.00
1999	$100.00	$700.00	$725.00
2000	$10.00	$80.00	$110.00
2000	$25.00	$230.00	$225.00
2000	$50.00	$350.00	$385.00
2000	$100.00	$700.00	$735.00

Platinum Coins

Year	Denomination	MS65	Proof
2001	$10.00	$80.00	$140.00
2001	$25.00	$230.00	$260.00
2001	$50.00	$350.00	$420.00
2001	$100.00	$700.00	$750.00
2002	$10.00	$140.00	$115.00
2002	$25.00	$180.00	$280.00
2002	$50.00	$350.00	$425.00
2002	$100.00	$700.00	$740.00
2003	$10.00	$85.00	$100.00
2003	$25.00	$170.00	$200.00
2003	$50.00	$350.00	$400.00
2003	$100.00	$650.00	$700.00

211

Bullion coins cannot be ordered directly from the mint. Over 1,000 outlets are listed in a special mint publication entitled, "American Eagle Buyer's Guide." This brochure can be acquired by calling 1-800-USA-GOLD. Also, the order form for U.S. Mint Sets mentioned above has a section for requesting the brochure by mail. Recent provisions in federal tax law allow for the inclusion of American Eagle bullion coins in a qualified Individual Retirement Account — the only tangible asset permitted by law in an IRA.

U.S. Gold Bullion Medal/Coins

The original attempt by the U.S. Government to compete for the millions of dollars that were being used to purchase foreign bullion gold coins was to issue the American Arts Gold Medallion. Complicated ordering procedures, medal-like appearance and the lack of legal tender status doomed the project almost from the start.

212

The medallions honored various persons from the arts, writers, etc. Issued in one-ounce and half-ounce sizes, the series lasted from 1980-1984.

Year	Size	Obverse Portrait	Mint State
1980	1/2 oz.	Marian Anderson	175.00
1981	1/2 oz.	Willa Cather	175.00
1982	1/2 oz.	Frank Lloyd Wright	175.00
1983	1/2 oz.	Alexander Calder	175.00
1984	1/2 oz.	John Steinbeck	175.00
1980	1 oz.	Grant Wood	350.00
1981	1 oz.	Mark Twain	350.00
1982	1 oz.	Louis Armstrong	350.00
1983	1 oz.	Robert Frost	350.00
1984	1 oz.	Helen Hayes	350.00

The price of medallions are, of course, bullion sensitive.

Chapter 8

WHERE TO FIND COINS

Was it easier to find interesting coins in circulation years ago? I have to think it was. In 1960, when I first began collecting, there was a much wider range of dates on coins in circulation. One could still find an occasional Indian Head cent or other coins dated before 1900. Almost all Lincoln cents could be found with a good deal of patience. Silver dollars from 1878 to 1935 were available at the local bank. No one seemed to want to carry them as they were quite hard on pockets.

When my paper route no longer provided me with enough change to search for that elusive complete set, I can recall riding my bicycle to the neighborhood savings & loan to obtain a bag (or two since it made more sense in terms of balance) of pennies ($50, 100 rolls, 35 lbs.)! I would bring these home to search for the dates I needed. Then, about 100 Lincoln cents dated from 1909-1960 were needed to complete the set.

Every so often a coin with a retail value of several dollars would be found. You can imagine that one such find alone was enough to guarantee another trip to transact a trade for an additional bag!

In one sense, it is amazing how patient my local banks were at the time. For them no profit was derived by catering to my desires. But even more

amazed, as I think back, must have been my parents when their son would be found occasionally searching through a bag of fifty-cent pieces. One thousand
dollars would have been transported without benefit of an armed guard to the family kitchen table. There is something to be said for having one's entire fortune within one's immediate grasp.

Those days are gone. Virtually every coin I touched then now sells for a premium over face, albeit in most cases a small one.

Are there finds that can be made today from pocket change or an occasional trip to the bank? Probably not. There are reports from lucky collectors who have been fortunate enough to have found a coin or two probably spent by a child from a parent's collection. Then, too, sometimes some silver coins get rolled up and deposited by someone unaware of their value. But I have to think such occurrences are extremely rare these days.

Coins in circulation, however, still provide a place to start. Try this experiment. Save your pocket change for several months. Then some evening take out all the coins you have saved to see what might be there. You can probably find most cents minted for circulation since 1959. You will find an array of Jefferson nickels from the 1950s through the 1980s, dimes and quarters from 1965 to 1993. No halves or dollar coins, although the bank may have a few. No Lincoln wheat pennies (before 1958), and, alas, no silver!

An error coin or two may come your way. A slightly double-struck coin, or one with a minute die crack may pique your interest along the lines of errors, freaks, and other oddities.

But at least you now have some idea of what is available from this source and what is not. That's the bad news. The good news is that many other coins can be obtained for a minimal amount over face. Their cost is so reasonable that it would have hardly made sense to search the coins in circulation for them.

Other more fruitful places to continue your search might be desks or bureau drawers and jewelry boxes. Almost everyone during their lifetime has set aside an interesting coin or two, received as a gift or kept as a little memento of an event now long forgotten. You will do well to ask other family members or friends concerning such small keepsakes. In most cases there will be an emotional attachment to the item, but at least you might persuade the

owner to let you find out about the coin. In some cases since the value will be
minimal, the owner may well decide that your new-found appreciation deserves to be encouraged. My father's cousin once gave me two nickel three-cent pieces on the condition that I would never sell them. Their value was quite small. But at the time, the sheer weirdness of such a coin opened up brand new avenues of awareness in my collecting.

Metal detecting is undoubtedly a hobby in its own right. But the obvious connection to coin collecting is evident with that initial find of a coin that is apparently one not currently found in circulation. Hobbyists of this ilk may soon find themselves researching county records that provide clues as to the sites of previous schools, businesses, and industries. The grounds of such places provide the opportunity to unearth coins that may be quite old, lost by playing children or customers and employees in a rush.

These more solitary pursuits, while rewarding, can take you only so far.

I recommend your next source be other collectors. Contact a family member whom you know is a collector or attend the next meeting of your local coin club. Be price savvy. Nothing discourages the desire to collect coins more than overpaying for the first few of them.

At about this time take a subscription to a numismatic paper or magazine. Get an idea of what is available, prices, condition, terms, etc., from the many ads that appear there.

Every collector has more duplicates than he or she will ever need. You may begin by buying a few wheat pennies or a circulated silver dollar or two. Your accumulation will grow surprisingly fast. But don't let it run too far ahead of your accumulation of information. Research your purchases. Find out everything you can about the peculiarities of each coin. Learn about where and how and why it was minted. Develop a consciousness with regard to its

215

value.

Other collectors cannot always provide the specific coins that you may wish to acquire. At that time you may wish to enlist the services of a dealer. There are thousands out there to help you. Some are willing to educate you as you make purchases, some are not. And, of course, as is possible in any business dealing, the opportunity to make a really poor purchase is forever lurking out there. In Chapter 13, I shall discuss in more detail suggestions for buying coins. There are some obvious things to do and avoid.

One last source, more for the acquisition of newly minted and specially struck coins, is the U.S. Mint itself.

Over the last two decades the Mint has struck coins commemorating the 250th anniversary of Washington's birth (a half dollar in 1982), the 1984 Olympic Games ($1 and $10 gold coin), the 200th anniversary of the Statue of Liberty (a half dollar, $1, and $5 gold coin in 1986), and the 200th anniversary of the Constitution ($1 and $5 gold coin in 1987).

216

The 1988 U.S. Olympic coins, to commemorate the Summer Games in Korea, were available (a silver dollar and $5 gold coin). The Bill of Rights and World War II commemoratives could be ordered from the Mint just last year. More commemoratives have been issued through 2002.

In addition, each year the Mint issues proof and mint sets along the lines of coins placed in general circulation for that year (some with special mint marks), various dated bullion coins, and even a number of medals (See Chapter 10).

Proof sets and special commemoratives are easily acquired and are beautifully struck. As I mention elsewhere, recent issues have not always held their value very well, but for a beginning collector the thrill of receiving these official coins directly from the Mint cannot be discounted.

Chapter 9

STARTING A COLLECTION

Many people who refer to themselves as "coin collectors" are really coin accumulators. I suppose this happens to most of us simply because we have no clear plan for the direction we want our collecting to take. We change our mind concerning what interests us. We tend to buy what is available or offered without much thought as to the scope of what we want to achieve.

A collection presumes order and direction toward a certain degree of completeness. Collecting by date and mint mark has traditionally been a way to assemble 19th and 20th century series.

For example, a Jefferson nickel set is composed of 180 pieces dated from 1938 to 2003 The "S" mintmarked coins from 1968 to the present exist only in proof and, therefore, must come from the proof sets of those years. They are not expensive but since they were not struck for circulation, acquiring them demands a purchase.

Throughout the rest of the set, there are just a few key dates. However, no coin retails for more than $6 in circulated condition. The entire set retails for about $50 although such a purchase would short-circuit the pleasure of assembling the set piece by piece. Also lost would be the knowledge acquired as an accidental feature of checking mintages and seeing the variety of conditions and pricing available.

More often today, collectors are more interested in acquiring coins by type, if for no other reason than the high cost of assembling every date and/or mint mark of some series. Essentially, this means picking a representative coin from each of the various series minted. Some series have fairly substantial design changes within them, so some decisions have to be made concerning how major such a change must be in order for the coin to be considered a different type. Changes in alloy complicate the matter also. The definition of the "type" might have broadened to include such changes.

A complete set of 20th century type coins (excluding gold coins) would make an interesting and fairly challenging "starter" type set. Such a set would include:

> $ .01 Indian (dated after 1899)
> $ .01 Lincoln (wheat reverse before 1959)
> $ .01 Lincoln (zinc-coated steel, 1943)
> $ .01 Lincoln (cartridge case alloy, 1944-46)
> $ .01 Lincoln (Memorial reverse after 1958)
> $ .01 Lincoln (copper-plated zinc, 1982-87)
> $ .05 Liberty (dated after 1899)
> $ .05 Buffalo (raised ground, 1913)
> $ .05 Buffalo (non-raised ground, 1913-1938)
> $ .05 Jefferson (copper-nickel alloy)
> $ .05 Jefferson (copper-silver alloy, 1942-45)
> $ .10 Barber (dated after 1899)
> $ .10 Mercury (1916-1945)
> $ .10 Roosevelt (90% silver, 1946-1964)
> $ .10 Roosevelt (clad 1965-date)
> $ .25 Barber (dated after 1899)
> $ .25 Standing Liberty (1916-1917)
> $ .25 Standing Liberty (redesigned, 1917-1930)
> $ .25 Washington (90% silver 1932-1964)
> $ .25 Washington (clad 1965-date)
> $ .25 Washington
>   (Bicentennial design dated 1776-1976, clad, 40% silver)
> $ .50 Barber (dated after 1899)

$ .50 Walking Liberty (1916-1947)
$ .50 Franklin (1948-1963)
$ .50 Kennedy (90% silver, 1964)
$ .50 Kennedy (40% silver, 1965-1970)
$ .50 Kennedy (clad, 1971-date)
$ .50 Kennedy
   (Bicentennial design dated 1776-1976, clad and 40% silver)
$1.00 Morgan (dated after 1899)
$1.00 Peace (1921-1935)
$1.00 Eisenhower (1971-1978)
$1.00 Eisenhower (1971-1978, 40% silver)
$1.00 Eisenhower
   (Bicentennial design dated 1776-1976, clad and 40% silver)
$1.00 Anthony (1979-1981)
$1.00 Sacagewan (2000-2003)

The alloy differences might well be ignored making for complete sets of considerably fewer coins. A much more expensive, although not difficult, challenge would involve collecting an example of each <u>denomination</u> of coin that has been minted—half cent to $20 gold. (15 coins in all).

Basic Coin Knowledge

However, no matter what directions your collecting interests take you, the most important thing you can do is to keep your knowledge of coins a pace with the monies spent on the coins themselves. Put together a small library as you go. Essential are the following:

A book on grading coins.
A comprehensive catalog.
A comprehensive almanac and history of U.S. coinage.
A weekly or monthly paper or magazine.
A volume on the aesthetic considerations of U.S. coins.
A volume on coin investing.

The following is a list of sources that would be suitable for such a beginning library: One item in each category.

1. ***Official American Numismatic Association Grading Standards For United States Coins.*** Kenneth Bresset and A. Kosoff. Western Publishing, Racine, WI. (1987). Price: $7.95

2. ***A Guide Book of United States Coins.*** R.S. Yeoman. Western Publishing Co., Racine WI. Commonly referred to as the "Redbook," this catalog has been published every year since 1947. Price: $6.95.

220

3. ***Coin World Almanac.*** The editors of Coin World, Amos Press, Sidney, OH. (Sixth edition, 1990). Price: $15.95

4. ***Coin World.*** P.O. Box 150, Sidney, OH 45365. (weekly) Price: $28/year.

5. ***Numismatic Art In America.*** Cornelius Vermeule. Belknap Press of Harvard University Press, Cambridge, MA. (1971).

6. ***High Profits From Rare Coin Investment.*** Q. David Bowers. Bowers and Merena Galleries Inc., Wolfeboro, NH. (1983). Price: $14.95

A more extensive list of sources will be found in Chapter 13.

Basic Coin Supplies
and Accessories

The coin board is an ingenious and inexpensive device for helping you bring some order to your ever growing collection. The task of filling the holes is at once finite and seductive. The most basic kind of coin board or folder costs about $1.95. Prices for more elaborate ones, usually purchased for better grade coins, can range up to $10 and even $50 for some of the fancy plastic holders.

Keeping track of duplicates and other coins you want to save can be done in a variety of ways. Small 2" x 2" coin envelopes and several styles of transparent holders are available. The most recent of these is called a "vinyl flip," actually two adjoining clear pockets, one for the coin another for inserting a small sheet for descriptions and pricing information. Retail they cost from $40-$45/1,000. Any of the above can be placed in specially made vinyl sheets or coin boxes.

Plastic tubes can be purchased to hold rolls or part rolls of coins of current denominations. These are priced at $.20 to $.25 each.

A good 10 or 20 power magnifying glass is a must for any sort of precise grading.

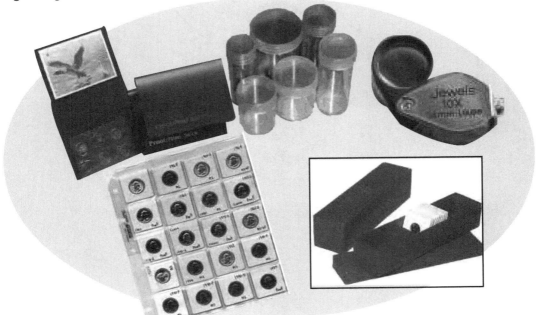

Chapter 10

HOW TO BUY COINS

Coin Shops and Coin Shows

Acollector's first exposure to someone from whom he will buy coins in any systematic way is likely to be his neighborhood coin dealer. Most coin shops these days have diversified into other collectibles including stamps, baseball cards, political buttons, and almost anything else you can think of. Some may even remind you more of precious metal and money exchanges. A few do considerable business in gold and silver jewelry.

With all this in mind, it is no wonder that a first experience with a coin dealer can be somewhat disappointing. If he or she is busy selling 10-ounce silver bars he may have little patience with a collector who wishes to pursue his stock of late date Lincolns. Don't be discouraged. Visit several shops. You will eventually find a dealer who is interested in bringing you along as a collector and customer.

Plan to educate yourself as you proceed to buy coins in his shop. Ask questions about grading standards. Compare prices.

If a dealer does not have the coin you are looking for in stock, suggest that he attempt to find one for you. Once you are reasonably comfortable with a

224

particular dealer, you might even supply him with a small want list of coins you are very interested in buying. Good etiquette demands that you give such a list to only one dealer at a time, since he will presume that if the coin meets your standards you will very likely purchase it. Obviously, you would not likely intend to purchase the same coin from several dealers.

Other collectors will also likely be willing to sell coins to you from time to time. And clearly you should be able to get a somewhat better price from a collector since he does not incur a dealer's usual costs of doing business.

Paying that lesser price, however, is a double-edged sword. Most collectors will be less willing than a dealer to allow you to return purchases. Also, you will not have near the leverage to satisfactorily clear up any dispute that may arise concerning a purchase. The law looks differently at private party transactions. You will do well to make very clear the conditions for the return of any coins sold to you.

Once you become a bonafide member of your local coin club, the club itself will open to you a variety of ways to purchase coins.

Other members can offer you duplicate coins from their particular specialty that even many dealers would have in stock on only a sporadic basis.

Some members will, in fact, be part-time dealers, sometimes called "vest-pocket" dealers. They will have no shop, maybe no business cards or pricelists. Seldom will they have a retail sales license.

The commodity they are selling is price. Often coins can be purchased from an entrepreneur of this sort at or near the prevailing dealer "buy prices"

(See Chapter 2 for a discussion and explanation of prices).

Making deals in such circles is probably best conducted by an experienced collector. A vest-pocket dealer, given his small markups, is considerably less inclined to spend a great deal of time educating his customer. At the prices he charges he can just as easily sell to a dealer and minimize any problems that arise due to the ignorance of the prospective buyer.

Coin clubs will also sponsor courses, where several, and sometimes up to hundreds of dealers are invited to set up tables and display their coins for sale.

Regular lists of the dates of these events are published in most coin papers. The benefits to the collector are obvious. Having so many dealers available makes for a much more efficient way to search for coins and coin knowledge.

Your first visit to a large "coin show," as they are sometimes called, will likely be an overwhelming experience. Millions of dollars worth of coins piled in display trays, bags of coins on the floor behind dealer tables, the unusual racket made by a machine counting junk silver, and armed guards everywhere are just some of the things you will see and hear. And here you will be looking for a 1950D nickel!

But don't return to your car in embarrassment. There will be someone on the floor to help you. Take your time. Get acquainted with a few dealers from your area. You may want to visit their shops at a later date, since in this environment it may be difficult to ask all the questions you want. Also, these dealers may very well have other things to show you that they did not bring along.

Peruse the tables to get a sense of grading and pricing by the various dealers. You will undoubtedly be startled by huge discrepancies on both counts.

Buying By Mail

For collectors who live in areas where there are no local dealers, and coin shows are quite difficult to attend, buying coins by mail is a relatively painless alternative.

Coin magazines and newspapers are filled with ads for every conceivable coin. Read them carefully and compare. Be aware of the terms. These will include costs for postage and handling, appropriate sales taxes, return privileges, the manner in which payment should be made, etc. Often a toll-free number will be listed for convenience in ordering.

Since there can be a considerable delay between the time an ad is placed and the time it actually appears in print, it usually does not hurt to confirm the prices of coins that may be of interest. This would be especially true of coins whose prices are bullion sensitive.

You may also wish to take notice of the professional organizations to which a dealer belongs. Membership is often prominently displayed in an ad. And such may well provide a safety net for any disputes that may arise concerning transactions. A significant drawback to buying by mail is having to buy sight unseen. This problem is magnified with an initial purchase since grading standards vary so. Showing a coin around to collector friends for other opinions makes sense. Trial and error adds to the expense of buying. But there is no real substitute for it.

Asking another dealer for an opinion concerning a coin you have bought by mail is somewhat more problematic. I think it puts a dealer on the spot and I do not recommend it for that reason. Any negative remark could be construed as sour grapes, as in, "Why not buy this coin from me?" On the other hand, positive comments could well be interpreted as encouragement to continue dealing with the other firm. What dealer wants to be put in such a dilemma?

Returning coins purchased by mail is not an inexpensive proposition, although the costs would certainly be less than a drive to the local coin shop.

The U.S. Postal Service offers two ways to protect yourself in mailing shipments of value. Postal "insurance" can be purchased in various increments to $5000. An amount of $500 costs around $8 plus postage. Registered mail runs around $8 plus postage for $500 and shipments of considerable value (up to $25,000) can be fully covered.

It is not quite clear what the difference is between the two services on amounts up to $500 except the price, of course. I have had no difficulty collecting for losses under either service. My experience has been that less than one in 1000 packages/letters has been lost or damaged. Both services are very reliable.

Returning or sending coins via certified mail makes no sense, although I know it is occasionally done. No insurance claim can be made for such delivery. "Certified" merely means that the delivery will be signed for. If it is damaged or lost, the sender has little or no recourse.

Other carriers, Federal Express, Puralator Courier, etc., will carry numismatic packages, but the insured limits are quite low, ranging from $50 to $500.

UPS says that it will not be liable for shipments of numismatic items (rare coins) or gold and silver bullion. These terms seem to permit the insured shipment of pennies and nickels having no numismatic value. Presumably, one could ship a bag of wheat pennies and recover at least the $50 face value should they be lost. However, the few times that I have put in a claim for a lost package, payment has been made with no regard to the fact that the contents were coins.

Mail Bid Sales & Auctions

228

Other popular ways to purchase coins include mail bid sales and auctions.

A mail bid sale allows a bidder to make an offer on a coin within the limits of any minimum bid. Some terms permit the seller to refuse all offers if he so chooses. Also, it may well be the case that some or all the lots are the property of the firm holding the sale. In other words, no consignments have been made to the firm by third parties. Auctions are quite similar to mail bid sales, except that with an auction the presumption is usually that the coin will be sold to the highest bidder over the minimum. And although some lots may be owned by the auction house, most are the property of the parties who have agreed to pay a commission (up to 10%) to have their coins described, cataloged, and sold. The buyer may also have a 15% commission added to the hammer price.

Auctions are typically designed to handle more expensive properties. In fact, major rarities often cannot be purchased in any other way. Terms vary from auction house to auction house. Great care should be exercised in submitting bids. They are binding and mistakes can be quite expensive.

Being present at an auction can be very exciting, especially if one is attempting to acquire a special, long sought after coin. The emotion of little bidding wars can easily catch up the most phlegmatic.

The purchase of common coins is more easily accomplished by a method of outright purchase. However, good bargains can be found at auction and a familiarity with prices realized is valuable information since it represents actual prices for which coins are trading—information to which a collector would normally have little access.

Buying Directly From the Mint

The U.S. Government has become the biggest dealer in the country. So, I suppose, no discussion of how and where to buy coins would be complete unless mention was made of this source.

Should you wish to purchase current mint or proof sets, bullion coins, medals, etc., you will find below an address where you can write to obtain the latest information on products available from the mint. Write to:

U.S. Mint
Customer Care Center
Lanham, MD 20706-4331

International Catalog
U.S. Mint's International
Division
801 9th Street, N.W.
Washington, DC 20220

In some cases a healthy premium over face value makes up the bulk of the price for the Mint's products. Some recent proof sets currently trade for less than the original price from the Mint. (The 1982 set, for instance, had an original issue price of $11. It currently sells for $6 retail.) So going to "the source" is no guarantee of preservation of value or price appreciation.

229

Mass-Marketed & Promoted Coins

As a note of caution, any number of firms have mounted campaigns to mass-market certain coins. Ads in popular, large circulation magazines and papers tout coins as sure-fire investments and sometimes attempt to leave the impression that the firm is some type of official issuing agency. The appeal of such ads is undoubtedly directed to the undereducated collector. I know of no serious collector who would even think of purchasing coins from such sources. Overpricing and overgrading seem to be the rule in this arena. I cannot stress too much the need for the exercise of extreme caution here. I have seen   instances of common silver dollars being offered for $25 each as "limited issues" when they were available at every coin shop for around $10. And worse, some "coins" offered never even experienced one transaction on a secondary market. They truly became "dead" issues. All the more reason to join a coin club. Get a good idea about price <u>before</u> you buy that first coin.

Chapter 11

HOW TO SELL COINS

A Day in the Life of a Dealer

To understand some of the dimensions of selling the coins we may have lovingly amassed over a lifetime, let us sit with a dealer through a typical day. Such knowledge may also have an impact on how we go about assembling our collection from the start.

Unlike you, a dealer need not be in love with the coins he buys. This gives him or her an entirely different attitude in any transaction. When he looks at the "deal," he wants to be virtually assured that a profit can be made. He must "feed" every coin until the day it is sold. Since his living is based on his judgments, he must "live" with his mistakes in a different way than a collector does.

For some dealers this means making the absolutely lowest offer for a collection that he thinks the seller might accept. Ethics aside, this works sometimes and indeed there are at least some positive things that can be said about such a strategy. I am not recommending this approach and I shall say more about it later.

Well what can a collector expect? The person on the other side of the counter has been in the office since 9 a.m. In the next few hours several calls will be received that are seemingly price inquiries.

"How much will you pay for a 1964 Proof Set?"

"Do you sell silver bars? How much are they?"

"I have a coin the size of a half dollar with a horse on it. What's it worth?"

These are typical. But care must be taken in answering them. Later the proof set is brought in but the coins have been neatly placed in a metal container. Silver has shot up 13 cents an ounce since the inquiry concerning the bars. The owner of the "horse coin" refuses to bring it in, declaring he "does not have the time."

Since it is so often a mistake to answer questions over the phone, especially those concerning price, most any dealer will invite you to come into his shop. There can be slight differences in the condition of even a 1964 Proof Set. There is nothing gained in explaining later that the coins in the set are scratched and, therefore, worth far less than the $10 originally offered.

The silver bullion customer might better have the dynamics of the metals markets explained to her so as not to be disappointed by daily or even hourly price changes.

"Horse coin" questions may be well-intentioned, but are often insensitive to even the barest concerns of etiquette.

Don't blame the dealer who is emphatic about wanting to "see it." It's his only defense. A mark of a genuine offer to sell a coin is to have brought it in. The one person every dealer appreciates is someone who makes it clear that he realizes the dealer's time is at least as important as his own. So if you have decided to dispose of those duplicates, how should you handle it? First call and make an appointment. Put together an inventory of what you wish to sell. A dealer may have no particular interest in what you have for sale. A glance at the inventory can save everyone's time.

Further, unless your intention is to sell the group of coins piecemeal, the question may arise as to what you want for the lot. If you have put together a total of the average retail prices of the coins then at least both buyer and seller have a place to start.

But now here is where things may get difficult. Whether you are paying for an appraisal or not, any offer made by the dealer has a value. It is worth something. For example, in negotiating a price with another buyer, it provides a degree of knowledge that would not otherwise be there. The seller can now deal from somewhat more a position of strength.

Consequently, many dealers are loathe to make an outright offer. Dealers rightly believe that should the seller decline this offer and then seek another, the chance to buy the collection will be lost. The next offer may top the original by some negligible amount. Some dealers respond to this by asking the seller to get several offers and then return. Sometimes it is to the dealer's advantage to make the last offer or at least have the opportunity to top any offers.

Another response on the part of the dealer may be to inquire as to what "ballpark" figure the collector has in mind. This can be a specific amount or percentage of retail. At least now the buyer will have an idea as to whether further discussion is worthwhile. Then too if the two parties are far apart, the dealer has not had to make an offer that proved offensive or ridiculous to the seller.

The situation is complicated when, as often happens, the seller is quite ignorant about the coins he wishes to sell. My advice here is two-part: (1) Ask a disinterested coin collecting party whether the collection or accumulation is worth an appraisal. (2) Assuming the answer is "yes," inquire as to respected dealers in the area and arrange for an appraisal only, as opposed to an offer.

233

Appraised Value and Worth

An appraisal can be done on an hourly basis or as a percentage of the appraised price. I would expect to pay \$20+/hour or anywhere from 2%-5% of the appraised value. Make it clear that you wish to know realistic retail prices. Sometimes an appraisal for insurance purposes can be substantially inflated since in such a case the intention will be to cover all possible replacement costs in full.

Now armed with an appraisal, the seller is not as quite at the mercy of any potential buyer. The "ballpark" figure can be given with some confidence.

And here the seller might expect to receive something around 40-60% for an accumulation of common coins, 65-75% of retail for an intermediate level collection, somewhat more for a specialty collection, up to 90%+ of retail if the group consists mainly of bullion coins. Damaged coins, of course, may sell for only a small fraction of their retail price, if at all.

Selling at Auction

Another avenue for disposing of a collection is through an auction. This method does not, however, shift all decision-making away from the seller. Most auction houses want lots that cannot easily be purchased anywhere else. Of course, these are just the sorts of items that usually make up only a small part of most collections. Run-of-the-mill items will be lumped together in "wholesale" lots, provided the auction house wants them at all.

On the other hand, truly rare items or coins in extraordinarily high grades should probably not be sold anywhere else but at an auction, especially where the seller is ignorant of the market. In such an arena the seller can be virtually guaranteed that the prices realized will be competitive. This is extremely important when condition is so critical in determining price. One "nice" uncirculated Standing Liberty quarter can be worth $150; another $2,500. The uneducated eye certainly cannot see the difference. Now the auctioneer and all those potential bidders make independent assessments. Their joint decision cannot help but be very close to the true condition/value of the coin.

As a seller at an auction, you can expect to receive the price realized on any lot less a 10 or 15% commission to the auction house. On very large groups or expensive rarities the commission can be negotiated. I have even seen consignments accepted for 0% commission. In these cases the firm conducting the auction is willing to forego the commission from the seller because that received from the buyer alone makes selling the coin worthwhile.

It is also not uncommon for an auction house to advance the seller a portion of the estimated value of the coins consigned. Then again, months can often go by between the time the coins are sent and the time when a final settlement is made.

The consignor should make himself very aware of the specific terms of the auction house, and there are considerable differences among them. Also, this may not be the preferred method of selling if quick payment is needed.

Buy Ads

A somewhat trickier method by which to sell coins is through the buy ads in collector papers and magazines. In some cases these ads are extensive and list prices and conditions wanted on a variety of different coins. At the very

least, familiarizing oneself with these prices will give a seller a good idea about what coins are being sought and the range of prices offered.

Such sources provide an outlet for quantities of similar coins that often make up an accumulation. A local dealer cannot always use multiples of the same issue.

Dealing by mail is however associated with a bit of apprehension. I do not recommend large initial shipments to buyers working out of a post office box. Better to gradually get a feel for the grading standards and dollar limits of the person at the other end. Many ads reserve the right to limit quantities. Others state that "overgraded coins will be returned at the sender's expense."

As a matter of practice, buyers of this sort are not always happy to receive lists of inventories to evaluate. Nor do they take kindly to a sender's demand to buy all or nothing from a shipment.

Do not be surprised should part of the shipment be returned and only a few of the invoiced coins have been purchased. In such a case you must decide if the buyer is engaging in a practice called "cherry picking," where only the coins at the high end of a grading range have been selected; or whether it is truly the case that those returned were overgraded and/or the buyer received too great a response from the ad and is now overstocked on some issues.

Only after dealing for a time in this way will you get a feel for the integrity or idiosyncrasies of the buyer. This method of selling coins would be more appropriate for a collector who intends to sell over a number of transactions. The one-time seller will be "shooting in the dark" with unhappy results.

Buy prices must be regarded by the collector as ephemeral. They represent a price that a buyer is willing to pay at some given period of time. Weeks pass before the ad appears in print. Financial positions change.

I think it always makes sense to give the advertiser a preliminary call. Ask questions about when payment can be expected, what quantities are being sought, what other items are needed. A $2 call can go a long way toward preventing the inevitable anxiety that arises when you've heard nothing three weeks after making a shipment.

Also, follow the normal good practices of securely wrapping the package. Remember coins are heavy and extra precautions should be taken. Include a copy of an invoice. Fully insure or register the package. (See our earlier discussion in Chapter 10 for mailing costs).

Undoubtedly it is aggravating to send coins in the mail and then weeks later receive most of them back with counteroffers. But the same sort of things can happen face to face with a dealer. I believe the best attitude to have is that if you think coin "X" is really worth $8 then there is no reason to take less for it. A buyer will certainly be discovered.

Advertised buy offers do tend to raise expectations since something like an actual price is being quoted. Maybe that is why a mail deal gone sour can be so upsetting.

236

Other Collectors

Some success is achievable by offering coins to collector friends, relatives, and club members. However, they may be willing to purchase only coins within their collecting interests. And, too, they are less likely to be in a cash position necessary for the purchase of a large collection or individual rarities.

Chapter 12

HOBBY OR INVESTMENT

History and Aesthetics

Some suggest that sooner or later every serious collector has to face up to the fact that his collection represents some considerable wealth. As the years go by, a casual inventory of a collection or accumulation can produce surprising results. Even if the coins purchased are able to be sold at only 65% of the price paid, putting aside any modest appreciation, your collection may be worth something in the thousands of dollars.

Although there is a tendency to ignore this accumulated wealth, it is nevertheless clear that the time can soon come when the collection must be understood as some sort of investment. Such a realization need not diminish the enjoyment that coin collecting brings. However, coin collecting is unlike other hobbies where the monies paid out are rarely recovered.

A photography enthusiast usually has no expectation of selling his photos, and, therefore, is even less concerned about any possible appreciation in the value of his productions. People who build and fly radio-controlled airplanes probably never sell at a profit. A more realistic expectation is that their work of several months will be destroyed on the runway someday.

Coins are different. The supply is fixed or diminishing. And the presumption is that with new collectors the demand for many coins will increase.

Since my own introduction to collecting in the early 1960s many "booms" and "busts" have taken place in the market. I can remember when uncirculated rolls of 1950D five-cent pieces were selling for $1,000. Now a roll might sell for $240. I can recall buying nice uncirculated Liberty nickels for $15 each and selling them 15 years later at $150 each.

Different series can be popular for years and then it seems almost as if no one is interested in them. Lincoln pennies, silver dollars, and gold coins have all experienced times when they were "hot" and times when they were "not."

The average collector may well pay little attention to such trends. And if one's collecting interests do not extend to uncirculated coins or coins costing over $50 or so, probably no great price is paid for being oblivious to the possible investment angle to coin collecting.

But, then, too, part of the joy of collecting can be found in selling coins at a profit. Since the 1960s, pressure has come from a variety of sources to treat coin investing as somehow analogous to the stock market. *Coin World* and many other publications and newsletters now have quite extensive coin "trends" sections. Some endeavors are made to plot individual price increases and decreases over as short a period as a week. Excellent books now exist on treating coins as long term investments much as one would buy real estate (See, for example, the Q. David Bowers book mentioned in Chapter 9).

Investment fever is not an uncommon phenomenon. Buying an extra roll or two of an item that is perceived as "underpriced" in the market is one response. And should the retail price of these items shoot up, the effect is seductive. Price appreciation can easily become the entire goal of one's collecting interests.

To avoid reducing coin collecting to nothing but dollars and cents, an effort should be made to see the coins in one's collection for their historical and aesthetic significance.

Interesting historical questions might include researching the various changes in the metal content of certain denominations. Why was the alloy for the Lincoln cent and Jefferson nickel changed during World War II? Was it a necessary change? Why did the Trade Dollar contain more silver than a regular silver dollar? Why are little chop marks often found on these coins?

Why do some coins have arrows next to the date? Why were weird denominations like three-cent and twenty-cent pieces minted? Why were no gold coins minted for circulation after 1933?

Coins can be viewed as miniature sculptures in limited editions. The sheer beauty of a lightly toned uncirculated Liberty Standing quarter can be breathtaking.

Studying a coin closely can bring to one's attention design features never really noticed. Studying the different patterns considered can give one an insight into the reasons for the design that an engraver finally selected.

An even closer inspection of a coin can often give clues concerning the conditions under which it was struck. Had the die cracked or been damaged in some other way? Had it been re-engraved as a shortcut in the striking process? Many coins have one date engraved over another.

Again certain metals seem to function as better mediums for the striking of the details of an engraving. Our recent clad coins appear dull and flat even before they can be circulated. They pale in comparison to high grade Barber coins. They make even a Franklin half dollar look like Michelangelo's *David*.

An appreciation of these sorts of considerations provides a depth to one's collecting interests. The question, "How much is it worth?" can be considered superfluous.

239

A Peek at the History of Coin Price Appreciation

On the other hand, I do not have any desire to disparage the investment/ speculation side to coins. This aspect may well be more easily abused and indeed for the average collector realizing a profit over and above that of more orthodox investments is undoubtedly difficult. But I will not deny that money can be made by the wise and patient.

In 1962 I convinced my father to lend me $500 to "prove" that coins were a good investment. He agreed and I promptly spent the entire amount on my next trip to my local coin shop. I recall purchasing, among others, an 1885 and 1886 five-cent piece in uncirculated condition for $140 and $80 respectively.

I held the coins until the early 1970s and sold them for a reasonable profit of something around triple what I had paid. Not too bad, all things considered. The inflation rate was low in those years, so few investment vehicles fared better over that time span.

During those middle 1960s, I, like everyone else, put away silver coins as they began to disappear from circulation (The psychological forces of the era were irresistible). Most of these I still possess. Let's say I saved $200 face in Washington quarters in 1967. And that I paid $300 for them. What would they have to be worth for me now to sell at a real profit? Real is defined as something beyond the rate of inflation. Would I have been better off in Series E Savings Bonds?

Well, if I were to sell today, 34 years later, I would expect to realize 3 to 4 times face value on the coins, or about $800. The Consumer Price Index now stands at over 6 times what it was in 1967, the base year. To have grown as fast as inflation that $300 would have to be worth $1,800+ now. Certainly, other investments have done worse and some better. And there were probably shorter periods of time over which I could have done a lot better in silver. But the point is that silver bullion coins have not been any easy path to riches. Accurately predicting price fluctuations is especially difficult if not impossible.

As I look back, many coins, especially the most easily acquired, the ones that probably form the nucleus of most accumulations, have not done particularly well over the years. Unless one is able to anticipate significant commodity price changes, the prospect of making money in ordinary obsolete coinage is remote.

On the other hand, assuming the ability to grade uncirculated coins and an access to coins that are truly rare, we may well have another matter.

The charts found below attempt to plot price changes of several typical coins over the years.

1. **Large Cent F (Coronet type coin)**
2. **1909S Lincoln Cent F**
3. **Liberty Nickel BU (Type coin)**
4. **1950D Nickel BU**

240

5. **1916D Dime G**
6. **1796 Quarter G (Type coin)**
7. **Bust Half F (Type coin)**
8. **Trade Dollar XF (Type coin)**
9. **1895P Morgan Dollar PR**
10. **$1 Gold VF (Type 1)**
11. **$20 Saint-Gaudens XF-AU (Type coin)**
12. **Isabella Quarter MS60**
13. **1950 Proof Set PR60**

The chart below sets out the value of each of these coins for the years 1962, 1975, 1988 and 2003. These years were within relatively stable periods for the coin market and give us, therefore, a reasonably accurate picture of how an investment might have performed over the past 40 years. The above coins were selected as a representative selection, with the exception of the 1895P Morgan dollar and the 1796 quarter, that would turn up in the average person's collection. This comparison also shows that the dramaticprice changes occurred in more expensive coins.

Coin	1962	1975	1988	2003
Large Cent F	$2.00	$5.00	$7.00	$18.00
1909S Lincoln Cent F	12.00	20.00	50.00	75.00
Liberty Nickel MS60	10.00	45.00	125.00	88.00
1950D Nickel MS60	5.00	9.00	8.00	6.50
1916D Dime G	40.00	80.00	325.00	650.00
1796 Quarter G	300.00	750.00	3100.00	3720.00
Bust Half F	4.00	20.00	35.00	48.00
Trade Dollar XF	12.00	70.00	150.00	150.00
1895P Morgan Dollar PR60	850.00	6000.00	15000.00	23575.00
$1 Gold VF	25.00	100.00	150.00	150.00
$20 Saint-Gaudens XF-AU	50.00	300.00	550.00	450.00
Isabella Quarter MS60	40.00	175.00	500.00	600.00
1950 Proof Set PR60	55.00	115.00	525.00	550.00
Totals	1405.00	7689.00	20525.00	30000.00 app.

Even if one were to assume a return of 75% of the above amount after commissions, etc., the original investment would have increased by roughly 20 times. If one were to remove the two most expensive items the investment would still have increased by 6 times. What other investments have performed so well?!

The promise of fantastic profits can always be established by looking selectively at the past. Indeed, some coins have done very well over the years. Logically, there is nothing that necessitates that this will continue to happen. The forces are largely psychological and, consequently, quite unpredictable.

One need only look at what happened to coin and metal prices in the wake of the stock market "crash" on October 19, 1987. Historically, hard assets have often leaped in value given uncertainty in financial assets. But, six months later, the drop in the market had not appreciably affected coin or bullion prices. If anything, both were somewhat lower.

My experience has been that those who come to coin collecting primarily as an investment vehicle soon leave greatly disappointed. They are preyed upon by investment promoters, take shortcuts instead of learning how to grade coins, and in virtually every case, leave the hobby in disgust.

Even for the proficient and wary, investing in coins is full of minefields. A number of years ago, the American Numismatic Association Certification Service drastically revised its grading standards, especially for uncirculated grades. And, of course, the standards were toughened, leaving many who had purchased supposedly MS65 coins holding very expensive MS63s.

Even now, when a coin is purchased which is certified as to its grade, the purchaser will do well to act with care. The year it was graded is a factor for deciding how it might currently be graded and priced. For example, some dealers advertise to buy 1982 ANA graded coins at 50% of what they will pay for those graded in 1986.

Such a change in direction does nothing if not shake the confidence of those who primarily hope to profit from the coins they have acquired. It also points up that grading is at its foundations an art not a science, and worse, an art dependent upon the supply and demand forces in the market.

When demand is high and the market is bullish the tendency is to push the limits of previous grading conventions. When a buyer's market returns, prices

242

fall and standards rise.

One beneficial role that investors play in the market is setting aside rolls, even bags, of current coinage for future generations. Unless there had been someone with an eye toward investment it is doubtful that we now could enjoy the variety of well-preserved coins at today's reasonable prices. If anything, over the long run, investors probably keep the prices of coins down.

Coin Investment as a Hedge

During the period 1977-1980, at which time the country was experiencing significant inflation, a huge run up in the price of gold and silver took place, and many predictions were made concerning the total collapse of financial markets.

Some suggested that silver and gold in coin form should be made a part of any thinking person's portfolio as a hedge against disaster.

In this scenario, paper money would quickly become worthless. The image of wagons of Marks, circa 1923, was useful. Bartering, initially at least, would be difficult since communications would be poor or non-existent. Consequently, what was needed was a reliable, negotiable, small unit of real value. Presumably gold and silver bars would need assaying. Obsolete 90% silver coins would become the perfect vehicle. A hedge against disaster.

243

To some this plan made sense, although planning for such an eventuality would have, by now, over 30 years later, involved considerable cost.

Decision-making in this area is reminiscent of good science fiction. I suppose the best one could do would be to make a reasonable estimate of the probability of a disaster of this magnitude. Then apply that probability in percentage terms to one's own wealth and security quotient.

For example, if one thought the chances of financial collapse were something on the order of 5% over the

next five years, then putting 5% of one's assets into disaster-oriented "hard" assets would seem appropriate. A one-year's food supply, a shotgun and shells, 100 cords of wood, and $500 face in Roosevelt dimes might be bought in for simple peace of mind.

But do coins make sense as a hedge in more normal times? My answer would be "yes," but only if I were speaking of a very astute buyer. This buyer would certainly have to know how to accurately grade coins. He or she would almost as certainly have to be able to make purchases at or near wholesale levels. Knowledge of the marketplace would be helpful but not an absolute necessity.

Coins, especially rare ones, can at times present a liquidity problem. They do not trade as easily as stocks and bonds due partly to their individual uniqueness. A buyer must be sought out. Even then prices are usually negotiated.

But for an investor willing to be patient and able to avoid any pressure for quick liquidation, coins provide an interesting but not easy alternative to more traditional and orthodox investments.

244

The easier path to coin investment, and a much more precarious one, is to turn over the decision-making process to a reputable coin dealer/investment advisor. The commissions charged with this approach are considerable. Breaking even, that is, price appreciation in an amount equal to the purchase charges, may take several years (Sales taxes present an additional hurdle to profit realization).

And remember all this is said within the context of reliance on a dealer's reputation. If one peruses the advertisers of 1963, very few names survive.

Further, most dealers are automatically in a conflict of interest situation. It is easier to tout coins that can be acquired relatively easily rather than attempt to buy for one's clients coins that are always in short supply.

And when you think of it, if any person, dealer or otherwise, really was convinced that a coin were going to perform extremely well over the next five to 10 years, why would he sell it? That unwillingness to take anything like the risk that the client is asked to take makes any advice rather suspect.

Chapter 13

WEB SITES

Following are listings of Retail Coin Collector and Coin Auction Web Sites, Coin Organization and Convention Information Sites, Coin Certification Sites, Hobby Publications and Numismatic News Groups which might prove informative and useful for both the beginning and advanced numismatist.

Retail Coin Collector & Coin Auction Sites

ANA Dealership A Listing:
American Numismatic Association Member,
Professional Coin Collectors and Dealers
This site contains an extensive listing of coin dealers in alphabetical order by state. All are members of the association. This prvodes some degree of safety in coin transactions. SITE: http://anamarket.money.org/index_a.html

Bowers and Merena
SITE: http://web.coin-universe.com/bowers/Have_a_Great_Time.html

Coin World Online
This site provides thousands of online classified ads for numismatic purchases.
SITE: http://www.coinworld.com/

Coin Universe
This site is an easy link to the home pages of many dealers.
SITE: http://www.coin-universe.com/

eBay Coins
Provides thousands of coin offerings and an online auction.
SITE: http://coins.ebay.com/

Heritage Rare Coins: Rare Coins and Numismatic Auctions
Heritage Rare Coin Gallery is the largest rare coin dealer in the world with
$20 million inventory specializing in US rare coins, world gold coins, and
buying and selling rare coins.
SITE: http://www.heritagecoin.com/

Jake's Marketplace, Inc.
SITE: http://www.jakesmp.com/

LEGACY—Rare Coins & Bullion
SITE: http://www.legacycoins.com/

Spectrum Numismatics
SITE: http://www.coincity.com/Spectrum/default.htm

Steinbergs Gold Coins
SITE: http://www.steinbergs.com/

The U.S. Mint
SITE: http://www.usmint.gov/

246

Coin Organization & Convention Information Sites

American Numismatic Association
The ANA, a non-profit, educational organization chartered by Congress is dedicated to the collection and study of coins, paper money, tokens and medals, and was created for the benefit of its members and the numismatic community. The organization provides a number of conventions with courses throughout the year. Check the site for dates and places.
SITE: http://www.money.org/

PNG
Professional Numismatists Guild 3950 Concordia Lane Fallbrook, CA 92028 (760) 728-1300 | FAX (760) 728-8507 E-mail: info@pngdealers.com. This organization has strict requirements for dealer members and includes a listing of these dealers.
SITE: http://www.pngdealers.com/buy/in-buy.htm

247

Coin Clubs
Lists coin clubs and shows by locality.
SITE: http://www.coinclubs.com

Coin Certification Sites

ANACS
P.O. Box 182141 Columbus, Ohio, 43218-2141, (800) 888-1861.
SITE: http://www.anacs.com/

Professional Coin Grading Service, Inc.
SITE: http://www.pcgs.com/

Independent Coin Grading Company
Independent Coin Grading Company (ICG), 7901 East Belleview Ave., is a company formed by some of the industry's top graders. Absolute unbiased grading.
SITE: http://www.icgcoin.com/index.htm

Numismatic Guaranty Corporation of America (NGC)
SITE: http://www.ngccoin.com/census_report.cfm

PCI, Inc.
SITE: http://www.pcicoins.com

Hobby Publications

Coin Dealer Newsletter
A serious resource for wholesale rare coin prices, bullion values and industry news, CDN publishes the Certified Coin Dealer newsletter, Bluesheet; the Currency Dealer newsletter, Greensheet; and the Numismatic Dealer Directory, Greysheet.
SITE: http://www.greysheet.com/

Coin World Weekly
Weekly numismatic magazine and marketplace for young and old coin collectors. Besides industry news, the site features forums, club links, convention and bourse dates, numismatic trivia and games.
SITE: http://www.csmonline.com/coinworld/

Numismatic News
Weekly numismatic newspaper includes coin ads and articles with an extensive classified section.
Site: http://www.Krause.com

Numismatic Newsgroups
Numismatic Newsgroups are discussion groups for various topics. You need a news reader, such as rn, nn, tin, WinVN, or NewsWatcher, to read and post to newsgroups. See ton of the EFF's Extended Guide to the Internet.
SITE: http://www.limunltd.com/numismatica/internet-resources/news.html

Chapter 14

SOURCES FOR REFERENCE

This chapter provides the reader easy access to the acquisition of numismatic information.

1. Coin Papers and Magazines

COINage Magazine
2660 E. Main St.
Ventura, CA 93003

Coins Magazine
Iola, WI 54990

Coin World
P.O. Box 150
Sidney, OH 45367

Hobbies Magazine
1106 S. Michigan Ave.
Chicago, IL 60605

Numismatic News Weekly
700 E. State Street
Iola, WI 54990

The Numismatist
818 N. Cascade Ave.
Colorado Springs, CO 80903

2. Books—General

American Guide to U.S. Coins. Charles F. French. Simon & Schuster, Inc., New York (1988).

Annual Report of the Director of the Mint. United States Mint, Department of the Treasury, Washington, DC 20220.

Coin Collecting Made Easy: Basic Knowledge for the Coin Collector and Investor. Staff of *Coin World.* Amos Press Inc., Sidney, OH (Fourth printing 1987).

Coin World Almanac. Staff of *Coin World.* Amos Press Inc., Sidney, OH (sixth edition 1990).
The Catalogue and Encyclopedia of U.S. Coins. Don Taxey. Scott Publishing Co., New York (1976).

250 *A Guide Book of U.S. Coins.* R.S. Yeoman. Western Publishing Co., Racine, WI (1988).

The Macmillan Encyclopedic Dictionary of Numismatics. Richard C. Doty. Macmillan Publishing Co., New York (1982).

Numismatic Art in America. Cornelius Vermeule. Belknap Press, Cambridge, MA (1971).
U.S. Coins of Value. Norman Stack. Dell Books, New York (1988).

U.S. Mint and Coinage. Don Taxey. Durst Numismatic Publications, New York (1983).

3. Books—Grading

Grading Coins: A Collection of Readings. Edited by Richard Bagg and James Jelinski. J. Essex Publications, Portsmouth, NH (1977).

A Guide to Grading United States Coins. Martin R. Brown and John W. Dunn. General Distributors Inc., Denison TX (1980).

NCI Grading Guide. James L. Halperin. Ivy Press, Dallas, TX (1986).

New Photograde. James F. Ruddy. Bowers and Ruddy Galleries, Los Angeles (1972).

Official American Numismatic Association Grading Standards for United States Coins. ANA and Western Publishing Co., Racine WI (1987).

4. Books—Specialized

American Half Cents. Roger S. Cohen. Wigglesworth & Ghatt Co., Arlington, VA (1982).

America's Copper Coinage 1783-1857. American Numismatic Association (1985).

The Comprehensive Catalogue and Encyclopedia of U.S. Morgan and Peace Silver Dollars. Leroy C. Van Allen and George Mallis. Arco Publishing Co., New York (1976).

The Early Coins of America. Sylvester S. Crosby. Quarterman Publications, New York (1983, a reprint of a 1875 edition).

Early Half Dollar Varieties. Al C. Overton. Colorado Springs, CO (1970).

The Early Quarters of the United States. A.W. Browning. Sanford J. Durst Numismatic Publications, New York (1977, a reprint of a 1925 edition).

Early United States Dimes: 1796-1937. David J. Davis, and others. John Reich Collectors Society (1984).

The Encyclopedia of United States Silver & Gold Commemorative Coins. Walter Breen and Anthony Swiatek. Arco Publishing Inc. (1981).

Encyclopedia of United States Liberty Seated Dimes. Kamal M. Ahwash. Kamal Press (1977).

The Fantastic 1804 Dollar. Kenneth E. Bressett and Eric P. Newman. Whitman Publishing Co., Racine, WI (1962).

251

The Morgan and Peace Dollar Textbook. Wayne Miller. Adam Smith Publishing Co., Metairie, LA (1982).

Penny Whimsy. William H. Sheldon. Quarterman Publications Inc., Lawrence, MA (1983, reprint of a 1958 edition).

Standing Liberty Quarters. J.H. Cline. Cline's Rare Coins, Palm Harbor, FL (1986).

United States Copper Cents 1816-1857. Howard R. Newcomb. Quarterman Publications Inc., Lawrence, MA (1981, reprint of a 1944 edition).

United States Copper Coins—An Action Guide to Collectors and I nvestors. Q. David Bowers. Bowers and Merena Inc., Wolfeboro, NH (1984).

United States Gold Coins, an Illustrated History. Q. David Bowers. Bowers and Ruddy Galleries, Los Angeles (1982).

The United States Half Dimes. Daniel W. Valentine. Quarterman Publications, Lawrence, MA (1975, a reprint of a 1931 edition).

The United States Trade Dollar. John M. Willem. Sanford J. Durst Numismatic Publications, New York (1983, a reprint of a 1959 edition.

The Walking Liberty Half Dollar. Anthony Swiatek. Sanford J. Durst Numismatic Publications, New York (1983).

5. Books—Errors

The Encyclopedia of Double Dies, (2 Vols.). John A. Wexler. Robert C. Wilharm News Printing Co. Inc., Fort Worth, TX (1978 and 1981).

How Error Coins Are Made at the U.S. Mints. Arnold Margolis. Heigh Ho Printing Co., Newbury Park, CA (1981).

Modern Mint Mistakes. Philip Steiner and Michael Zimpfer. Whispering Pines Printing, Indiana (1974-60).

Official Price Guide to Mint Errors and Varieties. Mark Hudgeons. House of Collectibles Inc., Orlando, FL (1985).

The RPM Book. John A. Wexler and Tom Miller. Lonesome John Publishing Co., Newbury Park, CA (1983).

6. Books—Counterfeits

Counterfeit Detection. (2 Vols.) Staff of the American Numismatic Association Certification Service. American Numismatic Association, Colorado Springs, CO (1983 and 1987).

Counterfeits of U.S. Coins. Larry Spanbauer. Service Litho-Print Inc., Oshkosh, WI (1975).

Detecting Counterfeit Coins. (Book 1). John Devine. Heigh Ho Printing Co., Newbury Park, CA (1975).

Detecting Counterfeit Gold Coins. (Book 2). John Devine. Heigh Ho Printing Co., Newbury Park, CA (1977).

7. Books—Investing

The Big Silver Melt. Henry A. Merton. MacMillan Publishing Co., New York (1983).

253

The Coin Collector's Survival Manual. Scott A. Travers. Arco Publishing Co., New York (1987).

High Profits From Rare Coin Investment. Q. David Bowers. Bowers and Merena Galleries Inc., Wolfeboro, NH (1983).

Investing in Rare Coins. Dennis Steinmetz. Steinmetz Coins and Currency, Lancaster, PA (1981).

The Investor's Guide to United States Coins. Neil S. Berman and Hans M. F. Schulman. Coin & Currency Institute Inc., New York (1986).

The Official Investor's Guide To Gold Coins. Marc Hudgeons. House of Collectibles, New York (1985).

Survive and Win in the Inflationary '80's. Howard J. Ruff. Warner Books, New York (1982).

254

8. Newsletters

The Coin Dealer Newsletter
Box 11099
Torrance, CA 90510

The Certified Coin Dealer Newsletter
Box 11099
Torrance, CA 90510

There are scores of other newsletters on the market. Often, however, these are put together by firms with coins for sale.

9. Professional Organizations and Associations

The American Numismatic Association
818 N. Cascade Ave.
Colorado Springs, CO 80903

The American Numismatic Society
c/o Secretary of the Society
Broadway Between 155th and 156 Streets
New York, NY 10032

Central States Numismatic Society
P.O. Box 223
Hiawatha, IA 52233

Combined Organization of Numismatic
Error Collectors of America
Route 2, Box 6
Andover, SD 57422

Industry Council for Tangible Assets
25 E. St. N.W. Eighth Floor
Washington, DC 20001

Liberty Seated Collectors Club
5718 King Arthur Drive
Kettering, OH 45429

New England Numismatic Association
P.O. Box 99
West Roxbury, MA 02132

Numismatic Literary Guild
P.O. Box 970218
Miami, FL 33197

Pacific Coast Numismatic Society
610 Arlington Ave.
Berkeley, CA 94707

Professional Numismatists Guild, Inc.
P.O. Box 430
Van Nuys, CA 91408

Society of Philatelists and Numismatists
1929 Millis St.
Montebello, CA 90640

Society for U.S. Commemorative Coins
912 Bob Wallace Ave.
Huntsville, AL 35801

10. Grading and Authentication Services

Numismatic Guarantee Corporation of America
P.O. Box 4776
Sarasota, FL 34230

Professional Coin Grading Service
P.O. Box 9458
Newport Beach, CA 92658

ANACS
Box 182141
Columbus, OH 43218-2141

PCI
P.O. Box 486
Rossville, GA 30741

Chapter 15

COUNTERFEIT COINS

Collectors and dealers sooner or later encounter counterfeit coins. Two kinds exist. One is made for circulation and intended to cheat the public. Coins of this sort are very crudely made usually from base metals and will more likely be higher denomination coins. You can realize that it would hardly be worthwhile to go to the trouble of illegally reproducing coins of lesser value.

In 30 years of sorting through coins from circulation I have only encountered two or three pieces that were counterfeits of this sort. My view would be that such coins are so seldom seen that they probably have some value as curiosities. I would think it silly to spend them. Having several specimens as examples is worth more than any monetary loss one would suffer for having accepted them.

Both ways of producing counterfeits of this sort are readily detectable. One process is to cast the coin by taking an impression of the genuine one and using that as a mold. This counterfeit has a soapy feeling, and under a ten-power magnifying glass you can see pit marks made by air bubbles.

The second process is to produce an electrotype, made by taking an electrolytic impression of both sides of the coin. The counterfeiter then has two shells which are glued together with a base metal in the hollow center. The type of counterfeit is detectable by the false ring which the fake coin usually has. Unless the job is very skillfully done, you can also see a line around the edge of the coin where the two halves were joined.

The other kind of counterfeit is intended to cheat collectors. These usually involve altering genuine coins. For example, should one be able to successfully remove the "D" mint mark from a 1922D cent, the coin might be passable for the much rarer 1922 cent produced without a mint mark due to a defective die.

Other coins can be altered by adding a mint mark. The 1909S VDB is a notorious example. And any collector should be careful in purchasing one.

With sophisticated minting facilities, coins of even moderate numismatic value have in the past and are currently being produced in order to dupe collectors. Purchasing gold coins has become something of a nightmare. Such coins as the $5 Indian have an incused design making them relatively easy to reproduce. Many gold coins are found in finenesses matching the genuine article. Thus the whole idea is to cheat the person willing to pay above the gold content value of the coin. The face value of these counterfeits is, of course, well below the gold value. When these coins were circulating there was little incentive to counterfeit them. Rather, one was more likely then to encounter a gold-plated Liberty nickel dated 1883 without "Cents." A change was made that year to place "Cents" on the coin so as to preclude a gold-plated version being passed for a genuine $5.00 gold piece.

Only experience will give you the ability to detect counterfeits. I do not mind saying that I have been fooled. After all, the counterfeiter keeps up on the state of the art and in some ways has a greater incentive to keep his skills honed. In the near future it is not inconceivable that the quality of the product could surpass that of the genuine article if predatory foreign mints are permitted to operate with no restrictions. Such attempts have already been alleged.

Chapter 16

SLABS

Two years ago I had several high-grade Lincoln Cents in inventory. I had priced them at MS63. One was a 1918s, which I had offered on my price list for $110. Every collector for over a year was hesitant to purchase because this coin was valued at only $50 or so in MS60. Eventually, I sent these coins and some others to Numismatic Guaranty Corporation (NGC). Surprisingly, all graded MS63 or better. The 1918s graded MS64 Red. An eager dealer customer purchased the coin by phone for $600. A 1923s graded MS65RedBrown and sold for twice what I had been asking for it. They were much more easily sold once the determination was made by an established third party as to authenticity and grade.

I think I would still have these coins in my inventory if it were not for the "slabbing"— or I would have sold them too cheaply. I simply do not see enough high grade Lincoln Cents to be confident of my own grading. A less interested third-party service is in my estimation not just helpful but at times indispensable.

Here is how these services work: When a buyer and seller meet and try to agree on a price for a coin, authenticity and grade are often at issue. Experienced buyers and sellers may likely have no problems in this regard. They have bought and sold enough coins to pretty much know whether a coin is genuine and what grade it will be given by a reasonable buyer.

However, a novice or intermediate collector or dealer may not have confidence in his ability to tell whether a coin is a counterfeit or has been altered. Grading, especially of mint state coins, takes years of experience. Large amounts of money can be at stake. That altered 1909SVDB Cent you purchased raw (unslabbed) for $450 has little or no value. Since this coin is a common target for alteration, my advice would be to never purchase it unslabbed. A Liberty $20 gold piece is common in AU and commands a price of about $460. In MS65 it can easily be sold for $3000+. The differences are subtle. Getting expert opinions makes good sense.

The process of submission to an expertising service is simple. Information on four services is found below. For PCGS and NGC, the coins must be submitted through an authorized dealer, unless one is a member of the American Numismatic Association. ANACS and PCI take coins directly.

When the coin reaches the service it is examined by several graders. The consensus opinion is the grade given to the coin. It is then sealed in a reasonably airtight plastic holder. The date, denomination, and grade are placed on the holder, as well as the logo of the grading service. I contend that the prices charged are very reasonable and range from $10.00 to $25. Express service can cost $70 or more. I further contend that the services have been a great boon to coin collecting, as it greatly reduces the possibility of fraud and overgrading.

That is not to say that there are not some disadvantages to slabs. 1. The grade is not a guarantee. Differences of opinion are still possible and I have seen coins in slabs that I believed to be overgraded. Knowledge of grading is still important, although probably less so. (Authenticity is another matter. Grading services will refund something approaching the dealer buy price for a coin later determined to be inauthentic.) 2. Copper coins especially are susceptible to changes such as spotting and corrosion even in a tightly sealed holder. My experience has been that the services will not guarantee the continued condition of such coins. This is important since the price difference between a red (brightly copper-colored) cent and a brown (chocolate-colored) one can be enormous. 3. Aesthetically, "entombing" a coin, as some refer to it, takes some of the fun out of collecting. An artificial barrier is created between owner and owned. Holding a gold piece in your hand is a different, and less satisfying, experience as compared to possessing it in a slab. 4. No albums currently exist that do aesthetic justice to slabbed coins.

The enjoyment of seeing that entire set of Bust Half Dollars in a book is lost.

On balance, however, the advantages of slabbing outweigh these small disadvantages. Certainly, I would advise having any coin slabbed that may be worth $200 or more, should there be any question about genuineness or grade.

One last comment on slabbing: A common practice among dealers and some collectors involves resubmissions of slabbed coins if the grade received is less than expected. Where prices take huge leaps on only slight grading differences, the incentive is very high to "crack out" the coin and send it in again to the same or different grading service. The fee must be paid again and there is the additional downside risk that the new grade will be a <u>lower</u> one. Those risks usually pale against the upside potential.

For example, I recently purchased an 1855 O $1 gold piece. The grade on the slab was AU58 — just slightly under MS60. The price difference between AU ($1000) and MS60 ($5000) makes the coin a virtual must for resubmission. If the grade were to drop to AU50 or AU55, the price difference would be less that $200 or so.

NGC and PCGS keep population reports on the coins they grade. The presumption is that these figures can be checked to ascertain the relative scarcity of coins in each grade category. These reports are helpful, but these figures may be somewhat out of line due to resubmissions. If my 1855 O $1 gold coin gets sent in time and time again it may look as if there is a large number of these coins when there is only one.

Following are four services that I would recommend.

ANACS
P.O. Box 182141
Columbus, OH 43218-2141
1-800-888-1861
Coins may be submitted directly to ANACS. Cost of encapsulation: Typically, $10-$21, plus shipping and insurance both ways. Turn around time (including shipping time): Typically 25 days. Advantage: ANACS will grade "problem" coins—coins that have been cleaned or damaged. etc., are given a net grade. NGC and PCGS return these coins ungraded.

Numismatic Guaranty Corporation of America (NGC)

P.O. Box 4776

Sarasota, FL 34230

NGC does not accept direct submissions. For a listing of the 1200-plus authorized NGC dealers who can submit your important coins, call 1-800-NGC-COIN. The American Numismatic Association has a special relationship with NGC. Members of the American Numismatic Association can submit their coins to that organization. The ANA then sends the coins to NGC. Submission forms are found in every issue of the ANA journal, *The Numismatist*. Cost of encapsulation: Typically, $15-$25, plus shipping and insurance both ways. Turn around time (including shipping time): Typically 30 days. Advantage: One of the two most widely accepted grading services.

Professional Coin Grading Service (PCGS)

Box 9458

Newport Beach, CA 92658

1-800-447-8848

262

PCGS does not accept direct submissions accept from members of the American Numismatic Association. For a list of authorized dealers call the number above. Cost of encapsulation: Typically, $25.00, plus shipping and insurance both ways. Turn around time (including shipping time): Typically 30 days. Advantage: One of the two most widely accepted grading services.

Photo-Certified Coin Institute (PCI)

P.O. Box 486

Rossville, GA 30741

1-800-277-2646

Coins may be submitted directly to PCI. Cost of encapsulation: Typically, $7.50, plus shipping and insurance both ways. Turn around time (including shipping time): Typically 19 days. Advantages: Price. Also, cleaned or damaged coins are slabbed in a special holder with a red seal.

GLOSSARY

Base Metal
Metal other than precious metal (silver, gold, platinum) used to manufacture coins.

Blank
A planchet that has been further prepared for the coining process.

Braided Hair Type
Middle 19th century type where hair of Liberty is worn up in braids.

Bullion Coin
A coin minted more for the exchange of units of precious metal than for the purposes of commerce.

Bust Type
Showing only the head and shoulder of a figure.

Cameo Proof
A proof coin where the contrast between the design and field is so remarkable that the design often appears to stand out as if on a black background.

Clad
Recent coinage, since 1965, composed of copper and nickel in a sandwich fashion such that the nickel gives the coin a silvery appearance somewhat like previous silver coinage it was meant to replace.

Classic Head Type
A style of the bust of Liberty used in the early 19th century.

Coin
A piece of metal, wood or plastic with a design and legend, intended for use as money.

Common Type
Refers to the least expensive date of a particular design.

Commemorative
A special coin, celebrating a person, place or event.

Condition
Usually refers to the amount of wear or absence of wear a coin has had. Also may take into account any damage or special eye appeal a coin may have.

Coronet Type
A style of bust of Liberty used in the early to mid 19th century.

Cull
Damaged or otherwise very low grade coin. May have bullion value or some numismatic value if it is rare.

Die
The form from which coins are struck.

Draped Bust Type
An early Liberty type where the bust is covered with a loosely fitting gown.

Field
The background behind the principal figure in a coin design.

Fineness
The proportion of precious metal to base metal in a coin.

Flowing Hair Type .
An early Liberty type coin where the hair is not braided or covered.

Fractional Currency
Paper money issued in amounts less than one dollar.

Inscription
All lettering that appears on either the obverse or reverse of a coin.

Impaired
Referring to a proof coin that has seen wear.

Lettered Edge
Inscription on the edge of a coin. Found especially on our early coinage prior to the use of reeding.

Liberty Cap
A bust of Liberty wearing a distinctive cap.

Liberty Seated
An allegorical figure of Liberty seated, used on our coinage throughout the middle portions of the 19th century.

Liberty Standing
An allegorical figure of the Goddess of Liberty standing, found on the quarter dollar of 1916-1930.

Liberty Walking
An allegorical figure of the Goddess of Liberty walking, found on the half dollar of 1916-1947 and the silver $1 bullion coin 1986-date.

Medal
A metal piece with no legal tender status used to commemorate some person, place, or event.

Milled edge
Parallel vertical ridges around the edge of a coin called reeds.

Mintage
The number of coins produced in a specified period of time.

Mint Error
Any of a variety of mistakes made by the mint in the production of a coin. See Chapter 4 for types.

Mint mark
Small letters placed on a coin to show the place of mintage.

266

Mint Set
A group of coins of a given year specially packaged or struck for collectors by the Mint.

Numismatics
The science or study of coins and coin collecting.

Obverse
Front of a coin, the side having the principal design feature. Also referred to as the "heads" side of the coin.

Overdate
Coin made from an altered die, showing traces of a different date.

Pattern
Experimental coin struck to experiment with different metals or designs.

Planchet
The blank piece of metal on which a coin design is stamped or struck.

Proof
Condition of a coin struck from a polished die, often giving the coin a mirror-like appearance.

Proof Set
A group of coins of a given year specially struck and packaged by the mint under the conditions mentioned above.

Relief
The relation of the design of the coin to the field. Bas-relief means the design features are raised with reference to the field. An incused design means the design features are below the field or recessed.

Reverse
The side opposite the principal design feature. Also referred to as the "tails" side of the coin.

Restrike
A coin made at a later date from an original die.

Symbols
Small additions to the design supplementing the main subject.

Token
A private coin-like piece made for advertising or propaganda purposes.

Type
The kind of coin as designated by the principal design.

Varieties
Minor variations in coins, such as size of letters, size of date, added dot, different metal content, etc.